Small Boat Cruising

SMALL BOAT CRUISING

*A practical guide to
moderately priced cruising boats
and their handling*

D. M. DESOUTTER

with line drawings by

D. L. JENKINS

New and Revised Edition

FABER AND FABER
3 QUEEN SQUARE · LONDON

First published in 1963
by Faber and Faber Limited
New and revised edition 1972
Printed in Great Britain by
Latimer Trend & Co Ltd Plymouth
All rights reserved

ISBN 0 571 09681 6

Contents

Contents

Part One

1

From dinghy to cruiser

It is about ten years since I sat down to write a book for the growing numbers of people I expected to be turning from dinghies to boats with 'lids' on. At the time it seemed obvious that the boom in dinghy sailing which was already well established would lead in turn to a similar boom in small sailing cruisers.

But the extent to which that expectation has come true has still surprised some people. Moorings now have a scarcity value, and new marinas have had to be built to accommodate the rapidly rising number of small craft.

The craft themselves are of a very much greater variety, and are made by a number of new firms, many of which have come into existence well within the decade and yet have thriven and grown. When I was writing that book, *Small Boat Cruising*, we were in the heyday of marine plywood construction, though one or two of the boatyards I visited were beginning to dabble in resin and glassfibre. One man who is now managing director of one of the larger boatbuilding companies in Britain remains clear in my memory as he was then, humping a bucket of resin in splattered overalls. The rate of change has been extremely rapid, but the demand for comfortable cabin sailing boats at modest cost remains the same as ever it was.

Though a sailing dinghy provides tremendous sport, it has its limitations. As people grow older and beget families they tire of wet bottoms and gymnastic feats to avoid a ducking. They want a boat in which the children can be dry and comfortable, where clothes, food, camera and so forth can be kept dry too. And they want a boat that can be lived aboard, not only because it saves the tedium of driving home on Saturday night and back again on Sunday (only the lucky few actually *live* near the water), but because it also gives opportunities to sail farther afield.

An even greater attraction, certainly for myself and I suspect for most others who turn to cruising, is the mere fact of living aboard a boat, of not going home at night but of finding instead an anchorage where one can enjoy the subtle beauties of water and sky, of dawn and dusk—perhaps even the magic of a full moon over the water while nightingales sing in the wood ashore. (A favourite sea creek of mine really does offer that unexcelled entertainment. . . .)

But whatever the cause, the great company of people who have started by sailing dinghies is almost certainly the major source of new recruits to the sailing of bigger craft. It is obvious that they are not all able to plunge in and spend £2,000 or £3,000 on a boat. The expenses of a home, a family and a car rarely leave much over for expenditure on that scale. Therefore, when I began *Small Boat Cruising* I tried to adopt a sensible approach to the scale of boating which most people might be likely to afford. I have done the same in this edition too, though in the meantime prices have risen, so that the *numbers* are bigger. But in real terms the sums of money involved are not really very different.

I shall have more to say about costs in a later chapter (Chapter 10), but for the moment let me offer a little moral reinforcement for the man and his wife who are contemplating the buying of a family boat. If one uses a little common sense in buying, and another dose of the same in looking after her, she can be almost an 'investment'. Looking through the small ads in the back of *Practical Boat Owner* I see that standard production boats eight to ten years old are being offered for sale at prices between 60 and 90 per cent of their cost when new. Compare that with the price you can get for an eight-year-old car. . . .

Compare, too, the value that a family may get from a boat if they use her for holidays. Many people like to take their holidays abroad, and though package deals can be cheap a figure of £50 a head can quickly be exceeded. Add on the bits and pieces of incidental spending for a fortnight, and it is not difficult to pay out £300 or even more for a family of four. And at the end of the fortnight all that money has gone for ever—even though it did rain half the time and little Angela was laid low with a tummy upset!

But money put into a boat is still there, after a fortnight or even after a year, so long as you insure her and look after her. You can have two, three or four weeks holiday aboard, plus as many week-ends as you wish. After three or four years you can probably sell her for only a little less than you gave. If in the meantime you have been able to save (by *not* going on those fabulous foreign jaunts?) you are well on the way to buying a bigger and more comfortable craft.

I don't want to overdo it—someone is bound to ask about the running costs, and to that question it is not easy to give a definite answer. So much depends on the place where you keep the boat; it's expensive to enjoy the benefits of a posh marina, and cheap to rent a mooring in a creek where the boat will settle on the mud at every low tide. And there's a big difference in the cost of having a yard tackle painting and minor repairs, or in doing the work yourself.

Nevertheless, even in these days of high costs there are some people who manage to run a family boat on fixed costs of around £50 a year, while many more do it for about £100. And by fixed costs I mean moorings, laying up in the winter, insurance, and necessary repairs. Fuel, food, fancy fittings if you want them can all cost as much more as you like, but I do know that many years ago when we had a small and inexpensive boat we found that our greatest expenditure for the season was for petrol to travel to and from the boat in our car.

Even so, the first cost of a boat can be pretty daunting, especially if you look at the prices of some of the new boats described in the second part of this book. If you do feel a bit deterred, may I recommend a thorough search in the second-hand market? For a start, many examples of the boats I described in the first edition are still around —indeed they'll be in service for many years to come. And with a second-hand boat one can often acquire quite a useful amount of gear and equipment 'in the price'. It's a matter of shopping around.

Nor is it essential that one should have all the latest gadgets right away. In the last twenty years boating has been 'improved' by all sorts of devices, ranging from echo-sounders to hydraulic backstay tensioners. Some are more useful than others, and indeed a few are really valuable. But it was not so long ago that we used a lead-line because echo-sounders were only for the very wealthy, and we did without sheet winches and used blocks and muscles instead.

Just as newly-weds begin to build a home, so one can start with a boat that is very simply equipped and add to her as you go along.

But let's assume that the reader is in fact thinking of fitting neatly in with my basic supposition—that's to say of moving on from dinghy sailing to something bigger. Because I assume this reader has knowledge of dinghy handling I shall make no attempt to present him with a primer of sailing. It is true that there will be certain manoeuvres that are not quite the same, and others which rarely occur in dinghies. Gybing in a bigger boat is not the wild slam-bang that is best in a dinghy—it is a controlled affair in which the boom is sheeted as close in to the centre-line of the boat as possible before it swings across, thus giving it less time to build up momentum and less chance to do damage. Anchoring, picking up moorings and heaving-to are less commonly done in dinghies than in cruising boats, but there is no basic point of sailing that will be strange to the dinghy sailor.

What may be strange, and something of a disappointment after the liveliness of a dinghy, is the stability and the slower rate of reaction of a bigger boat. In a dinghy the heeling force of the wind on the sails is counter-balanced by the weight of the crew; in effect they become 'live ballast', whose weight is quickly moved to new positions as necessary. But in most cruising boats the ballast is a fixture and the boat herself is intended to remain right way up without aid from the crew's weight. There are exceptions to this general principle, for in small boats (under 5 tons Thames measurement, say) the weight of the crew can have a considerable effect. In a Caprice, for example, with her displacement of about 1,200 lb., the combined weight of a couple of hefty crew (perhaps 300 lb.) is relatively quite large, and in any sort of breeze they will keep their weight up to windward, where it will do quite a bit of good. Even in a boat like an Alacrity, with a displacement of about 1,500 lb. and with about 550 lb. in her twin keels acting 1 ft. below the waterline, the weight of the crew is not inconsiderable. If there are four of them with an assumed total weight of 500 lb., the righting moment they can exert if they all sit well to windward will, in fact, be greater than that of the heavy keels so long as the angle of heel remains small. But the keels become more effective as the angle increases, while the weight of the crew has a steadily smaller effect. When a dinghy is right over on her beam-ends it is usually the last moment before a capsize, when the thing has gone so far that the weight of the crew can hardly exert a sufficient leverage to hold her up. It is just at this point that the fixed ballast in a cruising boat is doing its best work: it gets its best leverage when it has been raised to a horizontal position.

In short, for small cruising boats up to 5 or 6 Thames tons, the weight of the crew can be useful in keeping the boat upright while the breeze is not too strong and the angle of heel is not too great. But the safety of the boat does not depend on their agility: although it is sensible for them to get up on the windward side, there is no urgency about it.

The lack of urgency is apparent, too, in going about. This takes appreciably longer as the size of the boat gets bigger, and a dinghy sailor must make conscious allowance for it. Some of the tubbier cruising boats are a good deal more touchy about staying than the average dinghy, and if they are not to be got into irons the helmsman (and the foresail hand) must do his work with a certain amount of tact. The foresail will very likely be bigger than a dinghy's, so there is all the more reason to sheet it home for the new tack in the brief period while the boat is head to wind and it is flogging idly; but brief though this period may be, any dinghy sailor will find it plenty long enough in comparison with the sort of thing he's been used to.

Because tubby cruising boats can be fairly easily got into irons, especially in short, choppy seas which tend to take way off, the helmsman may find that he has to make a stern board more often than he would with a dinghy. The situation itself is no different, but at a slightly greater remove from the water the realization that the boat is moving backward and that tiller movements must be reversed, may be a little longer in coming. It is surprising how even with a very slight drift astern the correct (reverse) use of the rudder will bring a boat's head round, so don't delay in taking the correct action.

Heavier boats . . . bigger forces

If one has been doing a great deal of dinghy sailing it is quite easy to overlook the rather obvious fact that in a boat which may weigh a couple of tons or more the forces involved are very much bigger. If you come alongside a quay with a bit too much way on you may not be able to rely on the shock-absorbing power of a leg stuck over the side to make up for your error of judgement. Your wife may be able to snatch up the mooring buoy even if you do approach too fast, but whether she will be able to take all the way off a heavy boat before she dislocates an arm or tumbles into the water is another matter. In a dinghy muscle power can handle a good many situations which in a bigger boat can only be solved by the skilful use of wind, tide, engine power, or the stored energy in the momentum of the vessel herself.

Likewise, if your cruising boat has a centre-plate you will be wise if you take care not to bump it too violently on sand or shingle. A centre-plate can be a useful warning device, just as it can in a dinghy, but if it is a steel one and there is any sort of a sea running it may bend more easily than you thought when it checks the combined rolling and leeway of several tons of boat. The forces are so much greater.

The contrast between dinghy and big boat will be even more marked if you happen to run aground in a boat with a fixed keel. Even if the water is shallow enough to stand in, it is unlikely that muscle power will be enough to dislodge the boat from the nice little bed she has made for her keel. Until the water lifts her you'll very probably be able to make no effect upon her at all. If the tide is still making, you will soon be free (as long as you don't allow yourself to be blown farther and farther on as the water rises). But if the tide is ebbing, then your best chance is likely to be one or two nice big waves, perhaps the wash of a passing boat, which may free the boat for a few seconds—long enough, maybe, for you to get her a foot or two off the bank.

If our imaginary dinghy enthusiast should go in for something really big and heavy— one of those bluff-bowed Dutchmen, perhaps, which will make such a pleasant week-end home for the whole family—then the time lag in manœuvring will be a thing demanding careful attention. With a big craft of that kind there is a considerable interval between putting over the helm and the moment when the boat begins to change her course. Conversely the helm must be centred again when the bows have still to swing through another 20 deg. perhaps, before coming on to the new course. Turning a boat of that kind is a long process and decisions must be made in good time.

But in spite of the slowing down of the action there is something particularly satisfying about the motion of a bigger boat and about her response to the helm and the sheets. One has a different kind of sailing, with its own appeal. The lift of the boat to the sea seems stately and purposeful by comparison with the scudding and darting about of a dinghy. To watch the rise and fall of the bows, to be able to walk along the deck and look down into the cockpit: to go right forward and look down at the stem as it curls the foam aside, and then to look aft and see so much boat following you brings a new feeling of independence from the rest of the world. Your world now consists of your boat, the sea, and the sky.

Your boat is your home, too, and for the time being at least your whole fortune is tied up in her. As you sail and the boat lifts to the seas, life aboard goes on in a more or less normal way (whether more or whether less will depend to a large extent upon the motion of the boat and the sensitivity of the crew's stomachs). But while it does remain normal there will be excursions below to brew up, and to bring meals to the cockpit. Someone may be spinning for mackerel; mother may be washing clothes in a bowl in the cockpit, with the idea of drying them out from the shrouds before you get into the night's port. But the ordinary chores seem lighter than they do ashore—they even seem to have a certain attraction when they are done against the background of a sunlit sea.

Unfortunately the sea is not always sunlit and there are days when passages are made in driving rain—much wetter and more penetrating at sea than ashore—and there are others when the wind is cold, the sky is a layer of grey mist not far above the truck and the sea seems to be malevolently waiting for a chance to make you look foolish. But if you weren't prepared for that sort of thing you would never have taken up sailing in the first place.

Children in cruisers

Most children take naturally to boats and water, but their pleasures tend to be small-scale. Their fun is in the dinghy, or in a folding canoe if you have room to stow one aboard, pottering about the beach or the shallows. On a passage of more than a few hours children can quickly become disinterested, and they may even lie on their bunks reading books, emerging only for something really dramatic, such as a surfacing submarine, a school of porpoises or a tanker on fire. In bad weather children cooped up below decks demand special measures. It is worth keeping a variety of amusements aboard—playing cards, a travelling chess set, plenty of paper-backed books (especially some funnies), drawing materials and so forth. For those who take to fishing there is no problem. Bird-watching and identification is a rewarding pastime for all members of the crew, and the sea-birds are one of the especial pleasures of a waterborne life. Bird books are an obvious item on the inventory. References to yacht-club burgees and the house flags of the steamship lines are also worth while.

Although I would never take a child boating until it could swim competently, the ability to swim is not a sufficient safeguard. With small children the boat herself must be well equipped with rails or guard-wires, and the child should have a harness and its own personal lifeline. Children in dinghies should always wear life-jackets, and they should wear them, too, on passage, especially if they are to move about on deck.

Seasickness can make life a misery for children and adults alike. It seems to be an affliction that the body can gradually master if one is on board for more than two or three days at a stretch. Some people feel sick the first day out—others only when there is an early-morning start. Fortunately there are now drugs available which make one's stomach insensitive to motion. Hyoscine seems to be the most reliable to judge from the tests made by the Royal Marines and the Royal Navy. My experience, both personally and with members of my family, has been that hyoscine is effective. It is used in various proprietary pills, of which Kwells are probably the best known.

But generally children thrive on a boating life, with swimming, fishing, sailing the dinghy, or rowing ashore to fetch milk and water. And in the evening, if it's too cold to sit in the cockpit and watch the curlews and herons flying home to roost, there's no place so snug and friendly as the cabin of a small boat. I like the soft light of an oil lamp, even though I admit that a few battery-powered lamps are useful, especially over the galley stove. Still, with comfortable cushions, a bit of carpet on the cabin floor-boards, cream paint and varnished wood gleaming in the mellow light of the oil lamp, and the water lapping gently outside, the tranquillity of your own cabin is the best antidote to the cares of the modern world.

In effect a small cruising boat becomes your week-end cottage, and even if you cannot go far in miles between Friday evening and Monday morning, no place on earth can be so remote in spirit from the jangling pressure of working life. Bacon and eggs never smelled so good as they do on the water on a summer morning, when the sun is silvering the wavelets and you can just begin to feel his warmth.

Perhaps because she is your temporary home, perhaps because you are now part of the coastwise sea traffic, or perhaps because you are going to be on board for so much longer than one normally is on a dinghy, you will find a deeper involvement with your boat. One goes aboard a dinghy to *sail*, but one goes aboard a cruising boat to *live*. Sailing becomes a part of day-to-day life, not something separate like an excursion to the theatre or the tennis court, to be followed by a return to conventional shorebound life.

You are now more deeply concerned with tides and weather, the supply of milk and fresh water, the rule of the road, cooking and washing-up, anchoring and mooring, tracking down and stopping leaks in the deck, remedies for seasickness, running repairs, as well as sailing. In all these things you are very much more on your own. You must be equipped to give first-aid to either boat or crew when you are several days away from your home base. The man who has been used to racing will no longer be able to think of the rule of the road as something which can be chewed over later in the day before a protest committee; for a cruising boat the Collision Regulations are a means of keeping out of serious trouble, not a tactical weapon for putting it across the other chap. If he is sensible the skipper of a cruising boat makes all his manœuvres with a good margin of safety, for the consequences of a collision may be serious; and there may be legal consequences as well as physical ones. With the current rapid growth in the number of boats of all kinds the strict and intelligent observation of the Collision

Regulations has become all the more important, and for that reason I have given the subject a chapter of its own (page 73).

There is nothing difficult or onerous about them, and for a cruising skipper they become merely a routine part of sailing, but they must be known and obeyed. Like the sailing of the boat herself, they are part of the basic knowledge which forms the foundations for a boating way of life. When you go aboard on Friday evening it may be for a passage to France, or it may be merely for a pottering week-end with a visit to a nearby bathing beach, but whether the trip be long or short the basic knowledge by which it is achieved is just the same.

In point of fact that knowledge comprises quite a number of things. It is a store to which one is always adding, and in the following chapters I shall try to pass on some of the items which have accumulated from my own mistakes, during a lifetime of messing about in boats, both large and small.

2

On from dinghies, but not good-bye to dinghies

There are dinghies and dinghies.

Arbitrarily and conveniently one can divide them into two main groups: there are the dinghies which are pleasure boats in their own right, and there are the dinghies which are boats' tenders. The boat's tender type of dinghy is heavy in relation to her sail area (if any), and her beaminess makes her stiff and stable. She is designed to carry as much as possible within her waterline length, not to go as fast as possible. Her ancestor is the small open fishing or general-purpose boat.

The other kind of dinghy, which includes a wide variety of designs from Heron to Firefly, and from GP-14 to 14 ft. National, belongs to a large branch of the dinghy family whose ancestry in general is associated with racing and whose ancestors in particular were those 14 ft. Nationals which were unleashed by Uffa Fox on to a surprised world in about 1927. Usually these dinghies are too tender to be used as tenders (oh these nautical terms!), and they are not good load carriers for their length. A tender has to be as small and as light as possible, so that she can be hauled up and down the hard and perhaps be stowed on deck. At the same time you want her to carry heavy loads, and not to put her gunwale under when your guests come aboard with an ill-placed foot, so a yacht's dinghy has to be beamier and more stable than the other kind of dinghy.

Moreover, the dinghy that sails well is not likely to tow happily, and that is very important. Apart from being able to carry the necessary loads with stability, there is nothing so important in a yacht's tender as sober and steady behaviour while being towed. For that virtue, rather blunt and buoyant bows that rise up well and tend to lift over the seas are much better than narrow, straight-sided bows that tend to dig in and make a towed dinghy yaw from side to side. One knows those boats which, if they must be towed, are best towed stern-first; obviously that is not the kind of boat to drag behind you on a lumpy sea passage.

But there's no reason why a boat's tender should not be able to sail. She won't be a star performer, but if she can be sailed she will give a good deal of pleasure in the exploration of the shallower waters of one's various ports of call. In places like the River Dart or Poole Harbour, for example, there are wonderful opportunities for an evening's pottering in the 'ship's boat' if she is rigged even with a simple lug.

And if there are children among your crew, it is even more desirable that the ship's tender shall be sailable. It is easy to overestimate the amount of satisfaction that the children will derive from a cruising holiday, and the more that you can find for them to do the better. A dinghy in which they can potter about in perfect safety (they must be able to swim, of course, and they must also wear life-jackets) provides excellent training as well as a lot of fun.

Quite apart from the amusement which can be had from a tender with a sail, it can be of practical value in some harbours; going ashore for petrol and water can sometimes be a long and tedious pull, but it becomes a stimulating excursion when it is done under sail.

Wangling with one oar

Whether under sail or not, the oars and rowlock crutches must always be in the dinghy, of course. The particular bee that I have in my own bonnet is that one should have two pairs of each. Bucking wind and tide with the kind of load that most people seem to put aboard even for a few days is much easier with two people pulling. Moreover, with two pairs of oars and two pairs of rowlocks one is always better prepared for the day when one of either goes adrift. If children use the dinghy for their own amusement, it is even more important that there should be spares aboard: even if they are practised in wangling with a single oar over the stern, they are not likely to make much headway by that means if there is any sort of wind or current heading the boat.

Wangling, or sculling, with a single oar over the stern, is something that everyone ought to learn to do, especially if you carry only one pair of oars or rowlocks. Every boat's tender should have a notch cut in the transom for the purpose. The motion is a side-to-side one, and there is a corresponding tendency on the part of the dinghy herself to waggle from side to side in opposition. Dinghies of 10 ft. long or more have sufficient grip in the water to keep fairly steady, but the short tubby dinghies that so many of us have to use are not really well suited to this form of propulsion. Still, you can make them go when you have only one oar; and it's useful in crowded harbours, where there's sometimes not space enough to pull two oars in the normal way.

The knack of wangling depends upon two simple things: first, a clear conception of the kind of motion you want to impart to the blade; and second, the correct position of the hand on the loom of the oar. The hand comes to the oar from below, with the wrist and forearm below the hand. With one or both hands in this position, the right motion follows almost automatically. Clearly, the oar must be twisted at the end of each stroke, so that the leading edge on the next stroke will be slanting forward. As soon as you get the knack of turning the wrist at the end of each stroke so as to make the oar bite into the water on the next one, you will feel it pushing down into the notch and driving the boat forward.

If the angle of the blade is the same for both directions of stroke, the boat will go straight: but she can easily be turned by using a large amount of twist to the blade when it is moving in one direction and a smaller amount in the other.

The same method of propulsion can be applied to boats up to several tons, using a long and slightly flexible sweep from a standing position in the cockpit. In that case the sweep and its pivot are designed in such a way that the change in angle comes on almost entirely automatically; it is no longer a matter of a twist of the wrist but simply of pushing and pulling the loom athwartships.

But most people who go on cruising rely upon an auxiliary engine to do the work that would have been done in the past by a sweep, and although a sweep can have its uses it *is* rather cumbersome to carry aboard a small boat.

Outboard motors: safety precautions

Although it is generally admitted that an auxiliary engine is the sensible thing for a cruising boat herself, it does not necessarily follow that every tender must have her outboard motor. Unless you have moorings which are a very long way from the shore, or where the tidal current is very severe, it hardly seems worth the expense and extra weight involved. I suspect that a good many people decide to invest in an outboard motor simply because they have not woken up to the fact that it is senseless to have only one man pulling a dinghy which is carrying a couple of passengers as well as a load of stores. If there is only one man aboard then the load will be light: if there are more, then *two* should be pulling.

But if you do think that you need an outboard motor for your tender, please don't start off with the idea that it will necessarily cause you a great deal of trouble. Although my own experience of outboard motors is limited to only a few makes, and mainly to one (British Seagull), I am inclined to take the view that the main trouble with out-boards is the people who own them. The kind of outboard one uses for a small dinghy is nearly always a two-stroke, and as with other two-strokes there are two rules which must be followed: the first is to use exactly the mixture of oil and petrol that the maker tells you to use; the second is to keep the sparking plug in good condition. Always have a new plug and a plug spanner to hand: check the cleanliness of the plug and re-set the gap at frequent intervals. Following those two rules, and keeping the motor reasonably clean and dry, I have always had service from my Seagulls whenever it was demanded of them. But although I have always looked upon them as good friends, I have often wished, as with some other friends, that they could be a little quieter.

In using an outboard motor, I would stress two safety precautions. The first is for the motor itself; it always seems sensible to me to keep a short safety line attached to the motor with its other end made fast inside the boat. This can be of chain, wire or rope, but it should be as short as possible so that if for any reason the motor slips from your hands, or even jumps from its bracket, it cannot go far—and certainly not below the surface. Actually a motor which undergoes an immersion of only a few seconds is unlikely to suffer much, and it will probably run quite normally as soon as the area round the plug and the high-tension lead has been dried off. Even so there is a risk of corrosion, and if salt water has penetrated to the magneto it will leave some salt behind, and that will always collect moisture—not a good thing for any electrical device. The most sensible course is to ensure that the outboard cannot suffer a ducking.

The second precaution concerns the danger to people—from the propeller. It is surprising how easily this rather obvious danger can be overlooked; I have even seen a man driving an outboard-powered dinghy with a couple of children in bathing suits hanging on to the gunwales. Great fun, of course, but the chance that a foot should stray towards the spinning, sharp-edged screw is more than negligible, quite apart from the fact that one of these 'outside passengers' might lose hold altogether, slip under the boat and aft into the works. Somehow, people seem more conscious of the danger of the screw in a bigger boat, while the same danger from an outboard seems to be forgotten.

Any kind of boating seems to involve the risk of a fair number of bumps and bruises, but one might as well avoid as many as one can, so it is a good idea to warn wives and families not to put their fingers over the gunwale of the dinghy when coming alongside.

Problems with dinghies

When cruising it is better to bring the dinghy on board than to tow her. But like so many good ideas this is easier to say than to do. It is a matter of observation that most boats, up to the size of 5- or 6-tonners, tow their dinghies: there's no room on board to stow them. True there are the excellent Prout folding dinghies, but even when folded they still take up quite a bit of length. Even a folded dinghy lying along the deck of a small cruiser is likely to snag a foresail sheet or make a nuisance of herself in some other way. Some hardy yachtsmen will shove a folding dinghy down into the cabin, but even if the thing is dried and cleaned with the greatest care, it is not a method of stowage that is likely to meet with the approval of wives and families.

And then there are the pneumatic dinghies which can be deflated and rolled up. It always seems to me that they tow so lightly that it's not often worth going to the trouble of squeezing the air out of them, drying off and bringing aboard. Another reason for leaving an inflated dinghy in the water is that she is the only kind of small yacht's tender that is any use as a life-boat in the conditions where a life-boat might be needed. She will remain buoyant even when swamped and as long as you could hang on somehow you could expect to remain afloat. The rubber boat also has the advantage that she is her own shock absorber. You could watch her being driven into the stern of your boat by a following sea without the least concern: at night her silent nudging would cost no loss of sleep.

The rubber dinghy is easy to maintain, light to carry ashore and down to the water again, and she can be packed up and stowed on board or in the boot of the car, without much trouble. For a non-sailing tender all logic points to the use of an inflated boat ... unless one cares about the look of the thing. So hidebound can one be, I am bound to admit, that the second reason alone may well be enough to prevent me from ever doing the logical thing. Until their designers can make inflated dinghies look like boats I can't see myself using one: but that does not stop anyone else from doing the sensible thing!

As a matter of fact, observation of the boats around me leads me to suppose that many other people are of the same mind. The fact is that many of the smaller cruisers drag their dinghies behind them. Squat prams for the most part, modern tenders do what is asked of them and tow well. They do not swamp easily and they do not over-turn. All the same, the oars and rowlocks, which should always be in the dinghy at sea, should be firmly lashed in place. It would be bad enough to have a swamped or overturned dinghy, without losing oars and rowlocks into the bargain. If such a thing should happen, it will almost certainly be in, and due to, big seas, with the consequence that you may be unable to right the dinghy and empty her. Except in dead calm, towing a capsized dinghy is such a burden that even if the painters don't part of their own accord you will be obliged to cast them off so as to keep reasonable control of your own craft.

But with modern prams the likelihood is not so much of the dinghy swamping and capsizing as of an oar being simply rolled or bounced out of the boat in a lively sea (and even on a calm day the steep-fronted wake from a passing steamer is a possible cause). The rowlocks should be already secured by their lanyards; the oars can be most easily secured by lashings made of elastic cord with an eye at one end, and a toggle at the other. This kind of lashing, by the way, can be used for all sorts of jobs on board; it is quick to put on or take off, and it won't work loose. I think I am right in saying that the idea is due to the well-known yacht chandlers in Chichester, the Bosun's Locker; at least, they were the first people to offer them for sale, as far as I know. But anyone can so easily make them for himself that I suppose the unfortunate originator can only hope that he will get his reward in heaven. The bailer, too, should always be in the dinghy, secured by a lanyard.

It is a good thing always to tow a dinghy by two painters. I decided that I would always do so after the occasion when my own dinghy broke away on a calm summer's day, an escape which would have gone unnoticed by anyone on board had not the crew of a passing freighter made an altogether out of the ordinary chorus of whistles and yells, accompanied by a suitable pantomime. Because it was a calm sea and the dinghy was still in sight, she was easily retrieved.

The significant thing about that particular loss was that the painter was absolutely sound, *and* it was properly made fast. It was the ring bolt in the stem of the dinghy herself that parted, at a point about an inch inside the wood. As far as one could see from an external inspection there was nothing at all wrong with it, but the pleasant lop of a Force 3 day was enough to part it. It had probably been maltreated when it was being fitted.

Although I decided after that incident always to use two painters when at sea (made fast to different points of both dinghy and boat), I was less cautious in harbours and estuaries. But the next time I lost my dinghy was inside Chichester harbour, on a pitch-dark night. We had come aboard at dusk and were moving down to the entrance with the idea of catching the tide westward early the next morning. This time it was the painter itself that parted (probably due to fretting on the trot during the previous two or three weeks). Of course, one can't find a dinghy, even inside Chichester harbour, on a pitch-dark night, and by the time we had recovered her the next morning we had missed our tide. Following that incident, I had two precepts to follow:

1. Use two painters at sea. 2. Use two painters at night.

It seemed simpler all round to substitute the single rule of using two painters all the time attached to two separate points on the dinghy. The practice has the slight additional advantage that if there are two painters to be made fast as a matter of course, there is less likelihood that the tender will be left behind simply because the last person to come aboard didn't make fast properly. (That, by the way, I firmly believe to be the most common cause of a dinghy going adrift. There can be hardly anyone to whom it has not happened at some time or other.)

The only disadvantage to using two painters is that there are two of them to shorten up before going astern under power; and that raises a very important point. A helmsman must train himself so that it is second nature never to put the engine into reverse without making sure that the painters are not long enough to allow a bight of rope to be drawn down to the screw. When a rope does get wound on to a prop shaft it seizes so tightly that it usually takes a long time to clear. Traditionally a very sharp knife, or even a hacksaw, must be taken to it in a series of necessarily short underwater sorties. My only personal experience is with the knife method, but a correspondent in *Yachting Monthly* has said that a rope will usually come free if one member can get hold of the end and pull steadily, while another turns the prop shaft slowly in an *unwinding* direction. In other words, if the rope was tangled while the screw was running astern the shaft could be turned over by engaging 'ahead' and turning the engine over with the starting handle. Remember to switch off, or disconnect the plugs, so that the engine can't fire. This certainly seems a sensible suggestion that would be worth trying before beginning a process of submarine surgery.

By the way, if you have to go down to the screw, remember that it is dangerous to swim under the stern of a boat if there is even a small sea running. A couple of tons of boat rising and falling on quite small waves can give you a very sharp crack on the head (I know). The danger is not so much of a cracked skull, as of a temporary loss of consciousness and control, with the consequent possibility of being carried away and drowned. A lifeline is a sensible precaution if you do have to go over where it is too deep to stand.

Cure for insomnia

Dinghies go bump in the night. They do it persistently, determined not to let you sleep, and apart from the nuisance the constant banging against the stern of your boat is good for neither craft. Some people suggest hanging a bucket over the stern of the dinghy, so that the tide will drag her off; but the banging is usually worst at the slack of the tide. On bigger boats you can rig a spar over the side, and haul the dinghy 10 or 12 ft. off, where she is well out of reach. But for a small boat the best method of ensuring a quiet night, if you can't bring her on deck, is to moor her alongside, fore and aft. Make sure you have plenty of fenders between the two craft, and then don't give the dinghy more than about an inch of scope. If she can't move far away she can't get up any speed for the return assault.

Nothing to do with tenders, but definitely to do with sleep: keep your halyards clear of the mast. Their slapping will keep people awake and it will also wear the varnish off the spar. If you have an aluminium mast, please remember other people and lash your halyards clear when you leave your boat on her mooring: the sound of halyards clattering against a metal mast is depressing or irritating, or both, as it carries across what might otherwise be a peaceful stretch of water.

The dinghy dilemma

When you come to choosing a dinghy for a tender you will have a wide variety from which to choose. In general the bluff-bowed are the better for towing, and even if you have a boat which is big enough to take the dinghy aboard, the pram style still takes up the least length for a given carrying capacity. A stem dinghy is better for rowing and sailing, but to get her to tow well you will probably have to take special steps to keep her bows well up in the water. The towing eye must be as low down on the stem as is feasible, so that the painter lifts as it pulls; even then you may have to stow something weighty in the stern sheets to make her sit down aft.

Among the bluff-bowed dinghies there are three main kinds from which you can choose. There is the traditional pram, clinker-built, strong, rather heavy, with a slab-flat bow. You get those good qualities for a price which is lower than at least two of the other kinds, but you have a drawback common to all clinker boats—the extra work of scraping around all those lands and frames when she has to be revarnished.

The slab-sided, plywood version of the traditional pram is much easier to maintain, because one is dealing with large relatively flat uninterrupted areas. She will be lighter than the clinker-built boat, just as cheap, and equally strong; but she suffers aesthetically.

Moulded hulls in plastics or wood laminations are able to offer a rounded form of the blunt bow, instead of the flat slab of the clinker or plywood boat. With plastics, maintenance should be almost nil: weight and strength are high, and so is the price, relatively speaking. The moulded wood boat, such as the Fairey Duckling or the Souter Penguin, is directly comparable with the plastics boat in price, weight and strength. A good many people would say that moulded wood looks better, but if they want those better looks then they will have to accept the work involved in rubbing down and varnishing from time to time.

A few years ago I felt that the inflatable would prove to be the most popular form of tender for cruising boats, and these 'bags of wind' did in fact become widely used.

New Materials

But more recently a form of 'plastic' boat of very light weight and low cost has come into being. This results from the development of foamed or cellular polystyrene not unlike the packaging material used for china, glass, delicate instruments and the like. The hull that results from the use of the material is inherently buoyant, and as the publicity men delight to show it does not even matter if a boat of this type is cut into two halves—each portion will continue to float quite nicely and to support a good load.

The first polystyrene boats have certainly not been elegant, nor have they all been structurally sound. Though most of these boats have had sufficient strength when new, a few have suffered breakage, and the worrying thing is the lack of predictability about the material's performance. There are ways of enhancing the strength of which the first to show its effectiveness was an outer sheath of some material compatible with the polystyrene. But though such steps solved the problem of strength, they seem always to involve rather large penalties in cost and weight—cost especially. Thus the special merit of cheapness and light weight begins to disappear and one may finish up with a boat almost as heavy and almost as costly as a more durable craft built in conventional materials.

At the time of writing we are in the very early stages of using low density materials for hulls, and it is more than likely that superior materials will be formulated in the laboratory, or that polystyrene itself may have its characteristics improved by more sophisticated moulding methods. It is too early to say, but the inherent qualities of a low density material are such that it is obviously a worthy aim to pursue its development.

While developments may continue in polystyrene and similar materials, advances are also taking place in inflatables, where the rigid-bottomed boat with inflatable sides now seems to have a good future. But the now-conventional polyester resin reinforced with glass fibre is probably going to hold its place for a good many years yet because although heavy it is a durable material which requires little maintenance. Nevertheless, complete neglect is not to be advised, especially in winter when an exposed boat can be seriously damaged by water which gains entry into fine cracks in the gel coating and then freezes.

One merit of resinglass dinghies is that they usually have built-in buoyancy, and that is a very valuable thing. Any yacht's tender is the better for extra buoyancy; it is surprising how many accidents there have been with dinghies, perhaps due to a slip or the careless placing of weight when stepping aboard, or perhaps due to overloading so that there is too little freeboard in choppy water. At night, returning aboard from a party ashore, the risks of overloading and swamping seem to be greater, perhaps because people are then in a happier and more careless mood. As with other kinds of dinghy, the rule in such cases is to hang on to the boat, so if she has buoyancy so much the better.

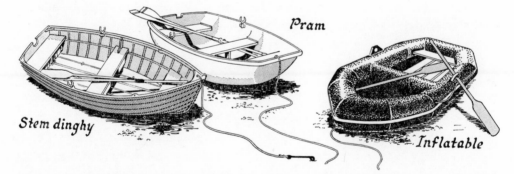

Figure 1. The clinker-built stem dinghy is probably the prettiest of all, but she takes a bit of looking after. The pram carries almost as much in a shorter length and tows better. The inflatable is lightest, can offer emergency buoyancy, and can be stowed in a locker, but does not give the pleasure of performance of a real boat.

A few other points: it is worth putting a strip of brass along the skeg of your tender, if the builder did not do so, otherwise it will wear very quickly from being repeatedly beached. Remember to paint the name of your vessel and your home port, or club, clearly on the tender: insurance companies usually require it. Since people sometimes 'borrow' other people's oars, you may find it worth while to paint yours with a bold and distinctive colour scheme: it discourages borrowers and helps you to spot your property if the discouragement fails. Every tender should have an all-round fender. This can be of the proprietary rubber kind, which is rather expensive, or you can make your own out of old garden hose covered in canvas—a cheap way if you happen to have some hose and suitable scraps of canvas.

Another very common method is to use a 6-in. grass rope. Traditionally this is 'stitched' to the gunwale with copper wire, which is passed *through* the rope and through holes drilled at either side of the frames. Obviously the wire must not go round the outside of the rope, or it will be likely to scratch your topsides. Personally I find that stout tarred twine is much more durable for this job than copper wire, and it can safely be taken right round the rope.

One disadvantage of the grass rope is that it holds a great weight of water, and moreover the surface begins to rot after a couple of seasons of constant wetting. When that happens it begins to make brown marks wherever the dinghy rubs against the topsides, even though the rope itself has several more seasons of useful life in it.

3

Navigation: equipment, tides and soundings

The problems of navigation and pilotage account for more than a small part of the pleasure and interest of cruising. Even though a passage may be no more than 20 or 30 miles, there is a great deal of satisfaction to be had from the efficient (more or less as the case may be!) completion of the various processes involved—finding one's way, using the tides, avoiding the various dangers and obstructions. For the dinghy sailor who has been used to racing the natural problems of passage-making may provide a stimulus to replace the challenge formerly provided by his human opponents.

For simple coastwise navigation the equipment that is required is quite modest: celestial navigation, on the other hand, demands a sextant, which is rather a costly instrument. One also needs astronomical tables, one of the excellent books of simplified methods which are now available, and a good deal of practice. For most people who start cruising, celestial navigation is something to be deferred for separate study at some future time when it will really be needed. It certainly is not needed by the majority of cruising skippers, and it is quite true that it forms a study in itself, because it is not a thing that one can tackle bit by bit. One needs the equipment, the tables and the practice all together to make any headway. The most important thing is to get the practice; but that demands the equipment, so that the real reason for deferment is the natural unwillingness to lay out about £50 or £60 on a sextant until there is some likelihood that it will really be needed.

So if we confine ourselves to coastal pilotage and dead-reckoning navigation, the minimum items of equipment are:

a watch or clock;
a chart of the appropriate area;
a pilot book;
a compass;
a 360 deg. protractor (preferably with pivoted arm);
a tide table for Dover (or some convenient standard port);

C

pencils and means of drawing straight lines;
a lead line.

That list represents the minimum. That there are various items which can be added to it goes without saying, and there are two in particular which I personally would add, because I consider them to be especially valuable. They are:

a pair of binoculars, and
a second compass for taking bearings of objects ashore.

In the standard textbooks of the past one will always find that a pair of parallel rulers is prescribed, but a more cumbersome device for use in a small boat it would be difficult to find, nor one more likely to lead either to errors or to exasperation. A 360 deg. protractor with square edges (such as the Douglas protractor) or a circular one which has north–south parallel lines scored on it (easily added to any ordinary circular protractor) is very much more accurate and much easier to use. I shall come back to this kind of protractor in Chapter 5.

Just as I omit the parallel rules from my minimum list, so I omit the tidal atlas. Tidal atlases show the direction and speed of tidal streams hour by hour; there are several of them, each of which covers its own particular area (Thames Estuary, English Channel, North Sea, etc.). They *are* very good, and I am not suggesting for a minute that you should *not* have them: on the other hand, they are not on my minimum list because you can get charts which include the necessary tidal information. Although it is not so extensive and detailed as that in the tidal atlases, it is usually adequate for the kind of navigation that the average cruising yachtsman is likely to do. Reed's Almanac contains a great deal of tidal information and, though not on the minimum list, is worth having aboard.

The charts which I have in mind are Stanford's: not only do they have the necessary tidal information, but they have a great deal of other useful information. For example, they have inset charts (at a larger scale) of all the creeks and harbours one might want to use in the area covered by the main chart itself. Take, for example, the chart *The English Channel from Start Point to Land's End*. This covers the coasts of Devon and Cornwall, from Dartmouth westward to Land's End and back on the northern shores as far as the River Camel and Padstow. The tidal flows are shown by small inset diagrams for twelve successive hourly intervals (6 hours either side of H.W. Dover). The time of high tide (in relation to that of Dover) is shown for twenty-eight major places together with the tidal rises for those places at springs and at neaps. The areas of land and sea which would otherwise be blank spaces accommodate separate inset charts at larger scale for the following places:

Avon River	Erme River	Falmouth Harbour
Fowey	Helford River	Looe Bay
Longships Channel	Mevagissey	Mounts Bay
Newquay Bay	Padstow	Plymouth Harbour
St. Ives Bay	Salcombe	Yealm River

In short one has many charts for the price of one, and since charts are quite expensive that is a consideration of some weight. It is a common experience to have to use a port that one had no intention of visiting when the cruise was planned. In fact, the only sensible thing to do when starting a cruise is to take charts of all the places which come within the area of the intended cruising waters, whether one *plans* to visit them or not, as well as a few which are on the fringes. If it is going to be a matter of buying a separate chart for every place, then you either spend a lot of money, or you try to economize by buying only a few. I expect I shall be believed when I say that it is the one that was *not* bought that will turn out to be the very one that's wanted!

Apart from the saving in money, there is an advantage in a small boat in having fewer charts to stow. On the other hand, I must in fairness say that if one is willing to have a separate chart for each place, that each will be to a much bigger scale, will contain more detail and will be generally easier to use. The man who has a larger boat with a large chart table and plenty of space is less likely to count the cost of ten or a dozen extra charts.

In 1970 Stanfords started a new series of charts which have pilotage information on the back of the sheet. This gives virtually all the information one requires for coastal passage-making and for entering the various ports shown as insets on the front of the chart. In fact, a Stanfords chart can save one the cost of a pilot book, though I suspect that many owners like to collect more such books than they really need because there is the chance that some extra item of useful information may be gleaned.

I have perhaps plugged Stanfords a bit heavily, so I must point out that they are not available for all the places where one might want to go. They are primarily concerned with British home waters, and they cover only the most popular areas of those. Hence it is likely that people in less heavily populated areas will turn to the Admiralty charts which, of course, are of the highest quality. Some Admiralty charts are drawn specially for yachtsmen, but most are not. Personally I find the standard Admiralty charts less easy to follow than either Stanfords or the yachtsmen's charts produced by Imray's, but I suppose that it is a matter of personal taste.

To see what Admiralty charts are available ask your chart agent (or yacht chandler) for a copy of the Catalogue of Admiralty Charts (NP 91) Home Edition. (Unless you want charts for other parts of the world.) At the time of writing it still costs a shilling (5p.), and is well worth the money.

Tidal information

In this and the following chapters we will see what this minimum list of materials can do for us, beginning with the chart. Evidently the chart is a form of map showing the relationship of places to each other in a two-dimensional form, but to the yachtsman some of its most valuable information concerns the third dimension—the depth of the water. These soundings are dotted about appropriately and are normally shown in fathoms (6 ft.), though in harbour plans they are often shown in feet. This can be a source of confusion, and it is essential to make sure what unit is being used in a harbour plan, because in entering over the bar, using the sea chart one may have been reading the figures '1' or '2' as fathoms, yet inside the harbour, using a larger-scale chart the same figures may well mean 'feet', plain and simple. On one chart the figure '2' (fathoms) means that one has plenty of water in hand, but on the next one the figure '3' may mean that one is hard aground. There is the further complication of the gradual change to the metric system, with depths shown in metres.

The depth of water shown at a particular point on the chart is the depth at low water—in other words the least depth you may normally expect to find there. That statement requires more careful definition, because tidal ranges vary from week to week, with the spring tides rising higher and falling lower than the neap tides. (In practice a spring tide comes around about every two weeks, and so does the neap, so that it goes neaps, springs, neaps, springs . . . roughly week by week.)

Now the modern chart datum, from which measurements are made, is the level of the lowest astronomical spring tide. There is the possibility of a lower water level even than that, due perhaps to the effect of a sufficiently strong wind. But that is not predictable, whereas the effect of sun and moon is predictable and therefore appropriate to charts and tide tables.

It is necessary to give a word of warning on the matter of chart datum, because the level has been changed in recent years. In the past it used to be the level of *mean low water springs*, which is not so low as the *lowest astronomical tide* which is now used. This might be misleading if you were using a chart whose soundings were based on the old datum with tide tables based on the new. For example, the current chart datum on a modern chart might show 3 ft. low-water depth at a certain point. On the old chart, where low water was assumed not to be so low, it might show 4 ft. for the same place. From your tide table you see that the height (or rise) of tide for the day and hour is 6 ft. This means 'six feet above the three feet depth of chart datum', but looking at an old chart one might take it to mean 'six feet above the four feet depth' shown.

In practice all that this means is that one must be careful. Of course the fact that a modern chart shows the least depths one is normally likely to meet is a comforting thing.

By the way, I assume that you will use one of the complimentary tide-tables, which many yacht chandlers prepare as a service to their customer and as publicity for themselves. These are usually sufficient for the practical purposes of coastwise cruising, but sometimes the tidal heights are omitted, which is a definite disadvantage, because the heights are a quick guide to the likely strength of tidal streams as well as giving useful background information for estimating the depth of water over shoals and the likely rise and fall alongside a quay.

Even where the tide heights are given in such a table, they will be shown only for the port of reference; for example, a table of the time of high water at Dover will have the corresponding tide heights for that port. Now, the actual rise of tide is a thing peculiar to each port or part of the coast: at Weymouth, for example, the spring rise is 7·5 ft.; at Mevagissey it is 18 ft. The value of having the actual tidal rise on one's tide-table is that it gives a better idea of the 'spring-ishness' or 'neap-ishness' of the situation than one could get from the mere knowledge that spring tides occur twice a month, one or two days after the full and new moon respectively. Tidal heights are given in feet and tenths of feet, by the way. This is a practice that was adopted a long time before there was any thought of turning from feet to metres for British charts.

Although it can be useful to have a 'local' tide-table in which the times and heights are those of one's home port, it is better to have a tide-table for Dover, since Dover is the chief of the 'standard ports' for information about tides in British waters. Pilot books will give the times of local high tide as so many hours before (minus) or after (plus) high tide at a standard port, usually Dover. Tidal streams are shown by reference to Dover, too, so that if you want to find out when the tide sets westward off the Lizard you will find the Pilot says:

'In the offing the stream runs west from −0345 Dover until about +0130 Dover. The rate is 3 knots at springs just outside the rocks ¾ mile from shore . . .'
and so on. All this is quite regardless of the fact that we are several hundred miles from Dover, have never been there and have no intention of going there. Similarly, you may see a note on the chart which tells you that the best time to round Portland Bill, westbound, is 'between about ½ hour before High Water Dover to 2½ hours after High Water Dover . . .'. No reference is made to high water off the Bill, which is, in fact, about 4½ hours earlier than HW Dover. Even when giving tidal stream information for entering ports the Pilot usually relates the tide to HW Dover; here's an entry for New Grimsby, in the Scilly Isles:

'In New Grimsby Harbour the stream runs in from −0010 Dover to +0115 Dover; it then runs out for 3 hours, turns and runs in for 4½ hours, when it again turns and runs out until −0010 Dover.'

So the obvious thing to do is carry a Dover tide-table; as far as your own port is concerned you will soon become accustomed to making the necessary mental correction. When it comes to cruising, the correction will be changing as you move along the coast from place to place.

Depths on the chart

I seem to have wandered a bit from the subject I began with—reading depths of water from the chart—but the point is that chart and tide-table have to be used together to get an idea of the depth of water. Obviously you must also know the date and the time of day, not forgetting any correction that may be necessary to account for the difference between Greenwich Mean Time and British Summer Time. Apart from that you have to have a method for estimating the depth of water at some time between high and low water.

Suppose one is concerned with a point on the chart where the figure has a line under it thus 2, indicating that the place dries out 2 ft. above datum. Suppose also, to make it easy, that it happens to be a time of ordinary spring tides and that the Pilot shows the local tidal rise as 16·7 ft. The first deduction is that there will be 14·7 ft. over that point at high water, but you want to sail across 3 hours before high water, or at some other intermediate time. The rate of rise and fall of tide is not steady, and the greatest rate of rise usually occurs in the middle period, half-way between high and low water. The simple guide for estimating the amount the tide will have fallen in a given amount of time since high water is the 'twelfths' rule. This says that in the first hour the tide will fall by one-twelfth of its range; in the second hour by two-twelfths; in the third and fourth hours by three-twelfths; in the fifth hour by two-twelfths and in the sixth hour by one-twelfth. This can be set out more clearly like this:

HOUR	RISE OR FALL
First	1 twelfth
Second	2 twelfths
Third	3 twelfths
Fourth	3 twelfths
Fifth	2 twelfths
Sixth	1 twelfth

It will be seen that the middle two hours account for a total of six-twelfths, or one-half of the whole range. It may be a help to mental arithmetic if I remind you that there are twelve inches in a foot, so that one-twelfth of a range of 16·7 ft. is 16·7 in. On the other hand, if you are not attracted by the inherent arithmetical amusement to be afforded by this kind of problem, I suggest that you make use of the 'Rise and Fall of Tide' table in Reed's Almanac.

This table can also be helpful when it comes to anchoring, partly because one needs to know whether the boat will be aground at low water (which you may or may not want), and partly because it affects the scope of cable allowed (see Chapter 6). But before you can begin to work out depth of water, you need to understand the difference between the 'rise' and the 'range' of the tide. Whereas you can easily work out the depth of water at springs by applying the 'twelfths' rule to the rise, this does not work for neaps, or for any time between. To understand this one must examine the diagram shown in Figure 2.

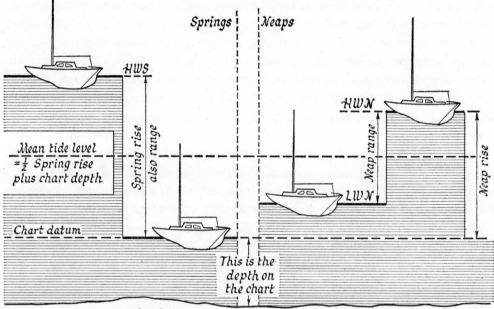

Figure 2. *A diagrammatic explanation of the meanings of tidal terms. Confusion often arises between the 'rise' and the 'range' of the tide, and as the drawing shows the two terms represent the same quantity only at full springs. At all other times there is a difference depending on the level of mean low water springs.*

The first point to note is that a neap tide does not drop as low as a spring tide. But, because the chart is marked with the figures for low water *springs*, the tidal rise is always shown as so many feet above datum. So the rise for high water neaps is not measured as so many feet above low water neaps, but above low water springs. In consequence the neap *rise* is a larger figure than the water actually rises: the real rise and fall of the water is distinguished by the term *range*. The *rise* is usually the important figure, because it allows you to calculate the depth of water from the datum point marked on the chart: the range, on the other hand, would be of significance if you were alongside a quay and wanted to get some idea of the amount of slack to allow in your warps and breast-ropes.

This business of rise and range can be a little confusing at first, but one is nearly always concerned with the rise, which is often called 'height' on tide-tables. 'Rise' and 'height' are often used as if they were interchangeable, though strictly speaking the 'rise' is the height at high water, whereas 'height' applies to any time. In practice it makes no odds, but the fact that there are two terms is confusing. The depth of water at high tide (neaps or spring) is found by adding the *rise* or *height* to the depth shown on the chart. For a date between neaps and springs it is necessary to estimate the proportional change. The time between springs and neaps is about 6 or 7 days (you can check from your tide-table), and it is not too difficult to estimate whether it is half-way between, or quarter or any other fraction.

One thing that may have become apparent from Figure 2 is that although the chart shows the depth of water at LW springs there is no immediate guide to the depth at LW neaps. The neap rise shows how far high tide will be above LWS, but it does not show how far LWN will be above LWS. If you need to know the answer, you can work it out. On the left of Figure 2 is a note concerning the 'mean level'. Notice that this average line goes right through the middle of the spring and neap ranges, and in each case the tide goes as far below the line as it goes above. It is a fair assumption to say that low water neaps will be as far below it as high water neaps is above.

The mean level can be found by halving the spring rise and adding that figure to the chart depth. You know the level for high water neaps (neaps rise plus chart depth), and if this is 3 ft. above the *mean level* you assume that LWN will be 3 ft. below *mean level*.

Thus if there is a point marked on the chart as 5 ft. and the springs rise is 18 ft., the mean level is $5+9=14$ ft. Then if the neaps rise is 13 ft., the depth at HWN will be $5+13=18$ ft.: this is 4 ft. above the mean level, so the depth at LWN will be $14-4=10$ ft. If you have a Reed's Almanac you can avoid working out the mean level, at least for some places, because it is shown in the 'Tidal Difference' tables.

In writing all this I have been conscious of the fact that it is all very tedious to follow, and that in any case there are thousands of people who cruise in small boats and never give a thought to rise and range. In real life one normally works on estimates which are on the safe side: if there's enough water to float you at LWS, then you'll be all right at LWN, and that's all there is to it. On the other hand, one can be misled by this business of *rise* and *range*, and the only way to get it clear in one's head is to work out one or two imaginary examples. A little exercise with the figures brings a certain familiarity; for example, it will become apparent that the neaps range is twice the difference between the mean level and the neaps rise. This is useful, because pilot books often give a figure for the mean level, as well as for the neap and spring rises.

Another way to find the neap range is to subtract the neaps rise from the spring rise, and then to subtract the answer from the neaps rise. Study of Figure 2 will show why that is so: the difference between the neaps range and the neaps rise is the same as the difference between LW neaps and LW springs. At least, it is approximately the same, though, in fact, the tide does not rise and fall in a perfectly mathematical manner. For one thing the wind has a very great effect, so that a westerly gale blowing up-channel, for example, causes higher tides at the eastern end and also prolongs the period of high water and delays the beginning of the ebb.

So all in all, these subtleties about tidal rise and range want to be taken with a pinch of salt. Know of their existence and then you can more or less forget them!

4

Pilotage: buoys and lights

Apart from indicating shoals, rocks and such dangers as submerged wrecks, remnants of piers and sewage outfall pipes, the main obvious use of a chart is to indicate the way from one place to another. Within harbours and estuaries the chart shows how the channels wind between the mudbanks, and to follow it is rather like map-reading on land. The difference is that you cannot see the actual lie of the land beneath the water, and that the appearance of what you can see changes so much with the rise and fall of the tide. Fortunately, one is helped by buoys and beacons of various kinds—and they certainly can be *various*: it often takes a bit of intelligence and imagination on the part of a cruising skipper to make out the significance of the withies, beacons and stakes, and buoys of various shapes and colours in the smaller, non-commercial harbours and estuaries. But since these places *are* non-commercial, and since the least commercialized are the most enjoyable to visit, one can only be thankful to those kind and thoughtful souls who use their limited means and time to provide some kind of indication to visiting yachtsmen.

In British home waters the system of buoyage is based on the idea that one *leaves* a buoy on one hand or the other. Thus a port buoy is to be left to port—in other words one passes to starboard of it. Coming back by the same route, of course, one would have to leave it to starboard. To resolve this obvious ambiguity the convention is that buoys are designated so as to be correct for a vessel moving in the same direction as the main flood stream. Since the flood comes from seaward, it follows that a port-hand buoy really is a port-hand buoy when you are entering a harbour from the sea. When you are going out again it is still a 'port-hand' buoy, but you have to leave it to starboard.

This directional system is fairly easily remembered, especially because the 'natural' sense of the phrases 'port hand' and 'starboard hand' is the one that holds at the most difficult time—when one is entering an unfamiliar port from seaward. On the other hand, there are occasions when the direction of the main flood is not so obvious as it would seem; some harbours have more than one entrance. Then there's a place like Poole, for example, which is dotted with islands, most of which have navigable channels passing right round both sides. At Poole the channels are, in fact, very well marked, but you still need your wits about you. In such circumstances the flood can come from an unexpected direction: still it all adds to the variety.

In general starboard-hand buoys are conical in shape, and port-hand buoys are flat-topped, as shown in Figure 3. Apart from the difference in shape, the port-hand buoy will be painted red, or in red and white chequers, or even in some other combination of colours. A starboard-hand buoy is normally black, though it may be a drab mixture of rust and nothing-in-particular: the important thing about it is that it is

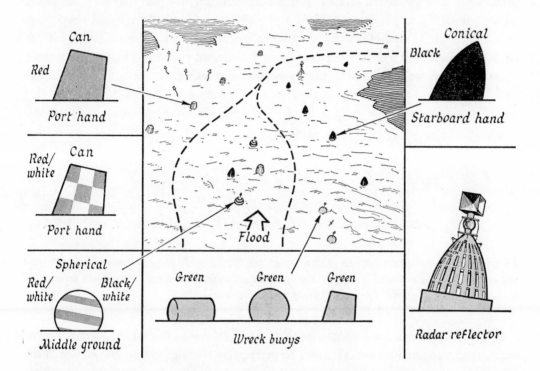

Figure 3. Buoys and other marks are 'port-handed' or 'starboard-handed' from the point of view of a vessel approaching in the direction of the main flood. Usually they are in their natural sense for vessels coming from seaward. In well-buoyed areas, where there is merchant shipping, the buoys are recognizable by both shape and colour, but in small harbours and creeks either the shape alone, or the colour alone, may be the only clue.

never red, nor is it chequered. The buoys lining a channel are often numbered, with No. 1 at the seaward end. Port-hand buoys bear the even numbers, the starboard-hand buoys have the odd.

When everything is perfect, these two main types of buoy are distinguishable by both shape and colour; that is the sort of standard in an area like the Solent or the Thames estuary. But lesser harbours have to improvise, so you may well come across a starboard-hand buoy that is just a barrel, with a port-hand buoy exactly the same shape a few cables away. If that happens the two buoys will be painted red and black respectively, and the distinction will be in the colour, and perhaps in the odd or even numbers painted on them.

In a creek you may see beacons which consist of nothing more than withies (beanpoles) stuck in the mud, and if there is any possibility of doubt about which row of withies marks which side of the channel you may find them decorated with the appropriate 'port' and 'starboard' shapes. The flat-topped effect for port may be achieved by nailing an old tin can to the top of the post, while the 'conical' starboard shape may be achieved with a triangle or diamond cut out of sheet metal or wood (Figure 4). If colours are used, red will be reserved for the flat-topped port-hand marks: sometimes green is used as well, to identify the starboard-hand marks.

Figure 4. Withies or perches are used to mark small creeks. If they are marked at all they are either painted red and green, or the 'port-hand' ones will have flat-topped topmarks, and the 'starboard-hand' ones will have pointed topmarks.

It is quite common for a wide channel to have a shoal in the middle of it, a sort of submerged elongated island. This will be marked by middle-ground buoys, which are spherical, and are painted with horizontal bands of red and white, or black and white. Where one channel is deeper than the other, the middle-ground buoys carry topmarks which indicate on which side the buoy should be left if you want to take the main channel. The topmarks follow the usual style: if they are pointed (diamonds or triangles) then they are to be left to starboard when moving in the direction of the main flood; if they are flat-topped then leave them to port. Of course, you may prefer to use the secondary channel to keep clear of the heavy traffic. The buoys were probably laid with big ships in mind and there may be plenty of water for your boat in both channels, and across the middle ground as well. The chart will tell you the facts, and you may be wise to keep to the shallows, where you will neither be an annoyance to bigger vessels, nor be frightened by them.

Wrecks are marked with spherical or can buoys which are painted green and often have the word 'WRECK' painted on them. Quite apart from these various navigational buoys, in harbours and estuaries there may be a good many others about: some will be mooring buoys, some may be telephone buoys at which a connection may be made to shore via a submarine cable (though not by any passing yachtsman!). Others mark the limits of naval training areas, firing ranges, practice mining grounds and so forth.

Fortunately all these various buoys (or nearly all) will be shown on the chart, so one knows what one is looking for. Unfortunately, the world being what it is, the colour or the topmark of a buoy may sometimes be changed without any amendment getting on to your chart. This can happen even though you may be very meticulous about arranging the supply of amendments from the chart agent and about entering them regularly when you receive them. But in spite of an occasional feeling of puzzlement because one is not quite as it should be according to the chart, buoys are extremely valuable to the coastwise yachtsman. They very often have their names written on them, so it is possible to confirm that you are in the very place where your navigation led you to believe you were (or not, as the case may be).

The colours of buoys are by no means limited to black and red (or green for wrecks) and the actual colours will be recorded on the chart in the following shorthand:

B, b	black
Bl, bl	blue
G, g	green
Or	orange
R, r	red
W, w	white
Y, y	yellow

The first two in the list are the only ones that you need to memorize: it is easy to fall into the trap of reading *Bl* from the chart as *Black* instead of *Blue*. Buoys may be painted in one or more colours, and patterns:

cheq	chequered
hs	horizontal stripes
vs	vertical stripes

From a distance the shape of a buoy can be more easily identified than its colour, and although charts often indicate the shape in a minute sketch, abbreviations are used, too:

con	conical
Ra, Ra refl	radar reflector

The radar reflector is a useful form of identification because of its distinctive shape. Even at that there can be confusion with the kind of buoy which has a special topmark in the form of a triangle or a cross to aid recognition from a distance.

Many of the buoys in main channels and harbour approaches show lights which can have a variety of 'characteristics'—the same applies to lights shown from lighthouses and beacons ashore. A light may be fixed—that's to say *on* all the time, or it may be flashing or occulting. With a flasher the periods of darkness are longer than the flashes of light; an occulter is the reverse, it shows short 'flashes of darkness' against longer periods of light.

A light, mounted on a buoy or ashore, can flash singly or in groups, and the time period for each cycle of flashes or groups of flashes is a key to recognition. Thus one may have a triple flashing red light every 10 sec., or a double flashing white light every 5 sec. The time shown on the chart (or in the lights list) is the time for one complete signal; for example, from the beginning of one group of flashes, through the dark period to the beginning of the next group of flashes. It is not the same as the interval between the two groups of flashes, and it is important to realize this.

To be able to identify a light by its period one must have some facility in judging the passing of seconds (a watch is not likely to be of much help for this purpose in the cockpit of a small boat at night). Most people have a 'one-second word', and it's easy enough to find a word or phrase for yourself that will occupy 1 sec. if spoken at your own normal rate: for example, '*Mississippi* one', '*Mississippi* two', '*Mississippi* three', was the formula used when I was at school to judge how many seconds one could swim under water, and it has been my personal formula ever since.

Lights may also be marked as *alternating*, which means that they show two or more colours successively, with or without intervening periods of darkness. Quick flashing lights, which flash at the same sort of rate as a car's trafficator, can also be *interrupted*, so that the effect is to 'flash' a light which is already quick flashing. Until you have become accustomed to it by experience, it is all too easy to misread 'F' on the chart as 'Flashing', whereas it, in fact, means 'Fixed'.

F	Fixed
Fl	Flashing
Q Fl	Quick Flashing
Occ	Occulting
Gp	Group
Alt	Alternating

Lights are often arranged to show different colours in different sectors. At Dartmouth, for example, to lead ships clear of dangers in the entrance there is a three-sector, green, white and red light (at Kingswear). This is indicated on the chart as

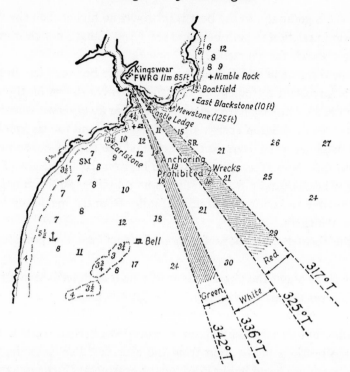

Figure 5. Light sectors are indicated by compass bearings in lights lists, but it is much simpler to follow what is meant if the sectors are actually shown on the chart. It is important to remember that the bearings quoted are as observed from the vessel, and not from the source of the light. This example shows the leading lights at the entrance to the River Dart.

F.W.R.G. On the chart which I use the sectors are printed in their actual colours, as is indicated in Figure 5.

As long as you see the white light you are on the track which passes between off-lying rocks on either side of the entrance. You must turn to port if you see the red light, to starboard if you see green. In addition to watching the lights you would also be following the compass course given in the Pilot: you thus have a cross-check.

Whereas the light I have just described shows a different colour in each sector, an *alternating* light shows a succession of colours in the same sector, or it may show all around. For example, it may flash red and white alternately.

In addition to showing the colour, grouping and periodicity of lights, the chart shows the height of each light above the low water level. That gives the maximum visibility of the light allowing for the earth's curvature, and the distance becomes less as the tide gets higher. At first it seems odd to suggest that one sees less far as one's boat rises with the tide because we are used to the idea of getting up high to see well. But the whole surface of the sea is going up, so the boat is relatively no higher than she was, whereas the light is lower in relation to both boat and sea. (And if that's not clear may I suggest that you make a sketch for yourself. . . .)

Obviously the distance at which a light is visible may be much less in rain or mist. Moreover, it is important to remember that the distances shown on the chart and in pilot books or Reed's Almanac have been calculated for an observer whose eye is 15 ft. above the water. In the kind of cruiser that we have in mind the cockpit sole is likely to be approximately at water level, and 'observer's' eye might be assumed to be at a height of about 6 ft. Now, the visibility to the horizon from a height of 15 ft. is 4·5 nautical miles, whereas from 6 ft. it is only about 2·8 miles. So for practical purposes we should remember to knock off a couple of miles from the maximum visibility of a light shown on the chart.

To make the further corrections for rise of tide tables are provided in Reed's Almanac.

A confusing thing about the characteristic of a light as described in a pilot book or a lights list concerns the arc of visibility. If the list says that a light is visible between 90° and 180° true, it does not mean that the light shines in a south-easterly direction from the lighthouse; it means that it shines in a north-westerly direction. The bearings as listed are the bearings of the light from the observer. For example, the lights at Dartmouth entrance are listed in my Pilot thus: '*red* from 317° true to 325° true, *white* thence to 336° true, *green* thence to 342° true'. From Figure 4 it will be seen that these are the bearings *from* the observer at sea.

For the man who owns a sextant, the height of the light can be used to derive the distance offshore, but there are relatively few coastwise cruising owners who own or use a sextant.

5
Navigation: distances and courses

Distances at sea are measured in nautical miles, and in tenths, or 'cables'. One nautical mile is 6,080 ft., which happens to be only a little more than 2,000 yd. A cable is therefore 608 ft., or 202·66 yd., so for practical purposes it can be considered as 200 yd. with an error of only a little over 1 per cent.

A chart is marked in degrees of latitude (up each side) and degrees of longitude (across the top and bottom). Each degree is divided into 60 min., and a minute of latitude can be taken as 1 nautical mile. For the kind of chart and the kind of cruising that we have been thinking of in this book it is easier to use the scale of miles printed on the chart, but if you want to use minutes of latitude as a scale of miles then remember to do the thing properly and measure from the latitude scale and from that portion of it which is abreast of that part of the chart where the measurement is to be made. The reason for doing this is that with the commonly used Mercator projection a degree of latitude takes more and more space on the chart as you move north or south of the equator: but this is not a matter of any significance until you come to make passages of 100 miles or more in a north–south direction. The real importance of latitude and longitude to the 'home-waters' skipper is their use as a system of reference to the positions of buoys, wrecks and so forth. When it comes to recording the position of your own vessel you will simply mark it on the chart in pencil.

Traditionally the way to lay off a compass course between two points on the chart is to lay a parallel rule with one of its edges joining the two places and then to shuffle it across the chart until an edge passes through the centre of one of the compass roses printed on the chart. A very much simpler method is to use a 360 deg. protractor with parallel north–south lines scribed right across it, and preferably with a transparent arm, as shown in Figure 9. The arm can then be laid directly between the points concerned on the chart. You must have some means of orientating the protractor, and the simplest way is to draw parallel lines of magnetic north from top to bottom of the chart, spaced at every 2 or 3 in. If you do that it will be quite easy to set the north–south lines of your protractor so as to be parallel to your pencilled north lines on the chart. Of course, magnetic north changes slowly all the time (the rate is shown on your chart), but not to worry, it will change by only 1 deg. in eight or nine years. Even 2 deg. is hardly worth bothering about, and before that happens you will probably be buying new charts anyway—or you can rub out the lines and pencil new ones.

By means of this simple chart modification the laying off of courses and bearings becomes extremely quick and simple. If your protractor is a circular one, then be sure that the north is boldly marked—it's quite easy to get it upside down. You may prefer to use a 'Douglas' protractor. This carries a 360 deg. scale, but it is square in shape, with a 'graph-paper' grid all over it. This, too, is very easy to line up with north. Douglas protractors, surplus to R.A.F. needs, can usually be bought quite cheaply from the dealers who specialize in ex-service equipment.

For coastwise navigation all the work can be done by reference to magnetic north. Stanford's charts, for example, show a number of ready-made courses all of which are magnetic. Some pilot books give bearings in magnetic as well as true, but even where they don't it's easy enough to add the variation shown on the chart (brought up to date for the passage of years). This variation, of course, is the difference between true and magnetic north, and even though you may adopt the practice of working only in magnetic there will come a time when you have to convert one to the other. There are various mnemonics which are supposed to be a help in remembering whether the variation should be added or subtracted—things like 'east least, west best' and so forth. I suppose it's all a very personal matter, but for my part I have never derived anything but confusion from these little jingles. If I am in doubt I look at the compass rose on the chart—it's easy to see at once whether true or magnetic is the higher number. In any case, as far as cruising in British waters is concerned there's no trouble. Seen from this part of the world the magnetic pole lies about 10 deg. west of the true north pole, so to convert a true bearing to magnetic you have to add 10 deg. To convert magnetic to true subtract 10 deg. (though you must use the actual local figure on your chart, of course). If in doubt look at the chart, or even draw a little sketch showing the relative positions of magnetic and true north, and all will become clear.

The advantage of working in magnetic is that while actually on passage you can use the steering compass and the hand-bearing compass without need of mental arithmetic. If conversions must be made, then they are best made while you are still at anchor, from true to magnetic; for example, if the pilot book tells you that you will have to enter your destination harbour on a true course of 283°, then the thing to do is to correct this to 293°M. before you start and when the time comes all you'll have to do is to follow that figure on your compass.

Compass deviation and swinging ship

In all this there is one important point that must not be overlooked—you want correct information from your compass, and it may be subject to interference from iron or steel built into the boat. The obvious items are the engine, iron ballast, a mild steel centre-plate, or a mild steel drop rudder. The first thing to do is to try and mount your compass at a point where it is least likely to be influenced by any built-in iron or steel. The position indicated in Figure 26 (Chapter 9) is usually quite a good one, as it is likely to be several feet aft of the engine installation. Or perhaps you are going to stow an outboard motor under the cockpit thwart? Well, you can make allowances for that, but remember that you will also have to make allowances for the occasions when the outboard is clamped on the transom. Similarly the engine may have a different effect when running, from when stationary, and the raising or lowering of drop plate or rudder may vary its magnetic influence on the compass.

When you have mounted your compass in the best possible position both for visibility by the helmsman and for freedom from magnetic effects, you will have to find out just what the effects actually are, and these will vary according to the boat's heading. On two headings the magnetic field of the engine, say, will be exactly aligned with the Earth's magnetic field, and it will not deflect your compass at all. But on other headings the engine's field will make various angles with the Earth's field and will deflect your compass by a greater or lesser amount. Only by experiment can you find out, and the experimental process that is usually recommended is 'swinging ship'.

Swinging ship is a process that is simple in theory, but not simple in practice. Here is the procedure: first you moor your vessel at some point where you can sight two objects ashore which are marked on your chart and will give you a definite magnetic bearing. Now, by tugging with the dinghy, or by judicious use of kedge anchor and warps, or by whatever means you can devise, you manœuvre your craft to a succession of different headings until you have completed a full circle. At each heading you have to note both the heading of your craft and the bearing of the sight line through the chosen objects according to your compass. Of course, the compass ought to show the two objects as lying permanently on the same bearing—if it does all well and good—but on some headings it will probably give a figure that's too high, and on others one that's too low. You can then prepare a neat 'deviation' card showing whether your compass reads too high or too low on the various different headings.

Apart from the actual manœuvring of the vessel, which ought to remain over the same spot while she is swung, the difficulty with this method is to get an accurate bearing of objects ashore from a steering compass. You may be able to rig up a sight for the occasion, but if the compass is fairly low in the cockpit it won't be easy to do, and over a large part of the circle the doghouse or the cabin-top is sure to get in the way.

Another way of swinging ship is to bring a second compass aboard and to set it some part of the vessel where you can be pretty sure that it is free from all undesirable influences (which includes the other compass). This second compass must be lined up with the centre-line of the boat; then you swing the boat on to successive headings, each time comparing the heading shown on your steering compass with that shown by the 'correct' compass.

My own preference is to take 'transits'—to get two known objects in line. This means searching the chart for pairs of fixed objects which can be identified so that you can steer the ship with her bow pointing right along that known line. You can find the correct magnetic bearing of the line from the chart, and record what your compass says.

It is also possible, but more difficult, to steer the boat directly away from the chosen marks, so getting a transit over the stern. To do that you need someone up forward in the boat, sighting centrally over the stern and telling you where to steer.

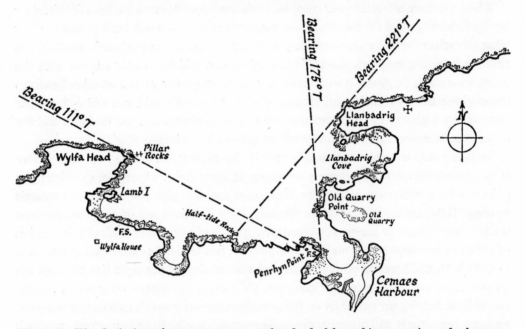

Figure 6. The deviation of your compass can be checked by taking transits—that's to say by steering the boat along the line between two recognizable aiming points. The true bearing on the chart can be converted to magnetic from the variation shown at the foot of the chart, plus any change due to annual variation. The final figure can then be compared with your compass reading.

It is obvious that you need as many transits as you can possibly get, and ideally one would have them at, say, every 20 deg. around the compass. That is not like real life, but it is possible to interpolate. My own method is to set out a column of bearings at every 10 deg.: 0, 10, 20, 30 and so forth up to 350. Now if I find a suitable transit on bearing 23 deg., for example, I enter that in a second column against 20. In the third column I put what the compass read on that transit, let us say 25 deg. Then in the fourth column I enter + 2.

As I collect more and more transits the holes in the pattern fill up, and it soon becomes possible to interpolate. One sees the error figure is rising towards a certain quarter of the compass and then falling off. Furthermore it is usually reasonable to assume that if the error is +2 on 23 deg. that it will be —2 on the reciprocal bearing of 203 deg. At least that is a reasonable assumption until one gets evidence to the contrary.

If your compass has very large deviations you ought to get a professional compass adjuster to come and set small compensating magnets round about—alternatively you can try to remove the offending magnetic objects or to re-site the compass.

What kind of compass?

Although some people still prefer to use the traditional compass notation of 'points' in which the 360 deg. circle is divided into thirty-two points of $11\frac{1}{4}$ deg. each, there is little to be said in its favour for anyone who is starting from scratch. It is true, of course, that one cannot expect to steer to an accuracy of a degree or so, even though each individual degree may be shown on the compass; but that need not stop one from trying. By working in 360 deg. everything becomes clearer and there is less chance of misunderstanding or of mental slips, because the scale is numbered in an orderly way that needs no special mental effort to comprehend.

Apart from the points system, and the degree system, there is a quadrantal system in which north-east becomes N45E, south-east becomes S45E, and so on. By comparison with the 0–360 deg. notation this again is merely an oddity. Of course, you may be in the position of buying a boat with perfectly serviceable compass already installed: in that case the thing to do is to use the one you have and make the best of it.

But if you are installing a compass of your own my recommendation is to use one of the ex-R.A.F. grid steering compasses, if you can get one. They are cheap and of good quality, and the grid method is ideal for a small boat. If you cannot find one of the R.A.F. instruments there are several other grid compasses on the market. The grid compass is arranged in quite a different way from the card compass, as I shall try to explain.

In the card compass the card on which the scale of degrees is marked is attached to the magnetic needle, and it therefore remains always pointing towards the north, while the boat turns around it. A lubber line, fixed in relation to the hull of the boat, enables you to read the boat's heading from the card. This is a simple scheme, with the obvious attraction of simplicity: the grid method is more subtle (see Figure 7).

In the grid compass the magnetic needle is attached only to a ⊥-shaped skeleton of fine wire (in some it is a cross), and it is this wire skeleton which remains north-pointing. There is no card: the scale of degrees is mounted on a movable ring around the outside of the compass bowl. This scale ring carries a sheet of glass on which is marked a ⊥-shape which can be made to coincide with the wire skeleton carried by the needle. Finally there is a fixed mark, or lubber line, which corresponds to the centre-line of the ship.

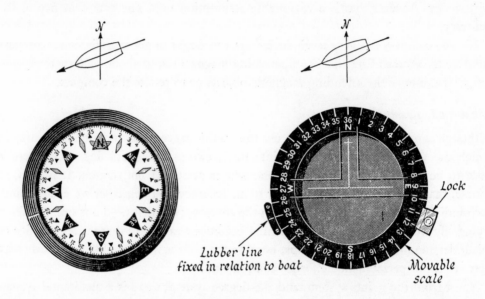

Figure 7. The old-fashioned card compass (left) was marked in 'points' of 11¼ deg. each. The grid compass (right) is marked in degrees, and even more important is the fact that it makes it very easy to hold a course. Once set it is not likely to be misread, and it is easy to see whether one ⊥ is inside the other from almost any angle.

To steer a course of 250°, for example, you first turn the scale ring until 250° coincides with the lubber line: there is a small locking lever to hold the ring in this position. Thenceforward you forget about the numbers and you simply steer the boat so as to keep one ⊥ pattern inside the other. This is very easy. Moreover, the actual setting of the ring is much simpler than I can make it sound—it is done in a couple of seconds.

Two important advantages result from the use of a grid compass: first the ⊥ within ⊥ pattern makes course-holding very much easier. So long as one skeleton ⊥ is kept within the other the vessel is being kept within 5 deg. either side of the desired course. That's to say she can be kept within say 237° and 247°, simply by setting 242°—no mental puzzles here. The second, and even greater advantage is that the form of presentation allows one to hold the course no matter where one is sitting in the cockpit.

Nothing is more misleading than to picture oneself on the bridge of a ship standing directly over a compass card: in a small boat you sit on one side of the cockpit or the other; usually you steer with a tiller and not with a wheel. The result is that the helmsman will normally have to observe the compass from the side, and square-on is the only way he will hardly ever see it. It is a very real advantage of the grid steering compass that it completely solves this problem.

With a sailing vessel it is often a matter of finding where the vessel will point close-hauled and then finding out what heading that happens to be: this is very different from the ideally simple book navigation which assumes that you have a motor vessel and can actually lay the course that you have taken from the chart. It must be admitted to be a drawback of the grid compass that before you can read off the boat's heading you have to turn the ring scale until the two ⊥s are in conjunction. Then the heading can be read against the lubber line. This again is very much quicker to do than to describe and for my part I have never found it any burden.

Bearings of objects ashore

It is sometimes said that the grid compass is not so good as the conventional card compass for taking the bearing of an object ashore, but that is not so. If one is using any kind of steering compass to take bearings, then the boat herself should be held steadily on course while it is being done. As long as the boat is on one course the scale ring of the grid compass can be turned until the two ⊥s are coincident: this means that the ring is correctly orientated so that 90° on the scale will in fact indicate the east. In practice it is easier to get a sight over the scale ring of a grid compass than it is over the card of a conventional kind: moreover, if you like making gadgets it is quite simple to make a 'sight' out of stout wire or brass strip which will stand on the scale ring and make it even easier to take a bearing. Even a sheet of card or thin plywood can be used—all you have to do is to stand it on edge and aim it at the object ashore while making sure that it passes across the centre of the compass scale.

Although all these dodges are perfectly feasible, the practice of taking bearings from the steering compass is not one to be recommended—it is far better to use a separate hand-held bearing compass, if funds will run to it (Figure 8). This is an instrument designed for the job, and one that makes it easy to get an accurate bearing of anything you can see. Obviously the hand-bearing compass must be kept well away from the steering compass—6 to 8 ft. should do, but it is best to make a test for yourself. It is not difficult to find out at what distance your two compasses begin to affect each other, and then to allow an extra margin for safety. The same kind of test should be made with a portable radio or any object which contains magnetic material: for example, you may use one of those battery-powered dry shavers.

The principle of fixing your position by taking cross-bearings on two fixed objects is quite simple and well known. If you get a bearing on a church spire which turns out to be due north of you, then you are due south of it. If you get a bearing of a pier-head a few seconds later and it lies due west from you, then you are due east of it. Draw a line due south from the church and due east from the pier and the point where they cross marks your position.

All too easy—especially when I choose such an impossibly simple example! But the point is that after you have taken the bearing of the object you need the reciprocal of it so as to draw the *position line* from it out to sea.

You could work out the reciprocal by adding 180° (if the bearing to the object was smaller than 180°): or by subtracting 180° if the bearing was greater than 180°. On the other hand, if you use a course-setting protractor like the one shown in Figure 9 the whole thing is done automatically. All you have to do is to put the centre of the protractor on the position of the church spire, or whatever it was, align it to magnetic north, and then turn the straight edge until the inshore end coincides with the observed bearing. The opposite end then runs through the reciprocal and provides your position line. The same result is achieved with parallel rules—for those who like 'em!

Naturally, a single bearing cannot give you a position; it can only give a line along

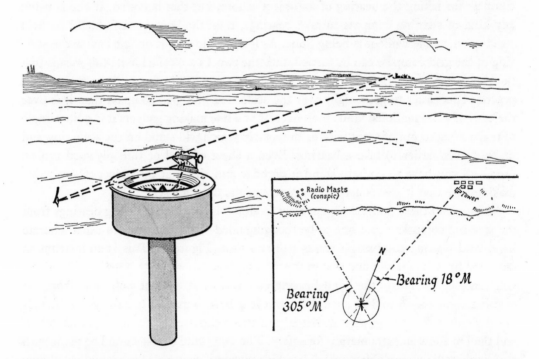

Figure 8. The hand-bearing compass provides the best way of getting the bearing of an object ashore. Back-bearings from two objects can be drawn on the chart to give an approximation of the boat's position (see Figure 9).

which your position lies, but even that can be helpful information. To get the best possible fix from two bearings they should be as nearly as possible at a right-angle, though the world being what it is there is not usually an ideal supply of easily recognizable objects in just the right position. Sometimes, in densely populated parts of the coast the reverse is true: where the chart shows a church spire, or a 'chimney conspic', there will be several spires and several chimneys, some of which may have even come

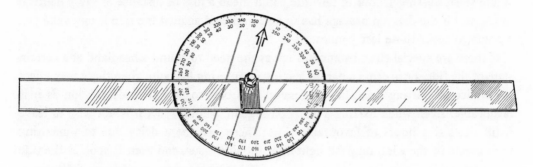

Figure 9. A course-setting protractor is much simpler to use than parallel rulers, so long as the chart is marked to show magnetic north. (See text.) Moreover, position fixing by back-bearings is done without arithmetic. With the protractor centred on the observed landmark, and with the shoreward arm of the protractor set to the observed bearing, the seaward arm must automatically lie along the reciprocal bearing.

on the scene since the chart was drawn and may be even more 'conspic' than the one the cartographer had in mind. I can remember taking a bearing on one of these conspicuous chimneys which put me about a mile ashore on the mainland. As usual, my first reaction was to doubt the compass, but after a little reflection and some searching with binoculars I discovered chimneys galore: the one that I had observed was just the most conspicuous one for miles around, completely dwarfing the correct one which was hardly noticeable, though much nearer.

Catching a fair tide

Nevertheless, in spite of the various snags, a fix by cross-bearings, or a position line by a single one, is a standard way of taking a departure—that is establishing the best fix that you can as the land is about to disappear from view. From that point on it will be a matter of dead reckoning. Now, this means either following the course you have worked out from the chart or, in a sailing vessel, of making the best course that the wind will allow. Apart from the need to clear headlands and other dangers, the primary considerations in laying off a course will be the effect of tidal streams. The tide will also have a great influence on the time of departure. If the whole passage can be made in the period of one tide, say 5 or 6 hours, then the obvious thing to do is to be out of harbour and ready to take the tide as soon as it turns in the favourable direction. *It is worth interfering with one's normal sleeping hours to do this.*

The important thing about tidal streams is that their speed can be high in relation to the speed of the boat. A 5-tonner will probably be making only 3 or 4 knots through the water, so a foul tide of 2 knots can reduce her speed made good over the ground to as little as 1 or 2 knots. A *fair* tide, on the other hand, can increase it to 5 or 6 knots. A late start, missing 1 hour of fair tide could mean a loss of distance of say 5 nautical miles, and if the delayed passage has to be completed against the tide it may take you 3 hours to cover those last 5 miles.

If there are special circumstances, such as the need to round a headland at a certain state of the tide, or to cross a bar on leaving or entering harbour, then these may affect the choice of starting time, but in general it is best to take the tide as soon as it is favourable. Even when making a short passage of 3 hours, say, it is not wise to leave it till the last 3 hours of favourable tide. There may be a delay due to something unforeseen, or the wind may fall light after the first hour, and then as soon as the tide turns everything goes into slow motion and the passage may take two or three times as long.

The actual effect that the tide can be expected to have on the progress of the vessel depends on its relative speed and its angle to the course being sailed. If the stream is dead ahead or dead astern the effect is quite obvious. If it is at an oblique angle, then the result can be found by a simple method. Thus if the vessel is sailing due west at 4 knots and the tidal stream is due south at 2 knots the resultant of the two velocities can be found by drawing first a line representing the vessel's westward progress due

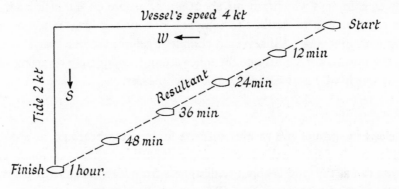

Figure 10. A simple example of the effect of a cross-tide on a vessel's track. The result of the southward tide is found by drawing a triangle in which two sides have lengths proportionate to the speed of the vessel and the tide respectively. The directions are the natural ones. The third side of the triangle will then have a length which is proportional to the actual speed made good over the sea bottom, and its direction shows the actual path of the vessel.

to her own speed, and the one showing her southward progress due to the tide (Figure 10).

The diagram shows the combined effect at the end of 1 hour: the length of the dotted line, *resultant*, is proportionate to the actual speed made good. In fact, it shows the distance travelled in 1 hour. Tidal streams are all the time changing in speed and direction so an hour by hour check is necessary. Tidal streams atlases do, in fact, show the changes on an hourly basis. Similar triangular diagrams can be drawn for any combination of speeds and directions, so long as the lines are drawn with lengths proportion to the speeds and at the correct relative angle. Here are some examples (Figure 11):

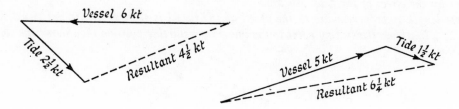

Figure 11. Two examples of vector diagrams, showing the effects of tidal streams at different angles to the ship's course.

All this shows so far is what the effect of the tide would be if one followed a certain course: the practical problem is what course to follow to get to the right point—or to make good the desired track. Going back to the simple example where it is desired to travel due west in a 4-knot vessel with a southerly tide of 2 knots, one can draw the diagram in another way. The effect of the tide is drawn first, displacing the starting-point of the vessel 2 miles to the south. From the real starting-point the desired track is drawn and then from the imaginary starting-point a line 4 units long is drawn to cut it, that being the distance through the water that you expect your boat to be able to sail in 1 hour. The angle of this line is the course to sail; you lay your boat's head on 300°, and she will, in fact, make good a track of 270°. The length along the westerly line shows the distance she will make towards her destination in the hour—3¾ miles (Figure 12).

These little vector diagrams show very clearly the effect that the tide can have, particularly the difference between a tide which is 'slightly foul' and another which is 'slightly fair'. Next is a diagram showing a 4-knot boat first with a 2-knot tide on the port bow and then with the same speed of tide at the same angle on the port quarter (Figure 13).

None of this should be taken too seriously, by the way. People who write books feel that it is necessary to put it all in, and it's quite fun drawing all the little vector diagrams.

Figure 12. Earlier diagrams have shown the effect of the tide on a vessel sailing on a given course. When it is required to know what course must be sailed to counteract the effect of the tide and to make good a desired track, a different approach is needed. The principle of the vector diagram remains the same but the method is to assume that the boat starts from an imaginary point, displaced from the real starting point by the effect of the tide. An arc 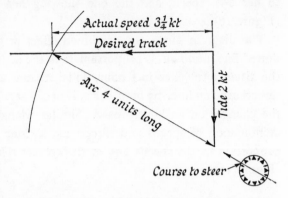 *whose length is proportionate to the speed of the vessel is then drawn to cut the desired track: a line from the cutting point to the imaginary starting position then shows the course to steer.*

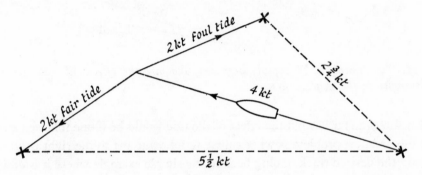

Figure 13. Because the speed of a small boat is so slow, tidal streams can have a very big effect. The upper part of this diagram shows what happens to a 4-knot vessel with a 2-knot tide on the port bow. The lower half of the sketch shows the effect of a similar tide on the starboard quarter.

But in real life it's often very different. In the first place you won't know the rate of the tidal stream very accurately: you have to interpolate between values at different points on the chart; you have to interpolate between springs and neaps; you won't be able to make an accurate allowance for the effects of wind and barometric pressure. As likely as not your own speed will not be constant, and there will be variations, greater or less, in your course. Probably the best one can say is that in trying to make an accurate assessment of the effect of the tidal stream you will finish up with a fairly good idea of the general effect of the tide on your track made good. The main thing is to be aware of the kind of thing the tide may be doing to you: take, for example, the common case in coastal waters where you can see the place you are aiming for: there is a headland, or a buoy, and the shore with all its features is abeam. In these circumstances few people would actually prepare a vector diagram: they would just point the bow of the boat towards the destination and unconsciously keep on correcting the course as the boat is carried off by the tide. What happens then is that the boat is carried off in a curve as this diagram (Figure 14) indicates. That's not so very serious, but if you do try to estimate what effect the tide will have and to lay the boat's head off accordingly, you will save quite a bit of distance and time. Moreover, the day may come when a mist blows up, so that a constant, curving course correction will not be possible.

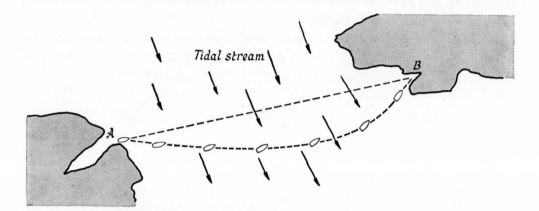

Figure 14. Even though you may be able to see your destination, it will save time if you make allowance for the effects of a tidal stream across your track. Merely heading the vessel towards the objective will result in a curved, 'homing', track, and the faster the tidal stream the greater the curvature.

There is another thing to be considered—the actual course you can sail in the wind that is blowing at the time. In Figure 10 the vessel would have done very well if she had been able to lay a course due west, but when allowance has been made for the effect of the tide the course she ought to sail becomes too close to the wind. Tacking in these conditions is going to be rather tedious. Figure 15 shows the total result of 2 hours' sailing—the boat has reached the point C, about 1½ miles from where she started.

If it is a short passage of an hour or two, the right thing to do is to wait for the tide to turn (or do it under power). If it is a long passage which will last beyond the turn of the tide, then you may make as far to the west as you can, letting the tide sweep you south, knowing that it will carry you northward again when it turns. There is a risk in doing that, because after 4 or 5 hours' sailing the wind may veer and head you just when you want to turn on to the northerly beat. The proper thing to do is always to take fairly short tacks on either side of your desired track, so that you are never far off to one side or the other.

But that is rather off the point I was trying to make, which was the effect the tidal stream could have on the possibility of laying the intended track. What looked like a fairly easy close reach was, in fact, not possible with the prevailing tide, and that fact was revealed only by drawing a vector diagram.

Real life can be even more difficult: the wind may not be constant in direction or strength, and although you know what course you ought to sail you are obliged to sail the best you can. In that case you can get some idea of where you have been if you note every course you have sailed and lay it off on the chart, allowing for the effect of the tide by making little vector triangles.

Cruising under power, you can decide what course you want to steer, and then follow it. There are times when you can do that under sail, too, but often you must lay the best course you can and find out afterwards where you have been.

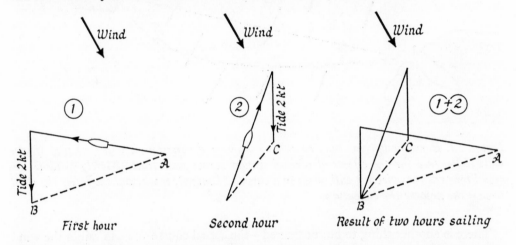

Figure 15. What may seem a quite feasible close reach may be made quite impracticable by a tidal stream running to leeward. In part 1 of this diagram the boat is carried south of her desired course by the stream. Trying to make back to the north on the other tack she in fact arrives at point C, as shown in part 2 of the sketch. Part 3 shows the combined effect of 2 hours' sailing, and it is an interesting exercise to see how much longer the passage will take if wind and tide remain unchanged.

6

Anchoring and mooring

Anchoring and mooring play a very small part in dinghy sailing—more often than not the boat is brought to a halt by running her into the shallows, or by coming alongside, grabbing hold, and hanging on. In general the dinghy helmsman gives more thought to techniques for making his boat go than for stopping her: to the cruising man stopping (and staying stopped) is just as important as making way.

Coastwise cruising men usually spend a great part of their waterborne lives at anchor. Many passages and holidays follow the routine of sailing by day and anchoring by night, and happy is the man who can lie in his warm bunk at two o'clock in the morning confident that his craft is secure in spite of a raging gale and a 5-knot current. It's no fun to find that the anchor is dragging when it's pitch-dark and the rain is coming at you like a horizontal waterfall; and it can be dangerous. At the other end of the scale, even on a calm sunny day, there's the sheer fool-faced embarrassment of coming into a popular anchorage, going ashore on to the beach and then seeing one's own craft drifting down on two or three others. Every season you can see one or two glorious tangles of that kind: the drifting boat's own anchor may collect the cables of others as she goes past, sometimes putting two or three adrift with an intimate mingling of cross-trees and shrouds, and bowsprits and bumkins.

If you have a good anchor and chain cable, and if you follow the correct drill, you will probably never wake in the night to the sound of a dragging anchor. On the other hand, you will often hear the *chain* dragging across the bottom: this comes at the turn of the tide, when the bight of the chain on the bottom has to be dragged round from one direction to the other. You may think that the noise is caused by the anchor dragging, but if *that* ever happens you will hear a quite different, bumpitty-bumping sort of noise. I can't describe the difference in words, but if it is only the chain, then you may *think* it's the anchor dragging: but if it *is* the anchor, then I am pretty sure you'll *know*. I hope that's understandable . . . and helpful!

59

Anchoring: a seamanlike procedure

There are many circumstances when the only course left open to the skipper is to anchor. Any circumstances in which the vessel cannot make way and may be carried into danger by a tidal stream demand the use of the ground tackle. Whether it's a case of an engine failure at sea in a dead calm with a rocky headland down tide, or whether it's a case of a fouled propeller (your own dinghy painter perhaps?) in an anchorage where there is too little space for prudent manœuvring under sail alone, the anchor and chain provide the only means of keeping your boat at rest and out of trouble until circumstances are more favourable, or until you can get things straight.

It follows that for coastwise cruising the bower anchor and its cable should always be ready for immediate use. The anchor itself should be lashed firmly on deck, of course, because in a sea it can bounce about and do damage, or it may even bounce overboard and start bashing the hull. From time to time one sees an anchor go overboard from a boat sailing past, followed by fathom after fathom of chain, followed in turn by the surprised look of the helmsman at the sudden rebellious behaviour of his boat. That kind of thing is such good entertainment—when you see it happening to someone else! But although the anchor must be lashed down as soon as it has been brought on board and washed free of mud, weed and shellfish, it must be lashed with knots which can be quickly slipped, even when they've been soaked with sea water and

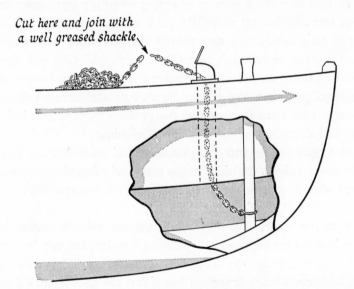

Cut here and join with a well greased shackle

Figure 16. The bitter end of the chain must be secure, but it is useful to be able to 'break' the cable—perhaps to bend on a warp for anchoring in unusually deep water. This sketch shows the best way to prepare a cable for easy breaking whenever the need arises.

your fingers are cold-clumsy. Tinkerers, handymen and genuine engineers will very sensibly make some mechanical kind of clamp for the anchor: if this is designed to be so simple that it cannot jam it is much better than a lashing. In any case, the anchor must rest in shaped chocks and those who are not very clever at gadgetry may make use of heavy-gauge rubber shock cord. This bungee rubber is a most valuable form of lashing on small craft, though it does tend to perish quite quickly when it's exposed to the weather, so that it usually has to be renewed each season.

Because it may be necessary to let go the anchor in a hurry the inboard end of the chain must be permanently made fast. This is called the bitter end, though a small boat rarely has bitts nowadays and the bitter end of the cable is, in fact, made fast to an eye-bolt in the chain locker. This eye-bolt is about as inaccessible as it could be, yet there will be occasions when you may need to unshackle the chain—perhaps to bend on a warp for extra length. The thing to do is this; shackle the end to the eye-bolt, then pull all the chain out on deck until no more will come. Now saw through a link about a foot outside the navel pipe, and join up again with a shackle. This provides a point at which you can break the chain whenever you like (Figure 16). The shackle itself has to be small enough to pass down the navel pipe, but it can be a relatively light-gauge one because you will never actually lie to it. At the other end of the chain the anchor, too, should be well shackled on. The shackle pin should be held against turning by a short length of copper wire passing through the eye and twisted round the body of the shackle. The shackles at each end of the chain should be freed and greased once each season, so that you can be sure of undoing them easily if ever you need to.

Choice of an anchor

There is a very wide choice of anchors available on the market, and there is a good deal of discussion about their relative merits. Unfortunately it is not easy to track down any simple, yet reliable, scientific measurements of their relative holding powers. But such tests as have been made indicate that the genuine CQR and the Danforth are by far the best. It is important, by the way, to insist that you get a *genuine* CQR, since there are other plough-shaped anchors which look similar, but do not perform so well.

If an anchor is any good at all (and some types do not even come into that category!) the thing by which its quality is measured is its holding power in relation to its weight.

Holding power takes priority; tidiness, convenience in stowing, appearance and so forth are of very slight importance. In the very smallest cruisers, where the weight of the ground tackle has a noticeable effect on the performance of the boat, it is imperative to get the necessary holding power at the smallest weight penalty. Above 6 or 7 tons, say, it becomes a matter of carrying the heaviest gear you can bring home by hand— unless you are going to use a winch. In either case you want the best holding power for the weight of gear you have on board.

E

It is generally accepted that $\frac{5}{16}$ in. chain is suitable for boats up to 7 or 8 Thames tons: thence up to about 12 tons $\frac{3}{8}$ in. chain would be right. Most people like to carry 20 to 30 fathoms of chain, but in craft under 5 tons it would be reasonable to carry say 12 to 15 fathoms, and to augment this when necessary with a nylon warp. (Nylon is best for the job, because in addition to strength it has elasticity and acts as a shock absorber. Terylene would be a second choice.) Whatever length of chain one carries it is always worth while to have at least one warp on board with an eye spliced round a thimble, so that it can be properly shackled on to your anchor chain. The actual weight of the anchor that you would use depends a good deal on the characteristics of your boat. If she is a slender 3-tonner with well-faired cabin-top and generally small windage, then a 15 lb. CQR might well be enough. But on the whole I would always prefer to have a few pounds more than the minimum. Above 5 tons I would certainly go for a 25 lb. CQR or Danforth, and at 10 tons 35 lb. would be more appropriate.

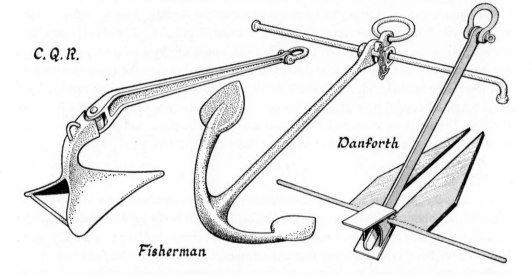

Figure 17. The three most common types of anchor. The CQR is the original 'plough' pattern and still the best. You can recognize a genuine CQR by the I-section shank— anyway it has the name on it. . . . The Fisherman is usually considered better than either the CQR or the Danforth when the bottom is covered with kelp or other weed. The Danforth originates in the U.S.A. and is a very good anchor.

In the case of the CQR in particular a few extra pounds of weight are well worth having, because its weakest performance is in getting started. Compared to the fisherman or the Danforth, it is a bit slow at beginning to dig in—it drags rather farther before starting. Moreover, while the CQR has excellent holding power in sand or mud, it does not easily penetrate through a layer of weed. Again, in loose shingle any anchor's performance is lessened and sheer weight has greater relative importance. The answer, therefore, is not to adopt the principle of carrying a CQR which is lighter than the fisherman you would otherwise carry, but to have one of the same weight and enjoy the extra holding power. In this way you will also get good performance in shingle or a weed-covered bottom. This is the point of my remark, above, that you might as well carry the heaviest ground tackle that you can handle, so long as you are not thinking of the very smallest class of craft. Apply the same philosophy in deciding the weight of your kedge—it is your stand-by which may have to do duty for the bower anchor.

Of course, no boat should set off cruising with fewer than two anchors. Many people use a CQR for the bower and a fisherman for the kedge, but there is little reason why they should not both be CQR. I myself use a fisherman as a kedge at the moment, simply because I happened to have a couple of fisherman anchors doing nothing—they were bowers of past boats which had been replaced by CQRs. But if I were starting from scratch I think I might adopt a CQR for the bower and Danforth for the kedge. The Danforth is a good anchor, whose performance is similar to that of the CQR. It has the advantage that it stows flatter than the CQR and is ready for immediate use, without the 'assembling' needed for the fisherman. Its flat, pointed palms should penetrate weed, and once in the ground there is no upstanding fluke to get foul of anything. As a kedge it should be easier to manhandle from a dinghy (but it can nip fingers), and to bring back into the cockpit than a fisherman, though not better than a CQR.

Whatever sort of kedge anchor you carry, don't be tempted to bury it in some locker beneath a heap of warps and fenders. As with the bower, the best place for the kedge to be is somewhere on deck, with a quick-release lashing so that you can bring it into use *quickly* if need be. One of the standard 'book' techniques for getting off again if you run aground is to get the kedge anchor out into deeper water with the dinghy. But on a falling tide each minute counts, and the skipper who can only get his kedge into action at the expense of a cockpit-sized earthquake with petrol cans, ropes, fenders and funnels flying in all directions does not stand much chance.

Letting go

Letting go the anchor is a subject about which there is an endless stream of articles in the yachting magazines. But really it is a matter of common sense, if one starts from a consideration of the way in which an anchor holds. Figure 15 shows an anchor and its chain cable at work. The important thing, of course, is to have such a length of chain that it hangs in a curve and ends up lying along the sea-bed with a horizontal pull. It is the weight of the chain that keeps it hanging like this. Apart from the fact that it can be frayed and cut by rocks and other underwater objects, rope does not have enough weight to maintain a full curve under the tugging of the vessel. Normally a scope of chain equal to three times the depth of the water produces a sufficient curve to give a horizontal pull; moreover, the weight of the chain acts as a shock absorber, rising and dropping back again as the seas cause the boat to jerk and snub. In very heavy weather extra chain can be paid out to increase the holding power of the anchor, and also to increase the shock-absorbing effect. There are other ways of increasing the shock absorption, of course: one is to increase the inertia of the cable by sliding a dead weight down it. The other is to make a spring of rubber shock cord from the chain to some strong point a few feet back—probably the mast. Traditionally rope would have been used for this job, but bungee cord gives a real spring. Naturally the chain itself must be made fast, so that it will take the strain if the rubber is fully extended, or in case it breaks.

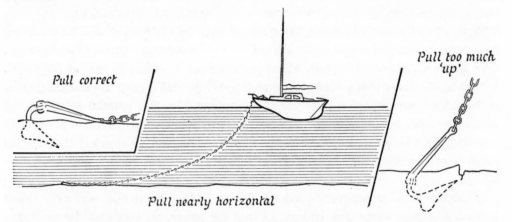

Figure 18. The length of the cable and its weight both help to produce a horizontal pull at the anchor. While a nylon warp makes a very good anchor cable, it is worth having 2 or 3 fathoms of chain at the end to lie along the bottom and keep the pull as nearly horizontal as possible.

If for any reason you are using rope as your anchor cable, then at least have 2 or 3 fathoms of chain at the lower end. Not only will this lie along the bottom and help to keep the pull horizontal, it will also be proof against abrasion or cutting. Beware, too, of chafe where your cable comes inboard, especially if your boat has a metal band on the stem or, even worse, a bowsprit with a wire bobstay.

Since the scope of chain should be three times the depth of water, you should mark off lengths of your chain with paint, or by tying a little bit of tape through a link, so that you can tell how much you have veered. Every 3 fathoms is practical. To know how much chain to veer you need first to know what depth you will be in at high tide. You take a sounding with the lead and then you allow for any amount the tide still has to rise. This may mean a bit of arithmetic; first you need to know the *range* of the tide: if it is springs, this is the same as the 'rise' or 'height' shown in the tide-tables. If it is neaps you may as well assume that the range is the same as the rise, even though it is not, because the error is on the right side. (This is dealt with in Chapter 3.) When you know the range you can apply the 'twelfths rule' to find out how much more the tide has to rise. (Also in Chapter 3.)

That's the procedure, but I must confess that I don't often do it myself, and I am sure that very few cruising yachtsmen ever do. Most will take a sounding, '3 fathoms', make a quick shot at the tidal rise, 'can't rise more than 2 fathoms now', add on a fathom for luck, 'say a maximum of 6 fathoms, so veer 18'. We don't usually get caught out . . . touch wood!

Whether you work it out with great care, or make a rough estimate, when you have decided how much to veer it is a good plan to range the correct amount of chain on deck before letting go.

The way in which an anchor achieves its holding effect immediately reveals two things about letting go. The first is that you must place the anchor some way ahead of the point where you want the boat to lie, and the second is that when you let go you must have the boat moving in a way which will help the anchor to dig in and settle down. The customary method is to take the craft somewhat beyond the point where the anchor should finally come to rest and then allow her to gather stern way (due to wind or tide) before letting the anchor drop. (There's no need to throw it, gravity will take it down fast enough.) As the boat goes astern chain is paid out steadily and is not snubbed until a length equal to about three times the depth of the water has been run out: then when it is snubbed it will give a good horizontal pull on the anchor which will dig in and hold.

If too much chain is paid out too quickly it will simply collect in a heap on the bottom, where it may get in a tangle or even get foul of the anchor itself (especially with a fisherman): on the other hand, if the chain is snubbed while it is too short it will simply pull the anchor upwards so that it doesn't even get a chance to start digging in.

It is perfectly possible to drop the anchor while the boat is still going ahead, though in that case 'ahead' should mean towards the point where the boat will ultimately lie: for example, with no wind, that would be *downtide*, so that the boat will overrun the anchor cable and then swing right round when she comes to the end of the scope. On the other hand, there's no point in letting go while the boat is going ahead *uptide*: in that case chain will be first of all dragged one way across the bottom, and will then be dragged all the way back again. If the anchor does dig in while the boat is still going ahead, it will be the wrong way round when she falls back, and although that will be the case when the tide turns, there's no point in starting off that way.

To come to anchor under sail one has to take into account the directions of both wind and tide. Generally a boat will lie to the stream of the tide, but if the stream is weak and the wind is strong she may (rarely) lie wind-rode. If there are other craft in the anchorage you can see how they are lying. When the wind and tide are in the same direction it is easy enough to beat up towards the point where you want to let go, luff up, and drop the hook just as she's beginning to gather stern way. The foredeck hand should be able to get the headsail down and muzzled while the boat is head to wind and losing way. This, by the way, is a time when a roller-furling headsail is such good value—if it doesn't jam up!

With the wind against the tide it is best to get the mainsail down first and run up against the tide under headsail alone. When the right spot is reached the sail comes down and the anchor goes down in quick succession. This is the familiar drill which is outlined in so many books, but nobody ever seems to mention the awkward situation when the tide is fast and the wind is weak: sometimes the wind is just not strong enough to carry the boat over the tide with just the area of the working staysail, or the headway you make is insufferably slow. In that case you had best run under main- and headsail to a point uptide of the right spot, then luff up and get the mainsail down; while you are doing that the boat will begin to drift downtide. You can either get the headsail off right away and drop the hook as the boat drifts (stem first) down the tide, or you can use the headsail to bring her round stern to wind, which in this case means head to tide. If you play the headsail sheets right and don't allow the sail to draw too much, you can keep directional control of the boat while the tide carries her, stern-first, upwind to the point where you want to drop the anchor.

This again is a situation in which a really reliable headsail-rolling device would be a boon. The trouble is that roller furling equipment sold by chandlers or made in boatyards usually seems to be of poor design.

The procedure for coming into anchor under sail is similar to that for picking up a mooring, so it will be as well to mention the fact here. In each case one wants to bring the boat more or less to a stop, with her head to the tide so that she will drop back from either the mooring chain or the anchor chain in a natural manner.

Coming to a mooring one can nearly always see plenty of other boats on moorings and from their behaviour it is possible to judge whether one's own boat will be wind-rode or tide-rode. As with anchoring, the rule is to *beat* up when wind and tide are together, but to *run* up under headsail alone when the wind is against the tide. As with anchoring, nobody ever mentions what you ought to do when the situation is not simple—when the tide is too strong for your staysail alone. You can't expect to sail upstream, lower the mainsail and drop back on the tide—it's not impossible, but it's not really practical in these modern times when moorings are so crowded. With roller reefing probably the best thing you can do is to reef the main right down as small as possible: its drive can be minimized if it is sheeted in close to the centre-line of the boat instead of being squared off. A gybe could spoil your aim for the buoy, but with a reefed sail in a light wind it may have only a slight effect. With this method you must sheet in hard as soon as the foredeck man has got hold of the buoy and get the mainsail down with a run. This, by the way, is a technique best reserved for light boats. Above 5 tons TM, if the wind will not allow you to breast the tide under headsail alone, then come up under power.

Strangely enough, very few people seem to think of handling moorings from the after end of the boat—yet when one is single-handed it can be a very practical method. There are occasions when one can bring the boat to a stop with the cockpit hard by the buoy; then all you have to do is to put your hand over the side and haul up. You may even lie by the stern for a time, while you stow sails and get everything shipshape —it depends on the directions and strengths of wind and tide, of course. Alternatively you may prepare in advance by making fast a good warp to the forward samson post, and then leading the warp aft to the cockpit *outside* everything. Then you can pick up the mooring from the cockpit, bend the warp on the chain and drop it back in the water. You haul up the chain at your leisure.

It can often be a help to drop a mooring from the cockpit, whether single-handed or not. Normally if the boat is lying head to wind on her mooring the mainsail is got up first, followed by the headsail. If, on the other hand, the boat is lying tide-rode, with her stern to wind, any attempt to get the mainsail up is going to cause trouble and confusion. The books all say that in such circumstances one should set the headsail only, drop the buoy, and run under headsail until there is room to luff up and set the main. I have had moorings in places where one would have had to run a couple of miles (under headsail only, against a 3-knot tide!) before there would be room to do that. But by transferring the mooring to the after end of the boat, so that she was lying stern to tide and head to wind, I have been able to get the main up right away. Single-handed, and in crowded moorings, there is great advantage in dropping the mooring from the cockpit; one hand is on the tiller, and you can choose your exact moment to let go.

Anchoring close inshore

Back to the subject of anchoring: in small boats it is quite common to anchor close in to the shore for convenience. If you do this, remember that where the shore is steep-to and the tide runs fast there may well be a reverse current close inshore. The reverse stream may be 20 or 30 ft. wide and where it meets the main current there will be a swirling popple. You will be all right if you anchor in either stream, but if you happen to position yourself on the boundary you will lead a merry-go-round existence for half an hour or so, as the boat gets caught first by one stream and then by the other. Ultimately the anchor will be screwed out and you will drift clear, which at least gives you a chance to anchor in some more settled spot.

Another thing to remember when anchoring close inshore is the possible result of a change in wind direction. I was caught like that when I once anchored a small craft in a miniature bay on a sandy shore. It was evening and low tide, but there was plenty of water to float us. As a good breeze was expected, we veered a long scope of cable. At low tide next morning, after a night of storm and thunder, we awoke to find ourselves high and dry on the beach. During the night the wind had veered and with our long cable we had blown into the shallows. After such a wild night it was quite pleasant to have a static boat on the warm, sunlit sand. If she had had a flat bottom or bilge keels it would have been even nicer. Still, it might have been mud, and we might have been due to catch the tide to somewhere instead of lazing the morning away on the beach.

In very narrow creeks, which provide some of the most sheltered and delightful anchorages for small craft, it is often worth while to anchor fore and aft. Not only does this keep the boat clear of the banks, which may be quite steep, but it may also give you the opportunity to arrange that the boat shall lie head to wind throughout both ebb and flood. This can be a real gain in a small boat in windy and especially wet weather. Sometimes there are places (the upper reaches of Wootton Creek in the Isle of Wight, for example) where the channel is very narrow and a boat lying to a single anchor can easily become something of an obstruction to other craft as she yaws about across the fairway; again a case for anchoring fore and aft.

The swinging room needed by a boat can also be lessened by mooring her, that is to say by lying to two anchors, well spaced out, but with a single chain to the bows of your boat (Figure 19). One anchor is the bower with her chain, the other is the kedge whose warp is bent on to the chain at about 6 or 10 ft. below the surface of the water (at a depth where the rope will not foul the hull as the boat swings above). The actual bending-on of the warp is done on deck, of course, the necessary 10 ft. or so of chain

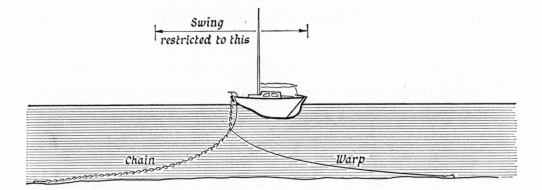

Figure 19. A boat moored with two anchors. This is a very secure way of restraining the craft, and it also reduces the swinging arc. The warp to the kedge anchor is seized to the bower chain, and then chain is veered until the seizing is sufficiently far beneath the water for the boat to be able to swing without fouling the warp.

being paid out afterward. The kedge can be laid out from the dinghy, or if you have enough chain you can fall back to the bower, drop the kedge and haul in the excess of chain again. Mooring like this is the most secure method of anchoring a boat, and she can safely be left to her own devices—a thing which one could not do with a single anchor. The most risky way to leave a boat on a single anchor is if you are using a fisherman—every time the boat swings with the tide there is a real risk that the chain will get foul of the upstanding fluke and drag the anchor out crown first. That this cannot happen is one of the advantages of the Meon and the CQR.

Still, even though mooring to two anchors is the best method, very few people do it when anchoring for a night or two. Moreover, although it is said that the reduced swinging arc means a reduced risk of collision with other anchored craft when the tide turns, the reverse is the case in a crowded anchorage if everyone else is lying to a single anchor. When all lie to a single anchor, all swing together: your anchor is likely to be immediately under the transom of the craft ahead, while under your transom is the anchor of the man behind.

Except when you are moored, when you may have to give thought to which anchor you will lift first, and how, weighing anchor usually presents no special problems. It may demand a certain amount of co-operation between the man at the helm and the man doing the job: under power the man at the helm can motor the boat ahead to take some of the load off the cable; under sail the man forward can help to make sure that the head of the boat pays off on the tack which the helmsman prefers. Only when the anchor gets foul of something below the water does any real problem arise. There are various answers:

1. You may have enough sense always to rig a tripping line to the crown of the anchor, so that it can be hauled out backwards with the chain slack. It is usual to buoy these lines, but in a crowded anchorage the lines are just another hazard to passing craft, and it has even been known for a boat to get her anchor buoy rope foul of her own screw.

2. If your anchor is foul of a cable or mooring chain you may be able to haul it up far enough to get a rope under the cable, or even hold it with a boat-hook, while the anchor is slipped free.

3. If you cannot bring the obstruction within reach you may be able to fish for it with some sort of home-made 'meat hook' with a rope doubled through it. The hook may have to be left on the bottom, of course, but if the rope is doubled you can let go one end and haul the other in.

4. With a CQR, or other stockless anchor, you may be able to slide an iron ring (with rope attached) down the chain and along the shank of the anchor until it reaches the crown. To do this the chain must be taut, of course; later it is slacked

off while someone goes off in the dinghy to try to haul the anchor away from the obstruction by the rope which (you hope) now leads to the crown of the anchor.

5. A good swimmer may haul himself down the chain hand over hand and try to deal with it in person.
6. You can haul the chain in short and cut it. But bend a buoyed rope on to the other end before you drop it back into the water, because nowadays there's a fair chance of finding an enthusiastic amateur frogman who would like a chance to make use of his newly acquired skill.

In spite of all the ingenious schemes for freeing fouled anchors, there have been many occasions when brute force has provided a remedy. If there is any sea running you can haul up short in the troughs, take a turn, and let the boat do the lifting as she rises on the next crest.

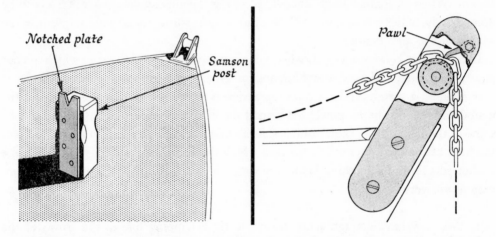

Figure 20. Two methods of holding an anchor chain while you rest your arms. A pawl in the stemhead roller, or a notched plate will allow you to take in the slack when it is available. Slight movements of the boat herself will do most of the work, including the breaking-out.

Mooring alongside other boats or against a harbour wall is a rather more elaborate business in a cruiser than in a dinghy. In the first place it is necessary to come alongside with the utmost gentleness—a leg may make a very good buffer for a dinghy, but it may not do so well if it gets between a 5-tonner and a jagged stone wall. In coming alongside you have to think what the wind and tide are doing. Normally one would choose to approach against the tide; then once a line is got ashore from forward the current will tend to press the after end of the boat inward. Always when there is any stream running it is the upstream end of the boat which should be the initial point of 'contact' with the shore, and the part from which the first line must be made fast.

Once the boat is alongside she can be made fast properly, and if she is to be there for any length of time lines should be arranged on the pattern shown in Figure 21. When mooring alongside other boats always run out your *own* bow and stern warps. Don't rely on the chap alongside: it's not fair to him; he may want to leave port while you are drinking on shore; if his warps aren't up to it you'll be in trouble, too, and it will be your fault.

When mooring between piles come uptide or upwind, whichever will have the most effect in pushing you back again until a line can be made fast to one pile. If you have estimated wind/tide effect correctly the boat will lie with her head to the pile while you arrange the warp in the most convenient way. If it is a long warp you may be able to let your boat drift back until you can reach the other pile from the cockpit or after deck, but usually there will be a cross-wind, so that you will have to take the warp over in the dinghy. Where there is much tidal rise and fall, piles are fitted with rings and sliders, so that the end of your warp won't be 6 ft. under the water when you want to cast off: make fast to the ring. If your warp is long enough, pass it through the ring and bring the end back on board so that you can cast off without leaving the deck, but beware of chafe between rope and ring and don't leave the warp unattended for a long time.

Springs — one to stop forward movement
one to stop aft movement

Stern warp

Bow warp

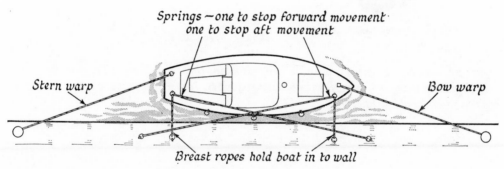

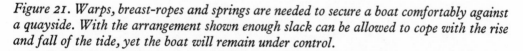

Breast ropes hold boat in to wall

Figure 21. Warps, breast-ropes and springs are needed to secure a boat comfortably against a quayside. With the arrangement shown enough slack can be allowed to cope with the rise and fall of the tide, yet the boat will remain under control.

If you come alongside an unfamiliar quay wall, give a thought to what might be under your keel—there is always a chance that the tide will drop you on to the stub of an old pile or something equally horrible.

Permanent moorings are usually laid by yards or harbour authorities, though some people lay their own. It is not unreasonable to make use of an unoccupied mooring, but one must use good sense in deciding whether the mooring was intended to hold a lighter boat than your own. Naturally one must not leave a boat unattended on a 'borrowed' mooring in case the rightful owner should come back while you are away.

To pick up a mooring the man on the foredeck should give hand signals, because the buoy will be lost to the helmsman's view as the boat gets close. Some people like to try to push the boat-hook through the ring on top of the buoy; others prefer to catch the buoy rope itself, sweeping the boat-hook in an arc beneath the water until it meets the hanging rope. Some people use the patent 'Grabbit' boat-hook ends which have a rope attached and hook on to the ring of the mooring buoy. A very simple method that is quite effective and easy for children is to string some small floats (cotton reels) along a Terylene cord. These will float beside the buoy and if you make a flat V-shaped hook of the kind shown in Figure 22, even the wildest swipe across the line of floats will result in a catch.

Figure 22. *One way to catch a mooring buoy. Bobbins threaded along a Terylene line allow a much greater margin of error for the boathook-swiper. It is useful to make a flat, V-shaped hook to catch a bobbin-line.*

7
The rule of the road

As sailing becomes more and more popular, and as coastal waters become more crowded, there is an increasing need for the owners of pleasure craft to know and obey the rules which govern the behaviour of all craft in tidal waters. There are certain inland waters which have special rules, but where the sea extends and where international traffic can move, there is one set of internationally agreed regulations. These rules have been framed with the intention of minimizing the risk of collision, which is not a matter to be taken lightly. That can be seen from the number of big ship collisions that are reported in the daily news, even though the vessels concerned have radar, radio telephones and every device they could possibly need. And you appreciate the seriousness of the matter even more when you are at sea in a 5-tonner and big ships are bearing down on you, one after another. Their high and sharp bows then acquire a specially malevolent appearance.

A man who has been used to racing around the buoys in a dinghy, or even in a bigger craft, may perhaps have regarded the rules as nothing more than the rules of a game, to be used to his own advantage and implying nothing more serious than a protest and perhaps disqualification if he breaks them. Quite apart from the fact that the racing rules are not the same thing as the 'Collision Regulations', the latter *must* be obeyed. If they are not, the result may range from loss of life and ship to a claim for damages.

Strangely enough, the title under which the rules are generally known is the Collision Regulations, whereas they are in fact the Regulations for Preventing Collisions at Sea. You can buy a copy from any branch of Her Majesty's Stationery Office for 4p., or 5p. by post, and I believe that every yachtsman should get hold of at least one copy and study it carefully. The language is the typical language of an Order in Council, and it does require a bit of effort to digest—still it is worth it, because you can then feel confident that you really do know.

The following pages are not meant to be a substitute for a thorough reading of the 'regs' themselves, but they may soften up the subject a bit in advance. Moreover, they give me an opportunity to make some comments which may be either useful or stimulating. I must emphasize that I have not attempted to deal with everything that is in the rules: much that concerns the lights and signals made by special purpose ships—those which are laying submarine cables, or sweeping mines, or trawling, for example—has been omitted. I do not mean to imply by those omissions that these things are not of importance to the yacht skipper. There are times when they may be very important. If the time comes when you see a vessel with either two or three white lights at her masthead it could be important to you to know that she is towing one or more vessels astern. If there are two white lights then the length of tow is less than 600 ft.; if three white lights, then it is longer.

For these special cases one needs the written information at hand, since it is unlikely that the 'week-end sailor' can remember all the rules. Something like the Skippers' Check Cards we devised for *Practical Boat Owner* magazine are useful for that purpose.

Lights to be carried between sunset and sunrise

A yacht under sail carries a white light showing astern, and green and red lights showing to starboard and port respectively. A yacht under power carries the same lights, plus an additional white light showing ahead. The rules stipulate that a vessel under sail must never carry the forward-shining white—a necessary provision since it is the absence of the forward white light that enables the skipper of a power vessel to recognize her for what she is, and to yield her right of way. Naturally a sailing vessel which has an auxiliary engine and is moving under power will show the lights appropriate to a power craft. Furthermore, if she is under both power and sail she is considered to be a powered vessel, and must act accordingly.

This stipulation applies for all the Collision Regulations, and that raises an interesting point—a vessel 'when proceeding under sail, when also being propelled by machinery shall carry in the daytime forward, where it can best be seen, one black conical shape, point downwards not less than 2 ft. in diameter at its base' (Rule 14). In fact small craft, under Rule 7g, may carry signals smaller than those prescribed, but I still don't see many yachtsmen complying with this regulation. Of course it's very irritating if you give way to a boat which you believe to be under sail, and then see the exhaust smoke from her engine as you pass astern. But one has to admit that with the modern sloop rig it is difficult to find a place to show this black cone in the forepart of the vessel, unless you fit a sprit or jackstaff on the stem for that express purpose.

But to go back to lights, which are shown in Figure 23. The stern light is to shine through an arc of 135 deg., or 67·5 deg. either side of the centre-line. The forward white light (when under power) shows over 225 deg., which is 112·5 deg. on either side. If you add these forward and rearward arcs together, it comes to 360 deg., which means that a vessel under power shows a white light over the whole horizon, whereas one under sail shows it only astern. The stern light is very important because (as we shall see later) an overtaking vessel must keep clear, and the sight of a white light is his sign to do so. And since we who cruise in small craft move much more slowly than the big ships the danger of being run down from astern is very real.

Much larger vessels carry two forward-showing white lights, both shining over the same arc of 225 deg. One of these lights is near the stem, and the other near the stern and set at least 15 ft. higher than the forward one. The relative positions of these two lights make a shape in the darkness which helps greatly in deciding the attitude of a big ship in relation to your own boat. The limit of size at which it becomes necessary to carry these two lights is a length of 65 ft. and over (Rule 7).

For many craft the port and starboard lamps must each show from dead ahead through an arc of 112·5 deg.—in other words the two together fill the same arc as the forward white light of the power vessel. Thus if you are coming up astern of any vessel you will see a single white light, and you are considered to be the overtaking vessel if you are in the arc where you *can* see that light. (More on that point later.) But if you are approaching anywhere within the forward arc you will see either a red or a green light alone, if she is under sail. But if the other vessel is under power you will see the red or the green plus a white light, or two white lights for a large craft.

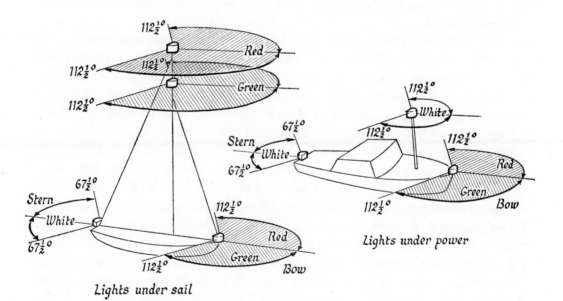

Lights under sail

Lights under power

Figure 23. The lights to be carried by a vessel under sail, left, and under power, right. The masthead red and green for a sailing boat are optional, furthermore, if the boat is less than 40 ft. long her red and green sidelights need not show through the precise angles indicated (see text). The angle of the stern light ($22\frac{1}{2}$ deg. abaft the beam) is of importance in the overtaking rule.

But the people who framed the rules made special allowances for smallish craft which cannot carry such elaborate gear as the big ships. Thus a vessel less than 65 ft. long, under power, may carry a combined green and red light, showing through the prescribed arcs and not less than 3 ft. lower than the forward white light. The forward white light should be not less than 9 ft. above the gunwale, though if the vessel is less than 40 ft. long it may be lower so long as it is at least 3 ft. higher than the red and green lights. Most yachts will come under this rule—at least most of those for whose owners this book is intended. Even though one owns a sailing cruiser, there will come a time when she is 'proceeding under power', and it is likely that she will be less than 40 ft. long, I imagine.

Now comes a curious point. Vessels under sail are also allowed to carry a combined red and green lamp, but when they are less than 40 ft. long, whereas for power craft the length limit is 65 ft. Furthermore, the combined lantern for a sailing craft is to be carried 'where it can best be seen' and 'showing a green light on one side and a red light on the other . . .'. No mention of any precise angles, you see, though the rule adds that the lantern shall be visible at 1 mile, and so fixed that 'the green light shall not be seen on the port side, nor the red light on the starboard side'. If it is 'not possible' to fix this light it must be kept ready for use and shown in sufficient time to prevent collision (Rule 7d).

Although this rule gives a vessel under sail more latitude in the arrangement of her lights than a powered craft, one comes back to the fact that nowadays we are all likely to be under power at some time or other. On the other hand, when you are under sail you do have a bit of latitude. In fact under these rules you would be perfectly entitled to use the method which a friend of mine has used with great success. He owned a sailing cruiser without generator or accumulators, and he was therefore obliged to use either oil or dry batteries for his lights. Knowing that neither would produce a sufficiently bright light in the ordinary way, he bought an ex-army signalling lamp which sends a narrow but very intense beam similar to that of an Aldis lamp. As it happened, the lamp came complete with red and green filters, though these could have been made for the purpose if necessary. Armed with this lamp my friend could show a very bright red or green light towards the centre of any approaching ship, and he was in no doubt that his signal was clearly identifiable over a distance of several miles. Evidently such a lamp as that comes within the rules if it is kept ready for use, and so long as the colours are only shown on their correct sides of your boat. Equally evident is the fact that by this method it is up to you to keep a sharp lookout, and also to aim the lamp accurately, since the beam is narrow.

Additional lights for craft under sail

A boat under sail may carry an additional set of lights if she wishes (and if she has plenty of spare battery power). Rule 5b says that 'a sailing vessel may carry on the top of the foremast two lights in a vertical line, one over the other, sufficiently separated so as to be clearly distinguished. The upper light shall be red and the lower light shall be green'. Both these lights are to show forward over an arc of 225 deg. This is the arc whose port and starboard halves are in any case covered by the usual port and starboard lights which must still be carried.

To make the point quite clear, both the masthead lights are visible over the whole arc, so that a sailing vessel fitted with them will show to port (reading downward) *red, green, red*. To starboard she will show *red, green, green*. If a sailing vessel chooses to carry these extra lights (the rules say 'may', not 'shall') she should be immediately identifiable as a vessel under sail. It must be admitted that the red-over-green array gives a more positive identification than the mere absence of a white light. On the other hand there are possibilities of confusion because the high-up red-over-green set will show up before the usual lights come into view and it may be difficult to know whether one is seeing the ordinary port and starboard lamps head on and relatively close-to, or the masthead lights farther off. A more serious criticism is that the use of additional lights on a sailing craft is undesirable since she must be relying on her accumulators. Usually, sailing craft tend to be short of electrical energy, which is one reason why their navigation lights are seldom bright enough. It would seem more sensible, if there is current to spare, to concentrate it into brightening the lights which *must* be carried, and not to dissipate it on others which *may* be carried.

Be that as it may, it is important to remember that the lights we have been talking about are those to be shown when the vessel is under way, which means that she is not anchored, or made fast to the shore, or aground. In the regulations 'under way' includes drifting, even though the vessel may not be making any headway through the water.

This is perhaps a moment to take breath and stand back from what is a rather complex situation—even though we have barely started! I will take the opportunity to point out that these Collision Regulations are agreed among many nations through the International Maritime Consultative Organization, but that I do not really understand what legal force they have. For example, to the best of my knowledge there is no policeman who will come alongside in a launch, take out his notebook and ask why it is that your forward white light is not the regulation 3 ft. above the green and red. I am no lawyer, so I cannot pronounce with finality, but I suspect that there is no punishment laid down in the Statute Book for anyone who fails to comply with the regulations. I take them to be in the nature of a valuable convention, and I take it that in the event of a collision or some other mishap the skipper and the owner of a vessel that was not properly lit, for example, would be held blameworthy on that account. Common sense tells us that we should obey the regulations to the letter as far as possible, and absolutely to the spirit.

The rule of the road

Lights and shapes when at anchor

After that digression let us get back to the matter in hand. When a vessel is at anchor she must show a white light visible all round the horizon. A vessel of more than 150 ft. in length must carry two white lights, one near the stem and the other near the stern. A smaller vessel *must* show one, but *may* show two if the skipper chooses. That is a rule I appreciate for, although some people are rather casual about anchor lights, I am not. It is rather unpleasant to be lying in your berth, suddenly wakened by the throb of approaching engines and to wonder if the so-and-so has seen you. One does not wish to be run down at any time, but there is something particularly unpleasant about the prospect when one is in bed.

According to Rule 7c, 'between sunrise and sunset every vessel when at anchor shall carry in the forepart of the vessel where it can best be seen, one black ball not less than 2 ft. in diameter'. Not many yachtsmen comply with this rule, I regret to say. Happily Rule 7g comes to our aid again by permitting small craft to show day signals smaller than prescribed. It does not say how much smaller, but common sense would suggest not less than 1 ft. in diameter. This tolerance, by the way, is extended to power-driven vessels less than 65 ft. in length and sailing vessels less than 40 ft. in length. The rules seem to me to be ambiguous when it comes to deciding whether a vessel at anchor is propelled by power or sails, when she is evidently being propelled by neither. But I deduce that a sailing vessel which is fitted with an auxiliary motor could take advantage of this dispensation to carry a smaller signal so long as she was not more than 65 ft. long.

Instead of splitting hairs—something practical: the black ball would not literally be a sphere. One cuts two circles of plywood, aluminium or some similarly suitable material, and one makes a slot in each from the edge to the centre. Then you drill suitable holes for a shackle, paint them black and you are all prepared to flaunt your superiority over all your friends! In fact, of course, such a sign is really quite valuable, for one often wants to know whether 'that boat over there is at anchor'. A naval vessel or merchantman will tell you at once by his day signal—regrettably a yacht seldom will.

When aground a large vessel has to show her anchor lights together with two red lights vertically one over the other and not less than 6 ft. apart and visible all round the horizon. By day she has to show three black balls, vertically in line, not less than 6 ft. apart and each not less than 2 ft. in diameter (Rule 11e). Power craft under 65 ft. and sailing craft under 40 ft. are excused from showing these signals (7g): by night they must either show the correct lights or *none at all*. To show an ordinary white anchor light would lead other people to suppose that your boat was afloat at anchor and might lead them to run their boats aground too.

To sum up, a yacht must show her navigation lights or her anchor light(s) by night, and by day she must show a black ball when at anchor, or a black cone if under both sail and power. As I have said, the day signals are very rarely shown, but that does not prevent anyone from setting a good example. . . .

In addition to those lights and marks, Rule 12 says that any vessel on the water may attract attention when necessary by showing a 'flare-up' light, or by making a detonating or other efficient sound signal which cannot be confused with any of the other signals prescribed in the regulations. As described later, there are special sound signals for use in fog. By a flare-up light is meant a white flare, though any other white light would do as well, and a flashing white masthead light is, I think, the coming thing. It must not be a red flare because that is a sign of distress and you will be alerting the Coast-guard and turning out the lifeboat if you show one of those.

I need hardly remark that it is not sufficient to know what lights or shapes your own vessel should carry. That is the first requirement, of course, but just as you should comply with the regulations so that other skippers know what kind of vessel yours is and what she is doing, so you must be able to recognize the signals of others. There are all sorts of different night and day signals for vessels fishing, for vessels being towed and so forth. For the week-end sailor there are too many to be memorized (at least there are for me). But at least one should have the details on board, and know where to find them when they are wanted.

Care in showing other lights

There are two final points concerning one's own lights. The first is that although they are normally to be shown between sunset and sunrise, they 'may' also be shown at other times when visibility is bad or in circumstances when the skipper thinks it necessary. The other point concerns the showing of lights other than those laid down, and as I have remarked before this is a matter which makes some people very cross indeed.

The regulations say that between sunset and sunrise 'no other lights shall be exhibited, except such lights as cannot be mistaken for the prescribed lights, or impair their visibility or distinctive character, or interfere with the keeping of a proper look-out'.

In spite of the fact that ocean liners sail along with lights blazing from end to end, coloured fairy lights (and a band playing full blast), some purists have come down heavily on yachts which carry working lights to illuminate the deck. In fact the rules do not forbid it, and all one has to ensure is that these lights which are usually fitted under the cross-trees or spreaders to shine downward, cannot be mistaken for some special signal. For example, a vessel towing or pushing another vessel shows two white lights, one vertically above the other: a vessel not under command shows two red lights: a vessel laying or picking up a submarine cable carries a white light with red lights vertically above and below it. These are just some examples of special light signals, but there should be no chance of confusion if working lights are properly shielded so as to direct their light down toward the deck.

Sound signals in fog or bad visibility

Fog is a great danger to yachtsmen, especially in the busy coastal waters where so many of us necessarily spend a good deal of our 'sea-time'. Right out in the Atlantic one would be pretty safe, but we seldom get there. Equally, if one can get into the shallows where bigger craft cannot go, that is a sensible thing to do. If that is not possible, hoist a radar reflector, make the prescribed noise signals, go very warily, and listen hard for other vessels' signals (or for the throb of engines). It will be easier to hear them if you do not run your own engine, so sail if you can: oddly enough, there is often a good breeze in a sea fog. If you must run your engine and it is a noisy one, as most boat installations are, then it will be a help if you can post somebody forward on deck where he can hear better.

A vessel of less than 40 ft. in length is excused from giving the fog signals laid down for other vessels (Rule 15c, ix). But she has to make 'some other efficient sound signals at intervals of not more than one minute'. The problem, of course, is how to make a noise loud enough to be heard at a distance by a man high on the bridge of some great ship. There's no doubt that it's best to carry a foghorn and a bell—the bell is not too difficult, but a powerful foghorn is not so easily found. Those which run from aerosol cannisters are quite good, but one wishes for a note both deeper and louder. I believe that the real answer may lie in an electronic foghorn. When one thinks of the ghastly row an ordinary transistor set can create it should be possible to generate a useful noise. . . .

Now let us look at the uses of horns and bells in foggy weather, but first it is necessary to make some definitions. In the regulations:

A 'short blast' is one that lasts about 1 sec.

A 'long blast' last from 4 to 6 sec.

From the point of view of yachtsmen the most important fog signals are the following, but there are special ones for vessels being towed, vessels not under command and so forth.

(1) A power-driven vessel making way through the water makes prolonged blasts at intervals of not more than 2 min.

(2) A power-driven vessel, under way but stopped and not making way through the water, sounds two prolonged blasts, with about 1 sec. between them at intervals of not more than 2 min.

(3) A sailing vessel under way sounds, at intervals of not more than 1 min.,

one blast if on the starboard tack,

two blasts if on the port tack,

three blasts if with the wind abaft the beam.

The rules do not say whether these blasts by a sailing vessel are to be short or long, but one assumes they would be short. Another rather ambiguous aspect of this rule concerns the right of way of sailing craft. As is explained later on, whether the boat is running with the wind abaft the beam has no bearing on right of way, although at one time under former rules it did. It seems that when the right of way rules were changed somebody forgot to change the sound signals to conform. But more of that in a page or two. The final rule for sound signals says:

(4) Any vessel at anchor must sound a bell rapidly for about 5 sec. at intervals of not more than 1 min. Very long vessels may have one bell forward and another aft. In addition you are allowed to sound three blasts in succession to attract attention to yourself if you hear another vessel approaching. These three blasts are in the form of the morse code letter R, or 'short, long, short'.

It is obvious that you must go carefully in fog, but there is a definite rule which says that any power-driven craft which hears 'apparently forward of the beam the fog signal of a vessel the position of which is not ascertained, shall, so far as the circumstances of the case admit, stop her engines and then navigate with caution until danger of collision is over' (Rule 16b). Moreover, Rule 16c makes a similar provision for a case where the vessel ahead is detected by radar.

Steering and sailing rules

The steering and sailing rules say which vessel has the right of way, and which must yield. The regulations make the overriding comment that 'in obeying and construing these Rules, any action should be positive, in ample time, and with due regard to the observation of good seamanship'. In other words, bluffing, or any pretence that you are not going to yield right of way in the hope that the other chap will weaken, is no more excusable at sea than it is in a motor-car on the highway. There have been occasions of that sort when a collision has resulted because at the last moment both craft have altered course, and the changes taken together have cancelled out. It is rather like the two gentlemen bowing each other through the door, and finally making up their minds to move at precisely the same moment. But if it were a gentleman and a lady there would be no doubt about the matter, the lady would go first and there would be no chance of a collision. At sea, each party must know who has priority and then there is no risk.

Most of these rules can be divided into those for power craft and those for sailing craft, always remembering that a boat running under sail and power simultaneously is considered to be a power craft.

One rule that applies equally to either form of propulsion is the overtaking rule (Rule 24) which says that the overtaking vessel must keep clear. Thus if you are overtaking a motor cruiser in your sailing dinghy, then you must keep clear. Obviously one does not always come up from dead astern, and there are other rules for boats whose courses are crossing. So there has to be a definition of 'overtaking'. Rule 24b says: 'Every vessel coming up with another vessel from any direction more than $22\frac{1}{2}$ degrees (two points) abaft her beam, i.e. in such a position, with reference to the vessel which she is not overtaking, that at night she would be unable to see either of that vessel's sidelights, shall be deemed to be an overtaking vessel; and no subsequent alteration of the bearing between the two vessels shall make the vessel a crossing vessel within the meaning of these Rules, or relieve her of the duty of keeping clear of the overtaken vessel until she is finally past and clear.'

There are some comments worth making on that rule. In the first place it reveals that the drafters had (not for the only time) forgotten about the small sailing boat. In an attempt to make the thing clear they say that you are overtaking when you cannot see either of the other chap's side-lights. But their own Rule 7d allows sailing craft under 40 ft. length to show side lights which do not fit in with the 'overtaking angle'. Had they taken the positive aspect of the matter, and said that you are the overtaking vessel when you *can* see the other vessel's stern light they would have been on firmer ground. Even though under Rule 10b a 'small vessel' (size not defined) need not show a stern light through a definite angle, she must show a white light to a vessel which is overtaking her. This may sound like splitting hairs, but for the most part the rules are precise and hair-splitting, as they should be. But where they can least afford to be imprecise and ambiguous is where they concern matters of right-of-way. Unfortunately that is just where they seem to be weakest. From a practical point of view, we who have to try and conduct ourselves by the rules must remember that we may be legally overtaking even when we can see the other vessel's green or red light, because she may quite legally show them through a larger arc than applies to larger craft. That ties up nicely with another paragraph in the overtaking rule which says that if an overtaking vessel is not sure whether she has approached within the prescribed angle of $22\frac{1}{2}$ deg. abaft the beam, then the skipper must assume that his is an overtaking vessel, and act accordingly.

My second comment on this rule is not another quibble (relief all round!). It concerns the bit about 'no subsequent alteration of the bearing . . .'. Obviously it would not do if the overtaking vessel were to come just forward of the 'overtaking' arc of $22\frac{1}{2}$ deg. abaft the beam and then assume the rights of a vessel on a crossing course. For example, if you were both under power, and she were to come up on your starboard quarter, then once forward of a line $22\frac{1}{2}$ deg. abaft the beam she would have right of way over you—*if* the rule had not been written so wisely as it has.

This brings us, slightly ahead of time to the rules for power-propelled craft which I will summarize as follows:

(1) 'When two power-driven vessels are meeting end-on, or nearly end-on, so as to

involve risk of collision, each shall alter her course to starboard, so that each may pass on the port side of the other . . .' (Rule 19).

The rule goes on to some helpful explanations about masts in line, whether both the red and green lights are visible, or only one of them and suchlike aids to deciding where there is in fact risk of collision. I would make the observation that this rule puts a duty on *each* vessel to alter course, whereas in other situations, only one of the craft must alter course. For example,

(2) 'When two power-driven vessels are crossing, so as to involve risk of collision, the vessel which has the other vessel on her own starboard side shall keep out of the way of the other' (Rule 19). Another rule explains that 'to keep out of the way' means to avoid crossing ahead of the other vessel, and, if necessary to stop, slow down, or go into reverse.

And now we come to the most frequently quoted rule of all: 'power gives way to sail'. This is Rule 20a, and it simply says that when a power craft and a sailing craft are on courses which involve a risk of collision, the power craft must keep clear. But Rule 20b explains that this does not give a sailing vessel the right 'to hamper, in a narrow channel, the safe passage of a power-driven vessel which can navigate only inside such a channel'. That seems only common sense, and most people would automatically keep clear of a large ship coming up the Solent, say. But there have been occasions when the skipper of a racing boat has thought that his chance of winning a cup was more important than the pilotage of the *Queen Elizabeth*.

Priority between sailing craft

The regulations about which I have been writing are those which were agreed at the International Conference on Safety of Life at Sea which was held in London in June 1960. Because it takes some time for governments to ratify such agreements, the rules did not come into force until some years later. Various changes were made at that 1960 conference, including a modification to the rules as between two vessels both of which are under sail. This is Rule 17, and I will quote it in full before making any comments. It says:

'(a) When two sailing vessels are approaching one another, so as to involve risk of collision, one of them shall keep out of the way of the other as follows:
  (i) When each has the wind on a different side, the vessel which has the wind on the port side shall keep out of the way of the other.
  (ii) When both have the wind on the same side, the vessel which is to windward shall keep out of the way of the vessel which is to leeward.
(b) For the purpose of this Rule the windward side shall be deemed to be the side opposite to that on which the mainsail is carried or, in the case of a square rigged vessel, the opposite to that on which the largest fore and aft sail is carried.'

This is a short, and apparently simple rule, but it is one that I have always considered to be badly framed. The first point is that if the 'windward side' is defined by the side on which the mainsail is carried, then it would have been more sensible to use those words in the rule itself. In fact that might have revealed more quickly what a bad rule it is.

It is easy enough to interpret in the simple case where two boats are beating to windward on different tacks. If their courses are crossing the boat which has her mainsail on the starboard side will give way. You will see, also, that she has the other vessel on her starboard side too, and thus the rule corresponds with that for powered craft on crossing courses.

But difficulties come when craft are running before the wind. If you are beating up wind and another boat is running down towards you, then she must give way if you both have your mainsails on the same side because she is the windward boat. But if you have your mainsail to starboard and she has hers to port, then you must give way. Of course, she may have had her sail to starboard a couple of seconds earlier, and it may have arrived on the port side by a sudden gybe. . . .

At night you would very possibly be unable to tell where that same vessel's mainsail was, or even if she was carrying a mainsail at all. Boats often sail under a headsail alone, or under jib and mizzen. Not only is it impossible to detect that sort of rig in the dark or fog, the situation is just as confusing in broad daylight. The word 'mainsail' is not defined, and with schooners, barquentines and heaven knows what other rigs one may come across the decision is not an easy one to make. Even the seemingly simple two-masted rigs are *not* always simple in practice. A ketch, whose after mast is the lower of the two, carries her mainsail on the forward mast. A schooner's mainsail is on the after mast which is the higher of the two. But I have seen boats with two masts so nearly equal in height that it was not possible to be sure whether the definition schooner or ketch should apply until you were square abeam—so there was no means of knowing in advance which was the mainsail.

A further indication of the muddle-headedness of this rule can be found in the sound signals for use in fog, which I have already described. These are not related to the side on which the mainsail is carried, and are in fact left over from a former set of rules with which they did harmonize. The sad thing is that it would have been so easy to make sailing vessels subject to the same, perfectly clear, rules that govern powered craft on a collision course. . . .

But the rule exists and we who sail must do our best to apply it, and even that is not always so simple as it sounds, as I shall try to explain.

Manœuvres to avoid collision

In spite of everything, collisions still do occur. One reason is that the rules are not always obeyed, another is that sometimes in the attempt to avoid collision the *wrong* manœuvre is made. Like two people trying to show politeness at a doorway, two ships can simultaneously turn to collide. If that sounds unlikely I will try to explain in a moment, but first let us see what the Collision Regulations have to say.

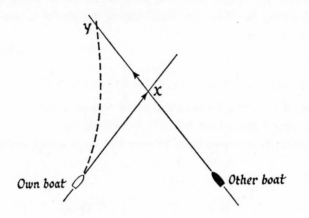

Figure 24. A perfectly safe situation can be made dangerous by the wrong manœuvre. In this case 'own' boat turns away *from 'other' boat and so creates a collision situation.*

Their first point (Rule 21) is that where one vessel is to keep out of the way, the other shall 'keep her course and speed'. But the same rule adds that if for any reason collision seems imminent the right of way vessel shall also 'take such action as will best aid to avert collision'. That sounds like common sense, but it raises the question of what *is* the right action. Some years ago Mr. E. S. Calvert of the Royal Aircraft Establishment at Farnborough made a close study of manœuvres for avoiding collisions between aircraft, but his findings were equally sound for ships. He found that there were two things the master of a vessel can do in taking avoiding action—one is to turn and the other is to change speed. Moreover, he showed clearly how a change of course and of speed could on some occasions make the situation worse rather than better, or even leave it unchanged because the actions cancel each other.

One has first to decide whether the two vessels are on a 'collision course'. The method is quite simple in theory, since one merely has to see whether the bearing of the other vessel changes or remains constant. If the other vessel remains at, say, 45 deg. on your starboard bow then ultimately your two boats will collide. As is indicated in Figure 24 the two tracks will ultimately cross—that is not in question. What one wants to know is whether the two boats will pass point X, the crossing point, at the same time. In the example shown, if the other boat is moving more quickly towards the crossing point than your own boat then her bearing will be swinging across your bow.

After a time it will change from a bearing on the starboard bow to a bearing on the port bow.

In such a situation as that, if you were to increase speed there is the chance that you might reach point X at the same time as the other vessel. Alternatively by turning away from her to your left, you might find yourself meeting her at point Y. It is important therefore to understand how one can avoid taking the wrong actions. Calvert's rules tell us precisely what to do:

Vessel on Collision Course on your Starboard Hand

1. If she is ahead of your beam—turn right and reduce speed.
2. If she is abaft your beam—turn left and reduce speed.

If the occasion arises where you have to give way to a vessel approaching on your port hand:

Vessel on Collision Course on your Port Hand

1. If she is forward of your beam—turn right and increase speed.
2. If she is abaft your beam—turn left and increase speed.

These rules are summarized diagrammatically in Figure 25. It will be seen that you turn to starboard for threats coming from forward of the beam, but to port for threats coming from abaft the beam. Likewise, if the threat comes from starboard reduce your speed, but if it comes from port increase your speed.

It is important to remember that these manœuvres are for collision course—that's to say when the other vessel remains on a constant bearing. If her bearing is swinging round ahead or astern of you then all is well.

Normally if you are under power you will be giving way to other power craft on your starboard hand, but to sailing craft crossing from any quarter. If both boats are under sail and beating to windward with crossing tacks, then you will be giving way to the other chap when he is on your starboard hand. But if you are beating to windward with your mainsail out to starboard and another sailing boat is running downwind and 'threatening' you on your port side, then you will have to give way. Thus it is necessary to know the right manœuvres for threats from either side. Of course, in a sailing boat speed alterations cannot be made to order. In that case you simply make the appropriate turn. There are occasions in sailing boats where that will naturally involve a change of speed; it is important therefore to take note of any natural speed change in case it is contrary to the Calvert rules.

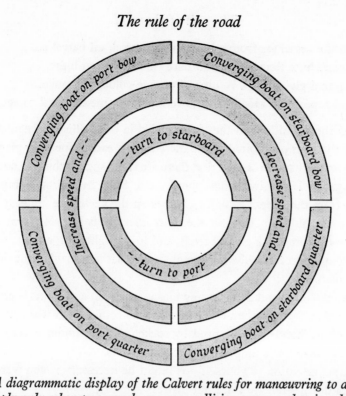

Figure 25. A diagrammatic display of the Calvert rules for manœuvring to avoid collision. The rules apply only when two vessels are on a collision course—that is, when the bearing of each from the other remains constant. The diagram should be read from the outside towards the centre. Thus if you observe a vessel on a collision course, and off the port bow, you should, (a) increase speed and, (b) turn to starboard. If the other skipper is meanwhile observing you over his starboard quarter, he should, (a) decrease speed, and, (b) turn to port.

Distress signals

Although frantic wavings and gesticulations from a boat may be interpreted as a cry for help by sharp-witted people ashore, you are likely to do better if you stick to the internationally agreed distress signals. Oddly enough, these are listed in the Collision Regulations as Rule 31. They are:

1. A gun or other explosive fired at intervals of about 1 min.
2. Continuous sounding with any fog-signalling apparatus.
3. Rockets or shells throwing red stars one at a time at short intervals.
4. A signal made by radiotelegraphy or by any other signalling method consisting of the group . . . – – – . . . in the Morse Code.
5. A signal sent by radiotelephony consisting of the spoken word 'Mayday'.
6. The International Code signal of distress indicated by NC. (Normally shown by means of signal flags.)
7. A signal consisting of a square flag having above or below it a ball, or anything resembling a ball.

8. Flames on the vessel (as from a burning tar barrel, oil barrel etc.).
9. A rocket parachute flare, or a hand flare showing a red light.
10. A smoke signal giving off a volume of orange-coloured smoke.
11. Slowly and repeatedly raising and lowering arms outstretched to each side.

I have given the definitions as they are worded in the Collision Regulations, which also has a rule that it is prohibited to use these signals except for their proper purpose.

Looking down the list one can see that there are some signals that are not easily made from a small yacht. Explosive bangs, morse code SOS by radiotelegraphy, Mayday (which comes from the French *m'aidez*), flames on the vessel are not easy for the likes of us. Perhaps the quickest, but not the most effective is the slow arm flapping—at least there's no equipment to go and fetch, and in daylight with a man overboard and other boats around you can make the signal at once without leaving the deck or losing sight of your man.

The fact that you can send SOS by any means is useful, and if one is going to sound continuously with a foghorn then one might as well sound SOS while one is about it. Signal flares, either hand-held, or fired by rocket to hang under a parachute can be bought from any chandler's shop. So can red star shells. (White flares, by the way, can be used to attract attention to yourself—as might be necessary if you were threatened with being run down—but they are not distress signals.)

The signal flags N and C can easily be carried aboard, and the square flag above a ball can easily be improvised. These shapes can be made up of anything—the ball can be a bundle of clothes. Better still, if you carry a black ball for a daylight 'at anchor' signal as one is supposed to do then only the square flag need be improvised.

In short there are plenty of distress signals which will be immediately recognized by a coastguard or a trained seaman, and by a good many yachtsmen. Therefore there is no need to try to get one's point home by any unofficial antics.

8

What kind of boat?

The man who wants to take up cruising nowadays has a very much wider choice open to him than we had before the war; the changes in designers' thoughts about cruising boats have been no less sweeping than they were with racing dinghies. Indeed, the revolution is not yet complete—the catamaran and the trimaran are developments which are full of promise; there is a great deal to be done with plastics; bilge keels have come to stay and are capable of further development. But even with all the developments that are still unfulfilled the difference that has come over the cruising-boat picture in the past few years almost passes belief. In Part Two there is a list of standard small cruisers, all of modest price—even as recently as 20 years ago I doubt if one could have compiled a list one-tenth as long.

One of the things that made this development possible was the development (originally for aircraft use) of resin-glued plywood, which is light, strong and impervious to water. In the period 1960 to 1965 (broadly speaking) plywood cruising boats appeared on the market in large numbers and were bought eagerly. But towards the end of the period, boats built in polyester resin reinforced with glass fibre began to appear, and since that time they have come to dominate the market in moderately priced family cruising boats. But although resinglass has achieved a dominant position, the customer still has a choice of structural material. The traditional forms of wooden building are still thriving and, if one troubles to go shopping in Holland, some excellent steel-hulled boats are available.

With such a choice the question is often asked 'which is the best material?' The only sensible answer one can make is 'that is the wrong question'. Each material has its advantages and disadvantages, so that one has to find out first what sort of boat one really wants, and for what purpose. One may find that although one's preference is, say, for resinglass, the only available boat that comes near one's ideal of size, layout and *price*, happens to be built in wood. Never mind: there is one thing one can say with reasonable certainty, and that is that a boat built properly in steel, wood, or plastics, is able to live at least as long as her owner, which is far more than can be said for most

89

motor-cars. To my mind that is a most pertinent point, to which it is necessary to add only that the boat must be well looked after if she is to achieve her maximum life. So the first thing when shopping for a boat is to list all one's preferences or desires, then see what is actually available on the market within your price limit.

There is something for every taste, which is just as well, because utility and efficiency are not by any means the dominant criteria in a man's choice of boat, any more than they are in his choice of wife. Sentiment and emotion play a very important role, often disguised and justified by a variety of carefully contrived 'reasons'. Thus however seaworthy and habitable catamarans and other multi-hulled craft may prove to be, there will always be people who remain loyal to the single hull—because it embodies their traditional idea of a boat. For similar reasons some men will choose a clinker-built hull, or a gaff-cutter rig in preference to a glass-fibre hull with aluminium spars and stainless-steel fittings. The one is emotionally satisfying, the other is far more practical and cheaper to maintain. Of course, there will always be the extremists, some of whom will stand by oak and tar and hemp regardless of cost or practical considerations, and the others who will dedicate themselves to efficiency, assessing all their boating in terms of weight, drag and speed. But most people are conscious of both sides of the matter and will have to balance the emotional attraction of something like a quay punt against the simplicity of a boat like the little Halcyon. I have even known some men swing from one extreme to the other, but most try to make a sensible compromise.

The one certain thing that comes out of all this is that there is no one kind of boat that can be said to be best: it all depends on the character of the owner and the kinds of thing he wants to do with the boat. If you are going to potter around the coasts of Britain, with an occasional sortie across the Channel, there's no point in modelling your needs on the experiences of someone who had a bad time in the hurricanes of the southern Pacific. In fact, if someone tells you that such and such a boat must be best because that's the type that Fred Fortescue used in his amazing 10,000-mile voyage from Oolomoloo to Parrioca, you can be sure that at least his reasoning is wrong.

Long-distance ocean voyages have been made in almost every *kind* of vessel you can imagine, open boats, catamarans, hard chine, round bilge, centre-board, bilge keel, fixed keel, sloop, square rigged, gunter lug and all the rest. And when you come nearer home it's no different: if you could take a helicopter over the Solent or some such place on a fine summer week-end you would get a bird's-eye view of craft of every conceivable shape, size and rig, all going quite well and all giving their owners a thoroughly good time. To hear some 'experts' talk at the bar you might suppose that all gaff-rigged vessels could only sail backward, or that any boat with a straight stem would be bound to sink as soon as the breeze rose over Force 3. But the more boats you see and the more you sail in, the better you appreciate the varied and different forms a perfectly satisfactory vessel can take.

Still, you will have to make some sort of choice, within the limits of your purse, and the main thing to decide is what you really want to do with your boat. If you have been used to dinghy racing, you may be attracted to the idea of speed, but quite different considerations apply with cruising boats; for example, if speed really were the primary aim, then the thing would be to go for as long a waterline length as you can afford. That is what will give you the highest real speed—that's to say the shortest time between two points. On the other hand, if you are thinking of racing your boat, then you will be more interested in *relative* speed, the speed of your boat in relation to other boats with the same handicap: you then find yourself in the maze of 'ratings' and you find yourself with a boat whose dimensions have been decided largely by the arbitrary arithmetic of some handicapping rule. It is not the place of this book to deal with the real cruiser-racer of that kind, which is usually a very expensive boat. This does not mean that racing is going to be impossible for the man who has only a modest amount of money to spend on a small cruising boat; on the contrary, there are ever-increasing possibilities for racing. This results from the popularity of the 'standard boat' in the last few years. There have always been standard boats, of course, but never in such numbers as there are now; what is more, the numbers are climbing steadily and this makes it possible for clubs to organize class races for small cruising boats. There can be few cruising centres where it would not be possible in any summer now to organize a class race for Silhouettes, Caprices, Tridents, Kestrels, Vivacities and many other types. Each year as more and more people take to the water with standard designs, so the opportunities for class races grow.

One result of this trend is that even for the man who very much wants to use his boat for racing, the way is still open to base his choice of craft on its other qualities. And now, what are those other qualities?

Seaworthiness is without doubt the overriding quality that is desired, and next to that comfort. To a large extent these two qualities go together, for they both tend to improve with increasing size. Remembering that we are in any case thinking mainly of the very small craft—all of them below 10 tons, the merits of size are in the extra freeboard, the increased waterline length and the relatively smaller area of open boat that is represented by the cockpit. With increasing size, other things being equal, there comes a steadier motion and a greater ability to make headway against seas. Working aboard becomes easier with more deck space to move about on, and this is important, because the greatest weakness is, in fact, likely to be the seaworthiness of the crew: anything that helps to improve the crew's own performance is worth while . . . here again there is a close parallel between seaworthiness and comfort.

The benefits of sufficient size

It follows that, so long as we are talking of *small* boats, the bigger the boat you can get the better. There are many excellent books to which the serious reader may have turned for advice which warn against the dangers of buying too big a boat; in fact, in times past the advice was usually to look for the smallest boat that could possibly satisfy your needs. All that advice was very sound in its time, but times have changed and the boats of today are very different from the ones that those authors had in mind. They would have been thinking of heavy, slab-sided ex-fishing smacks, or pukka yachts with long overhangs fore and aft, and hollow volumes of wasted space below. That was a time when at least one paid hand would always be aboard, and spars and canvas were very much larger and heavier, boat for boat, than they are today. Then a big, old boat could likely be bought at a very low price, but the subsequent maintenance costs would be high and the work aboard would be heavy without the help of paid hands.

The soundness of going as big as you can (up to 8 or 10 tons) will easily be recognized if you have the opportunity to go aboard a few craft of different sizes. If you have a chance to compare living aboard, say, a 3-tonner and a 6-tonner for a week or so in each, so much the better. It is perfectly true that designers are able to work four berths into a waterline length of 16 ft., but *living* aboard a boat demands more than a bunk's length for each passenger. There are a great many things to be stowed, oilskins, dry clothes, cameras, first-aid, cushions and bedding, shoes, books and charts, sails, warps and fenders, loaves of bread, tins of corned beef, bottles of milk, a wireless receiver, plates and cutlery, tools and oil lamps, petrol cans and water breakers. . . . The list can go on and on, and although some people are very weight-conscious and impose an iron discipline on the crew to prevent them bringing their knick-knacks on board, most people find that the amount of gear grows steadily as the season progresses. What's more the next season seems automatically to *begin* at a higher level, so to speak, and to rise from there in the usual way. The thing to remember is that whatever amount of gear *you* are going to permit for two, or four people, the bigger the boat the less she will notice it. Although a bigger boat may entice people to bring more gear aboard, the number of cushions, mattresses, blankets, knives and forks and so forth will remain the same and any increase in the total weight of gear on board will be proportionately less than the increase in the size of the boat.

In a very small boat those on board need to be well disciplined. Undressing for bed in what amounts to a box about 6 ft. square and $4\frac{1}{2}$ ft. high has to be done one at a time, almost 'by numbers'. And when everyone is settled, if there is a minor emergency, such as a dragging anchor half-way through the night and someone has to scramble over semi-conscious and slightly rebellious bodies, the lack of manœuvring space makes itself apparent.

For people with children (and a high proportion of people who are turning from dinghy sailing to something bigger will be doing so *because* they have children) the need for as much space as possible below decks will become even more apparent as soon as foul weather blows up. Thanks to the conservatism of those who control our educational system, August remains the primary holiday month for people with children, and this is the month of worst weather. If there are no gales there will almost certainly be days of blustery winds and continuous rain. The prudent skipper will have heard and recorded all the B.B.C.'s shipping forecasts (and the mainland forecasts, too), so if the weather is really bad it's a hundred to one that he will be snugly at anchor in a sheltered creek. But it is not likely to be the sort of place where the children can find bad-weather amusement ashore, so the day will be passed in what amounts to a small box, with steamed-up portlights and rain beating steadily on the deck above. This is such a common situation in our climate that I thought it worth while to mention in an earlier chapter some of the more obvious things that one can do to pass the time, but plenty of room below is obviously a good thing at such times.

Deep draught, or shoal?

Perhaps this seeming digression has helped to show the kind of consideration that is especially important in choosing a boat for cruising. Unlike a dinghy, which one may use for an afternoon's sail before returning to the warmth and comforts of a home ashore, a cruising boat has to be one's home for quite long periods of time. It has to do far more than just act as a wind-driven waterborne vehicle. For that reason one has to ask oneself, not only 'How will she go?' but also 'Where will she go?' This is where draught and the shape of the underwater hull become of so much importance. There have been many arguments upon hull shape and about shoal versus deep draught for sailing boats, but there are certain facts that are indisputable:

1. A shoal-draught boat can go wherever a deep-keel boat can go, and a good many other places besides.
2. A flat-bottomed boat, or one with bilge keels, is just as comfortable when aground as when afloat. (In some circumstances even more so!)

In recognizing these facts it has also to be admitted that many of the places which are impossible for a deep-draught boat are the very ones which are worth visiting. Now, I know that this is a matter of temperament, but I believe that there are a great many press-on types who devote their efforts to beating from one port to another at high speed and in clouds of spray, who do not know what they are missing. Sailing a cruising boat is only half the story—the other half comes in the quiet of some lovely creek, secluded from both sea and shore, where one hears nothing but the chuckle of the tide round the resting hull and the haunting calls of the marsh birds. I know quiet creeks of gurgling mud where I can find peace and thank heaven that I have not had to moor to the trots in Cowes, or some similarly overcrowded, urbanized marine parking lot. This is not to say that a busy little harbour never has its attraction—a few miles from Cowes, for example, is Yarmouth, which everyone seems to like to visit once in a while. But the fact is that as cruising becomes more and more popular the obvious anchorages grow more and more crowded and the shallow creeks become more and more valuable to those who can use them. Not only does the ability to creep into shallow water add greatly to the number of lovely places one can visit, it also frees you from the worrying business of trying to squeeze into an already overcrowded anchorage without giving some other fellow a foul berth.

But it is not just a question of draught—it is the vessel's ability to take the ground comfortably that is the controlling factor. It is one thing to be able to explore the extent of a shallow creek, it is quite another to have the confidence to do it. With a deep-keel boat you can sound your way around some very interesting places, but you need to have a foot of water always in hand: with a boat which will take the ground comfortably you can use the last inch . . . and a little more. You can freely anchor in a spot where you know you will be aground for an hour or two at low water, but by then you may be asleep, or sitting in the cockpit smoking your pipe and letting the peace soak into your soul. You may even have rowed the dinghy up to the head of the creek and while your boat is sitting comfortably on the mud you may be sampling the local ale.

I have stressed these points at some length because there are these two distinct choices of hull bottom and they do lead to two quite different kinds of boating. It cannot be disputed that the keel boat will have a superior performance to windward, though over the bilge-keel boat in other than the lightest airs the superiority may prove marginal. Although it may seem that the keel boat would be inherently stiffer and that the shoal-draught boat might be more likely to capsize there is really very little in it. A properly designed shoal-draught boat usually has more initial stiffness than a deeper draught vessel—she is given extra beam, and it is beam coupled with a firm, full bilge that does most to provide a righting moment in the earlier stages of heel. As the boat heels and the bilge is immersed the centre of gravity of the vessel has to rise and this provides a righting moment. In the early stages of heel the faster boat with her slighter beam and her ballast deeper down has little righting moment because the ballast rises but little.

On the other hand, the deep keel really comes right into its own when the vessel is on her beam ends, which we hope she never is. Then the leverage of the ballast keel is at its most effective.

These rather theoretical considerations may make good material for discussion round the bar, but it is the designer's job to make sure that the boat is sufficiently stable. In real life one does not see any capsized cruising boats, and arguments about how one boat or another might fare in a hurricane off the West Indies are for most of us, alas, purely hypothetical. The short answer is that the deep-keel boat is the answer if you are determined to carry the maximum of sail on a hull of given displacement; on other counts the shoal-draught boat has the advantages.

That the truth of this is being more widely recognized can be seen from the increasing popularity of bilge keels in particular, and of centre-boards too, for craft up to 10 tons. In the U.S.A., of course, the centre-board has for long been well established in craft of much more than 10 tons, and the sea-keeping qualities of shoal-draught boats are generally appreciated there.

In British waters there is one final point favouring the owner of a boat which can take the ground comfortably—you will be more likely to find a permanent mooring. Moorings in all the accessible places around the coast have become extremely scarce in the last few years, but it is still easier to get one if you can accept a spot which dries out at low water. Drying-out moorings are usually cheaper, too. If the boat is to take the ground regularly, more than just the shape of the bottom is involved—you must be sure that the structural strength of the hull is going to be up to it. In the first place you should ask the builder whether the boat is intended for that kind of treatment: secondly, you can make inquiries at boat yards and clubs where similar craft are on drying-out moorings; thirdly, you can use your own judgment in deciding whether the construction of the hull is too light. With bilge keels, of course, the skin of the hull itself is well clear of any large stones or similar objects which might pierce it, but there is bound to be some strain each time the weight of the hull (and all the gear and stores on board) comes on to the keels. This happens twice every 24 hours, and may not always happen gently, especially in a rather exposed anchorage where there may be a bit of a lop and the boat may be yawing about her mooring chain. Still, there are thousands of boats in tidal moorings which do take the ground regularly and it is very rare to see one come to any harm from it, so one should not overstress the possible risks.

Structural materials and methods

Nowadays there is quite a wide choice of materials and methods of construction in metal, wood and resin. For practical purposes we may ignore the metal-hulled boat, though there is a steady trickle of excellent steel-hulled yachts from Holland. There are great merits in the steel hull and one or two enthusiastic and nautically minded engineers in Britain have given serious thought to setting up in business and producing steel hulls here. But the day for that is probably too late; glass-reinforced resin is now the established alternative to wood, and if you really want steel you had best look to Holland where there is a seductive selection.

But even in wooden boats modern resin glues have made possible big changes and improvements in structural methods, and to the traditional carvel or clinker-planked vessels there are now added two other forms, those made of sheet ply and those of moulded ply. Perhaps it is worth saying a word about one of the oldest of the traditional forms—clinker (or clencher). This is a method of boat-building which is stronger, weight for weight, than a carvel hull. Each plank overlaps the next and they are riveted together along their edges, whereas the carvel planks are not joined to each other—they are simply joined to the timbers. In small boats the planking can be thinner with clinker construction, because the planks are joined to each other between the frames: moreover, a carvel boat may have to have planking which is thicker than she needs for strength, because thin planks will not hold their caulking. Similarly, a carvel boat may have to have her frames more closely spaced than a clinker.

People often seem to think that a clinker hull is more likely to make water than a carvel: actually there's not much to choose, but probably the reverse is true, assuming that both versions are well built. The most likely place for a leak in either kind of boat is above the waterline, where the planks may have dried out in the sunshine which was shining all the week while you were in your office. Then when the boat starts sailing hard and is pulled over by her mast and shrouds until her gunwale is in the water there may be slight leaks due to straining of the hull. In either case the planks will probably take up as they become damp. Naturally, as with any form of construction, a clinker hull must be *well* built, which means among other things that the builder must not have skimped on his copper rivets. These in effect stitch the planks edge to edge and on their number and tightness depends the strength and tightness of the hull. They should be spaced at not more than 2–2½ in. apart.

Some people do not like the look of a clinker hull, others do. It's a matter of taste. But one fact about which there is no dispute is the *noise* that a clinker hull can create. At anchor in any wind over Force 6 the noise made by waves hitting the lands of the planks makes conversation about as easy as it is on the Underground Railway! Another drawback to a clinker hull is that she takes more time to rub down and paint than a smooth-skinned boat. Yet the lands (or edges) of those planks keep water down off the deck, and off the crew too, when going to windward, so it's the usual mixture of *pro* and *con*.

Resin-bonded plywood construction

The first great change in boat construction of recent times came with the perfection of resin-bonded plywood. The resin glue that holds the laminations together is completely waterproof, and the same goes for the complete material itself, as long as the edges of the wood are adequately protected. Even though the glue is proof against water the wood itself will absorb it through the end-grains, if it is not covered and sealed. One need hardly say that plywood, with its successive layers having grains running across each other, is much stronger than simple wood. It has made possible in boat design the use of the stressed-skin techniques that are used in aircraft. This means that the outer skin of the boat does much more than provide a covering to keep out the wind and water—it actually contributes to the strength of the hull. This is something that carvel planking does not do, and clinker planking does to only a limited extent. Thus a plywood-skinned boat can use fewer timbers (or frames) than the traditional boat, and she can still be stronger and lighter, as well as being more watertight. There are far fewer joints in such a hull than in one of traditional construction, so there are far fewer opportunities for leaking: in fact a properly designed and built ply boat should never collect any water other than rain and spray.

Obviously the quality of the plywood is an all-important factor. The *minimum* quality that should be used for boat-building is wood to British Standard Specification 1088, but some yards use a superior grade and this is really worth having if you can get it.

As with any other form of construction a plywood boat must be both well designed and well built. The design ought to make use of the strength in the skin, and the designer ought to know all about the need to protect the edges of the sheets. The builder must be thoroughly competent in the art of gluing, for where the older kinds of construction depend on bolts and screws and nails, the stressed-skin boat depends on glue which spreads the stresses over large areas instead of concentrating them at points, as mechanical fastenings do. The two main points that have to be watched to get really good glued joints are the temperature in the workshop (cold can be deleterious) and good contact between the parts to be glued. It is not easy to be sure that there is really close contact between an 8-ft. sheet of ply and a curved stringer.

Moulded wood hulls

The more advanced form of plywood construction is the moulded hull in which the finished material is plywood just the same, but the builder lays up the laminations to the shape of a mould instead of working from ready-made flat sheets. Not only does this method make possible a fully curved hull, it also achieves an exceptionally good strength-to-weight ratio. The Atalanta and other Fairey hulls are outstanding examples of this form of construction. They are built by tacking thin strips of mahogany veneer in criss-cross layers on a mould, with glue coats between. Then the whole thing is enclosed in a large rubber bag from which the air is pumped out so that the atmospheric pressure presses the bag down on to the veneers and squeezes them against the mould. To 'cure' the resin glue between the laminations the whole thing is pushed into a large oven, where it is baked until the veneers and the glue have hardened into a complete, homogeneous shell. This is without doubt the best way to make a boat hull from wood. Cold-moulding is a similar process (without the use of the oven) and it too produces a very strong and light shell which is completely watertight.

But whatever form of hull construction is used, if wood is the material it will have to be cared for in just the same way. Even if modern polyurethane paints are used the owner will have to do quite a lot of scraping and painting, unless he can afford to pay someone else to do it for him. With a glass-resin hull, on the other hand, maintenance work is reduced to the minimum. In this case the hull is made by laying up layers of glass cloth or glass mat and bonding them together with a resin which sets hard. The glass reinforces the resin in rather the same way that tie-bars reinforce concrete. As with moulded wood hulls, the glass-fibre boat can be moulded hot or cold and with the use of an evacuated rubber bag to create pressure. As a rule hot moulding does not seem to be worth the extra trouble and expense.

Glass-resin hulls are not cheap, although many people think they ought to be. One cause of high cost is the resin itself, the other is the expense of building the mould. Obviously this item represents a relatively smaller part of the cost of each hull if many units are built. Proper control of temperature and humidity are necessary to get a sound result, and laying up the glass is a skilled task which has to be done conscientiously. For that reason one would prefer to buy a glass-resin hulled boat from a firm with adequate resources and discernibly good engineering standards.

It would be misleading to suggest that a glass-resin hull will always look as bright and shiny as it did when it was rolled out of the factory. In fact, the outer coat of resin, which provides a smooth finish to cover the glass mat or cloth, will eventually deteriorate—not sufficiently to make any difference to the structure, but enough to take the gloss off the appearance. Fine hair cracking, or crazing, of the surface is the usual trouble, and how soon and to what extent this happens will depend a good deal on the skill and care of the builder and on the grade of resin used for this outer coat. The surface can be restored by rubbing down and painting with a polyurethane paint, but the job is not nearly so arduous, nor so frequently recurring as it is with a wooden hull.

In some of the early glass-resin boats 'fillers' such as powdered chalk were used to bulk out the resin and so to cut the builder's costs. This is most inadvisable in marine practice, however acceptable it may be elsewhere; fillers tend to absorb water and they cause brittleness in the outer gel coat which quickly leads to crazing.

It is a sign of a well-built plastic boat if parts are bonded on to the skin of the hull, and not bolted through. Bolts tend to crush the plastic, and if they must be used pads of metal or plywood should be placed under head and nut so as to spread the pressure. Whereas wood tends to swell and grip a bolt passing through it, glass-fibre remains 'as drilled' and the result is that moisture tends to seep along a bolt.

Plastic hulls are quite suitable for amateur repairs; it is simply a matter of cutting away any damaged part and then laying up glass cloth with resin to make the required thickness. Using common sense and allowing sufficient overlap, the repair will bond firmly to the hull and become an integral part of it.

One quite real drawback to a plastic boat is that it is not quite such a simple matter to make one's own alterations to fittings below—lockers and suchlike—as it is with a wooden hull. It is very much more difficult to find anything to screw into. The practical solution is to bond in a wooden batten by overlaying it with a layer of glass cloth and resin. A few spots of Evostik or some similar glue can be used to hold the batten in place while the resinglass is laid up and sets.

But all in all the advantages of glass-resin hulls are sufficient to gain them general acceptance. The Admiralty favours this form of construction for its own small craft, because of the lightness, strength, and freedom from rot and water absorption, so there is a reliable precedent for any yachtsman who opts for a 'plastic' boat.

One advantage of a glass-resin hull is the extra amount of usable volume inside the hull in comparison with a framed wooden hull of the same outside dimensions; this results from the absence of frames. Although it is only a matter of 2 or 3 in., in a small boat the difference is quite noticeable. In most plastic-hulled boats the deck, cockpit and cabin-top are also moulded in glass-resin; this is efficient, light, strong and water-tight, but it can result in something of a 'bath-toy' appearance. A wooden super-structure achieves a more attractive appearance, but it means varnishing, so it's come back to a matter of weighing up the pros and cons.

Glass-resin allows a designer to use his intelligence: for one thing the most highly stressed parts of the hull can be given enough strength by laying up an extra thickness of material. This means that the structure of a boat can be made in a really efficient way, with every part tailored to the loads it has to carry. Another thing that a clever designer can do is to incorporate such things as a water tank, a sink, or shelves in the main mouldings. This approach is well exemplified in the Kingfishers which are built at Poole by Westfield Engineering.

When glass-resin hulls first began to appear, a number of firms without experience in boatbuilding tried their hand at this seemingly simple job of moulding. As a result some less than satisfactory hulls were produced, and official bodies felt it necessary to lay down standards of construction. Among the schemes developed was the Lloyds Series Production Certificate. For many years the best-quality hulls had been built under Lloyds' supervision, but for modestly priced boats all built on a production line to a common mould individual supervision would be too costly. The Series Production type of supervision requires Lloyds approval of the structural design, of the workshop itself, followed by regular inspections of the premises and of a proportion of the hulls produced. In this way the maintenance of good standards of work is pretty well assured.

But a word of caution is necessary. I have been told by enthusiastic, but perhaps not deliberately deceptive, salesmen 'this boat was approved by Lloyds' where in fact the hull only was one built under the Series Production scheme. Apart from the fact that that particular hull was very likely not actually examined by a Lloyds surveyor, there is the more important aspect that the scheme covers *hulls* only. The engine installation, sea-cocks, gas and fuel runs, deck fittings, mast and other important components do not come within the compass of the Series Production Certificate. And experience shows that these items are far more common causes of trouble than a weak hull.

9

Living aboard

A cruising boat is a compressed home, and just how home-like you will wish to make her is a matter of personal preference. There are some whose idea of a cruising boat is nothing more than a large dinghy aboard which it is possible to find sufficient shelter against the rains of an English summer and the chill of the small hours. Such a craft is the Seafarer. Whereas a conventional cruising boat has a decked-over hull and an open cockpit, Seafarer approximates to an open boat with a covered cuddy. Perhaps this kind of boat does not fit the usual conception of a cruising boat, yet for the man who is loath to give up dinghy sailing she does have the advantage that she will really perform. It is possible to sleep and cook aboard such a boat, but no concessions are made to comfort, and little can be said about possible permutations of the interior arrangements.

Indeed, it is possible to cruise in an open boat with the simplest of weather protection—after a summer's night of thunder showers I have looked out of the hatch in the morning to see a gentleman fully rigged in dressing-gown and slippers, step cautiously out from a tent slung over the boom of an open dinghy no more than 16 ft. long! But for most people a cruising boat is one which has the best provision for sleeping, cooking and sanitation that is possible within her dimensions: and size is, after all, the governing factor. It is in the smaller sizes of boat that it becomes a problem to find space for two, three or four people, and a good deal of ingenuity is, in fact, shown by designers in making use of the space. But in a boat which is less than 20 ft. long the possible arrangements are few and as a rule the internal dispositions in a boat of this size will be according to one or other of the basic patterns shown on the later pages of this chapter.

In very small boats, say up to 22 ft. in length, any attempt to accommodate more than two people is likely to result in the use of quarter berths; this is, in fact, the most practical solution and it is one which is used to good effect in much larger boats, too. It is the logical way to make use of space along the sides of the cockpit, since this is lengthwise space, and the problem with sleeping bodies is primarily one of length.

Apart from the fact that it is geometrically the right solution, the advantage of the quarter berth is that it is permanent; there is nothing to pack up or fold away. Many people have designed ingenious contrivances which form a berth at night, but pack away in the daytime, and though such schemes seem to give the best of both worlds I would suggest that very careful thought should be given before adopting that kind of solution. There is more to a berth than just the structural part—there is some kind of mattress, a sleeping-bag perhaps, a pillow, pyjamas, too (unless you insist on turning in all-standing), and all these must stow away when the berth folds up. With a quarter berth there is at least one little bit of territory which is the private realm of one member of the crew—a place where he can leave a jersey or a book. And when it comes to the business of actually going to bed or getting up, the quarter berth causes no trouble or confusion. The pipe cot, the extendable bunk, or the table top that drops down to fill the gap between the two seats, all such gadgets mean a deal of shuffling and manœuvring, bending and bumping of bottoms in a very confined space.

The truth is that the biggest limitation of the small boat is the lack of space to flex arms and legs in the processes of dressing and undressing, which include the putting on and off of oilskins on the one hand or of bathing-suits on the other. The times when most volume is needed below are when the weather is bad outside and people are going to bed or getting up: the idea of the folding berth is that it provides plenty of room for the rest of the day, but that is hardly ever a real problem. If it is fine, then the cabin is rarely more than half occupied—if it is foul enough outside to keep everyone below, then four people sitting down to read or play cards take up very little space. In such conditions the quarter berth is the more convenient; it is a place where one chap can doze or read without creating any disturbance to the general life aboard.

A typical arrangement with quarter berths is that of the Four 21 shown on page 137: on each side of the vessel the forward berth is separated from the quarter berth by a space of about 15 in. This allows room for a cooking-stove on one side of the boat and for a chest of drawers and a hanging space on the other. A flushing w.c. is fitted at the fore end of the cabin between the two berths. Another solution is that of the Crystal (known as the Halcyon in her modern version), which is a couple of feet longer than the Westcoaster. In this case there is no space between the innermost (head) ends of the two berths along either side of the boat, and in consequence the cooking installation has to be immediately in the way of the main hatch.

This particular position of the cooker certainly seems awkward, but it is not unique. Somewhat similar is the Kingfisher glass-fibre sloop but she has a sink immediately under the hatch. If reports be true, very few Kingfisher owners seem to have had trouble with people stepping straight into the washing-up! Both the Crystal and the Kingfisher have good w.c. accommodation, though they achieve it in different ways. This is obviously most important: in some very small boats everyone else must move out into the cockpit when one person needs the privacy of the w.c. That kind of shuffling around may not be too bad when there are only two aboard, but with four not only is the number of people who have to move increased, but so is the number of occasions when it will be necessary. Here is another example of the fact that the limiting factor to the number of people who can comfortably live aboard a boat is not the number who can be stretched out straight on bunks.

The moral is to try to avoid cramming too many people into too small a boat. That, of course, would be easy enough if one always had the money to spare at the right time, but there are many other expenses to be met, especially for the family man, who is the very one who most needs to accommodate four or five people. Still, in these small sizes of boat it is worth choosing the one that allows that extra couple of feet, other things being equal. At 21 or 22 ft. overall length, for example, it becomes possible to have a separate w.c. compartment, a forward cabin with two berths, and main saloon which will seat four, as well as a galley and ample hanging space. To achieve that the beam should be 7 ft. or more. Above that length it no longer becomes a problem to accommodate four people. In fact, the 26 ft. Centaur can sleep six below decks and still have a separate w.c. and ample galley space.

On centre cockpits

Although in larger boats, say of 5 tons Thames measurement* and upward, the problem of accommodation becomes progressively easier, it is only too easy to waste space, and there is still need for more thought by designers on that matter. The Atalanta (which is no longer in production but still giving satisfaction to many owners) is an example of a boat which not only has a cockpit of ample size, but also gets the maximum utilization out of all the volume below. She gains, of course, by having a 'centre cockpit', a term which means that there is accommodation aft of the cockpit rather than that the cockpit is actually at the centre of the boat. This is an arrangement that is certain to become more and more popular as designers are faced with growing numbers of people who expect a boat of, say, 26 ft. overall length to give them something more than two berths and a galley. That benefactor of yachtsmen, Mr. David Hillyard, knew all about this years ago, of course, and it is worth comparing the accommodation arrangement of his 6-ton centre-cockpit sloop with the more conventional arrangement which he provided in the same hull. The use of the last few feet in the stern end of the boat to accommodate two people's legs and feet has made possible a much more satisfactory w.c. compartment right forward as well as making it unnecessary to run the foot end of the port saloon berth under the galley flat. What's more, the after cabin is pleasantly isolated, and it has advantages equally for children who must go to bed early or for adult guests who should have a bit of privacy.

* See *A note on Thames tonnage*, Chapter 12.

For the helmsman the 'centre' cockpit gives a better view ahead, because the sole in such a cockpit can by the nature of things be higher than one in the conventional position. When coming up alongside a harbour wall, or at mooring piles, or in any such manœuvre at close quarters the commanding position of the centre cockpit really proves its worth. There is also the very satisfying feeling of security when one is running before large seas; or should it perhaps be described as the absence of the feeling of insecurity which can easily arise when there is not much boat between oneself and those piled-up masses of water. Probably the gain in actual security is not really so very great, because pooping with any sort of boat seems to be a very rare occurrence. Nevertheless anything that relieves even an unjustified anxiety can be a very real advantage, because it puts the helmsman at his ease and allows him to concentrate on important matters—his pilotage, for example. The reassuring effect on the other crew members (and this will probably mean wife and children) can also be worth while.

Looking through plans in the yachting journals and in brochures collected at the Boat Show one can see many boats which are so arranged that the last few feet aft of the cockpit is virtually wasted space. This is not the ideal place to stow too much gear, since this tends to concentrate weight in the wrong place. On the other hand, two pairs of legs don't weigh very much, and in any case they need only be there when the boat is at anchor: if it is a matter of night sailing, then the weight of the sleeping half of the crew can be forward in the saloon.

In many small boats the designers have taken a good deal of trouble to keep the cockpit as far forward as possible, so as to keep the weight of four people near the centre of the boat: the after cabin achieves that aim automatically.

Below-deck arrangements

There are two completely opposite schools of thought about the best way to lay out the interior of a small boat: some hold that there should be a minimum of bulkheads and divisions and that the ideal is to have the whole space clear from end to end. (A slight exaggeration perhaps, but that is the underlying thought.) These people say that a boat is a very small volume anyway, and that cutting it up into smaller bits simply makes one feel cramped. On the other hand, one has to remember that it is the bulkheads and divisions that provide the opportunities for a variety of useful fittings. One needs bookshelves, a stowage for the radio, and plenty of hooks to hang odds and ends on. In practice one comes once again face to face with the fact that in a small boat the problem is not so much to get bed-length for, say, four people: stowing all the things they bring with them is a far more difficult matter. Of course, you can take a stern line and say that there must be no books, no newspapers, no tins of humbugs, no packs of playing cards and no cameras: but you will still need your binoculars, and your pipe and tobacco; and sun-glasses and sun-hats must be handy, just in case. You will need first-aid equipment, knives, matches, some rubber bands, spare torch bulbs, pencils and dozens of other odds and ends. These are not galley equipment—that has its own stowage—nor are they the tools and chandlery that is properly in the bosun's locker somewhere aft in the cockpit, they are the purely personal oddments that most humans seem to collect around them, and for which there is hardly ever enough stowage space. Moreover, every bulkhead, or partial bulkhead, is a potential position for a hanging space, and places to hang jackets and skirts and trousers are nearly always too scarce in a small boat. The clothes one wears aboard may be as rough and crumpled as personal tastes allow, but for shoregoing everyone will want to have at least a pair of flannels and a reefer jacket, or an uncreased frock or skirt: the best way to stow these more presentable items of clothing is to hang them up. Oilskins, which may be wet, should have a place of their own, of course.

Finding stowage for everything

In contrast to those who like the 'wide open spaces' kind of layout below decks, my own taste is for plenty of division and plenty of fittings; and the smaller the boat the more the need to use up every inch of space with stowage for something or other. Even in the cockpit it is worth having either small shelves, or perhaps deep fiddles at the outer edges of the cockpit seats, so that binoculars, cameras, or mugs of tea can be immediately available, but will not come sliding down every time the boat heels (see Figure 26).

In small boats there is usually space for stowage beneath the berths, but it is better not to stow things right down in the bottom of the boat, where there is always at least a chance of some bilge-water, and in some boats the certainty of it. It is quite a good idea to fit shallow trays under the berth mattresses—these should stop short of the skin of the boat, and just in case their lower corners might be damp from time to time they should be made in marine ply, with glued joints and well painted both inside and out. Trays like this make a good stowage for clothes as well as for tinned food.

A good place to build small lockers is shown in Figure 27. A berth that is wide enough to sleep on (27 in. usually) is too wide to make a comfortable seat, but with a cupboard of the kind shown in the sketch there is something to lean one's back against: it should be 7 or 8 in. in depth and there should be 8 or 9 in. clear below.

Sleeping-bags make the best bedding on board. In the daytime they can be rolled or folded and stuffed into home-made covers to make cushions—something else to lean back against.

Water in a small boat is usually carried in separate containers of 2 or 3 gal. capacity, and nowadays there are excellent ones available in plastic: the semi-transparent kind are best, because it is easy to see how much water is left. Also with this kind it is easier

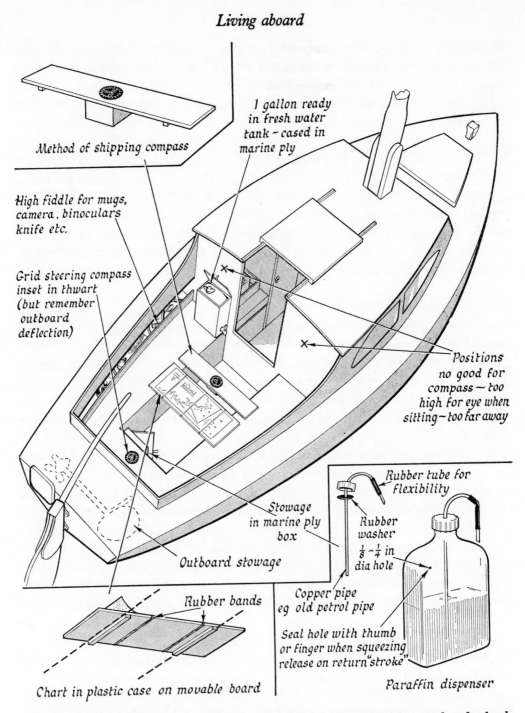

Method of shipping compass

1 gallon ready in fresh water tank ~ cased in marine ply

High fiddle for mugs, camera, binoculars knife etc.

Grid steering compass inset in thwart (but remember outboard deflection)

Positions no good for compass ~ too high for eye when sitting ~ too far away

Rubber tube for flexibility

Rubber washer

$\frac{1}{8} \sim \frac{1}{4}$ in dia hole

Stowage in marine ply box

Outboard stowage

Copper pipe eg old petrol pipe

Rubber bands

Seal hole with thumb or finger when squeezing release on return "stroke"

Chart in plastic case on movable board

Paraffin dispenser

Figure 26. Finding places for everything in a small boat is a problem that can be solved only by the skipper himself. The sketch shows some useful ideas for chart, compass, water supply and paraffin dispensing.

to see when they are getting dirty inside—it is usually a rusty deposit which originates in the mains supply. Cleaning out is quite simple (even if one cannot get a hand inside) by tying a dish-mop on to a piece of stick and using a little detergent.

But even though these plastic barricoes are very handy, it's not much good trying to fill a kettle from one. It is possible to get a plastic water pump which will fit some of them, but it's probably easier to have a small ready-use tank of about a couple of gallons, fitted with a tap and stowed in some convenient place. The forward end of the cockpit is a good position in many boats (see Figure 26), and if this tank has a good-sized filler cap in the top it is quite simple to keep it topped up from the plastic barricoes.

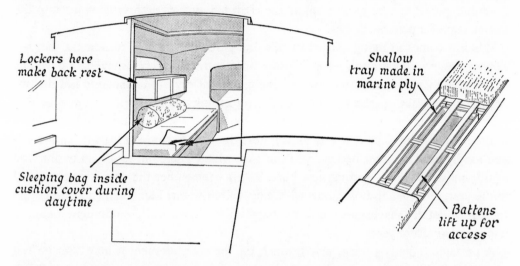

Figure 27. Stowage below decks is rarely adequate in small boats. There is plenty of space under the berths, but it can be wet down there so it is a good idea to make shallow trays to keep tins and clothes above the bilges.

To save fresh water, sea water can be used for washing hands. Liquid detergent, carried in those handy plastic squeeze bottles, is very good for sea-water ablutions. Crockery, too, can be washed up in sea water, but not in the sort of stuff you find in the Thames Estuary or the Solent: too much untreated sewage and other pollution goes into the water in those areas. It's no good washing clothes in sea water because the salt remains behind and always absorbs water from the air, so that the material remains permanently damp.

Talking of squeeze bottles reminds me that it is possible to make a 'pump' out of almost any plastic bottle or barricoe by fitting a pipe through the stopper and down to the bottom: then all you have to do is to squeeze. Each squeeze produces about a cupful of water, and then the plastic must be allowed to spring back so that the air can come in to take the place of the water: for a properly designed system there should be a one-way valve to let the air in, but for some purposes there is a simpler solution than that. In Figure 26 there is an example of the kind of thing that I use for filling paraffin lamps; in this case there is simply a hole near the top of the bottle and this is closed with finger or thumb as one squeezes. With a piece of rubber tube to make a flexible nozzle, this takes all the awkwardness out of filling paraffin lamps, and makes a funnel unnecessary. With this scheme an accidental kick will not pump paraffin out of the bottle (unless the kicker is so accidentally skilful as to block the air hole with his toe!). Nevertheless, just to be on the safe side, and for neatness' sake, I prefer to house my paraffin squeeze bottle in a small wooden box with a door that can be closed over it. A similar gadget can be used to inject the right amount of methylated spirit into the starter cup of a paraffin cooker.

When it comes to living aboard there's one particular item of equipment that the skipper deserves for himself—one of those little battery-powered shavers. I have one which uses a single U-2 battery: surprisingly, one battery can be made to last for two or three weeks, but I prefer to keep it lively and I think that 4p. spent on a new battery each week is fair enough. This is not a quick way to get a shave, but you'll have plenty of time at the helm. The best way to use these things is to shave at least twice a day— you hardly need a mirror because you can hear what's going on, so it's quite practical to tidy up when you're getting near port. When I remember the cuts I have suffered in the past, crouched in tiny cabins with mugs of hot water, I am inclined to think that these little battery shavers are one of the biggest advances in yacht equipment that have happened in recent years!

A portable radio is a must, not so much for the entertainment it may offer on wet nights, as for the shipping forecasts and gale warnings which come over the B.B.C.'s 1500-metre wavelength. (Radio Two.) It is therefore essential to have a receiver which covers 'long waves'—some of the pocket-sized transistor sets receive only the medium bands. The times of shipping forecasts are given in the *Radio Times*, or may be found in a booklet called 'Your Weather Service' which can be obtained from branches of Her Majesty's Stationery Office for $7\frac{1}{2}$p. This little booklet is worth getting, by the way. Not only does it fill in a good deal of background about weather forecasting, it also lists the met. offices from which one can get a local weather forecast by telephone or telegram. There are about forty of these places scattered about the country, and all you have to do is to ring up, ask for 'the forecast office', and tell them what you want to know: I have always found them most helpful, whether it was a matter of the risk of gales in the Channel or the likelihood of snow in the Alps.

If you buy a copy of this little pamphlet, it will probably be among the various books you take aboard: obviously you will choose a dry spot for your bookshelf, but it's still a good idea to cover books in polythene sheeting, as public libraries do. Pilot books are not the only ones which will be taken out into the cockpit and exposed to splashes and spray.

Polythene bags, the kind that drapers sell for storing blankets, are good for protecting bedding and clothes which are to be left on board. The interior of a small boat is always rather a damp place, especially when she is closed up and left for a week or two. There may be deck leaks, there may be condensation running down the inside of the skin, which is cooled by the sea water outside, and there may come a time when there is more bilge water than you expected. Excess bilge water can wet carpets, items stowed in low-level lockers, and even bunk mattresses if your mooring dries out and the boat lies over when she takes the ground.

Apart from leaks, most water is carried in by the air, especially if ventilation is slight. Moisture-bearing air comes in during the day, at night the temperature drops, and a certain amount of dew is formed. This is not easily picked up by the air again, unless there is a really good flow of it passing through the boat. So arrange the maximum possible amount of ventilation for your boat when she is locked up and left on the mooring. You can either buy patent ventilators, or you can make your own. In either case you must be sure that air can get in while water can *not*.

10

Gear . . . and odds and ends

The man who buys a small cruiser nowadays will probably be buying a production-line article, and such things as the design and material of the spars, the standing rigging and even the type of auxiliary engine may well have been decided for him. The limit of his choice may, in fact, lie between, say, one of two kinds of engine, both of which have been accepted as satisfactory by the designer and builder. Still, there are other things in which he can exercise his choice—the type of cooker, of ground tackle and so forth. In times past, on the other hand, when yachts were built on a one-off basis (as the more expensive are still), the prospective owner could have a good deal to say about the structural materials, the rig and so forth. In a book such as this, intended for those of us whose finances make a standard boat the best buy, it would be unrealistic to go into long discussions about things we cannot really hope to influence. Nevertheless there is always the choice between one standard craft and another, and even when a boat has been chosen there are opportunities for further selection. It may be possible to have either a petrol or a diesel engine, for example. If they both come from makers of equal repute, then the wise thing to do would be to opt for the diesel, if it is not too expensive. There are several reasons: in the first place diesel fuel is very much safer than petrol—petrol vapour and bottled gas are the two most likely causes of an explosion aboard. Secondly, the fuel costs for a diesel are lower than for a petrol engine, and this can be an important consideration. The engine in a 5-tonner may consume a gallon of petrol in an hour and, whereas you will travel 30 to 40 miles in that time in a car, you will cover only 5 or 6 miles in a boat. Finally the diesel does not use electrical ignition, and although modern marine petrol engines are very reliable, electrical devices are susceptible to the humid, corrosive atmosphere of the sea.

For a small boat there is a great deal to be said in favour of an outboard motor as an auxiliary. It will be very much cheaper than an inboard installation, a fact which is made clear on several pages of the second part of this book. Second, with an outboard there is no need for a stern tube or for other skin fittings. Third, the screw can easily be lifted right out of the water to eliminate the drag when sailing. Finally, the engine can easily be removed and taken ashore for overhaul or repair. This ease of removal also has its advantages when it comes to disentangling a rope which has wound itself around the screw.

Choice of sail material

Another choice that may well be left to the buyer of a standard boat will lie between cotton or Terylene sails. For economy, sailing efficiency, resistance to rot and mildew, choose Terylenes. Although they are a little more expensive you don't have to worry about drying them before stowing on Sunday night. If, on the other hand, you let your tastes rule your head, then you may prefer cotton, as I do. I prefer the feel of cotton and I think it looks much more attractive: it can be proofed against rot and mildew, and if treated with reasonable care cotton sails will last for many seasons.

You may also be offered a choice between galvanized or stainless steel wire for your standing rigging, and most people will say that you should choose stainless. Galvanized rigging has to be well looked after if it is to last, and few of us nowadays seem to have time enough to give thorough and complete attention to maintenance work.

It's often easy to decide what is the best buy, but it may not always be possible to indulge in it, because an accumulation of small extras can so quickly put the bill up by a large amount. It's all very well to say 'Have stainless wire, it's only a few pounds extra . . .', but one tends to say that for everything. To show what can happen I will list a few typical items which can make the bill for a new boat something of a shock. Let us suppose that the prospective owner is interested in an attractive little sloop which is advertised rather 'bare' with a price-tag of about £1,000 including a suit of two sails. On looking into it a little more closely he may find that he needs the following extras in order to be able to start using the boat:

	£
Four bunk mattresses	45
Marine w.c., installed	50
6 h.p. inboard engine with electric start	400
Anchor and chain	20
Compass	10
Canvas cockpit cover	20
Pulpit and lifelines	40
Calor gas cooker and cylinder	15
Bilge pump, fitted	15
Fire extinguisher	5
Four fenders	5
	———
	£625

That little list has put up the cost by more than 50 per cent. But all those things are likely to be needed (to put it mildly), though the owner might do without his inboard engine and buy an outboard such as a Seagull Century at a cost of only about £75, which means a really large saving. But the boat must be suited to outboard propulsion, of course.

He could do without the marine w.c., and use a bucket instead. On the other hand the list does not include many other things the owner is almost certain to want: a boat-hook, three or four good warps, leadline, ensign staff and ensign, water carriers, anchor light and navigation lamps, a genoa staysail, lifelines round the cockpit . . . need one say more? We come back to the point when we were saying 'Of course it's worth having stainless steel rigging—it's only £5 extra and cheaper in the long run. . . .' That's true enough, but the buyer may not be worrying so much about the long run as about his need to get a boat as soon as he can. The prospect of having to renew galvanized standing rigging in ten years' time may not be so important against the immediate problem of finding enough money to get afloat.

Please don't think that I am trying to frighten you with tales of endless expense. That is not my point at all, I just want to make clear that it is worth sitting down and making a tally of likely costs involved in the buying of any particular boat before you commit yourself. In real life the picture can be very much brighter if you buy a secondhand boat because she will often include a great deal of gear and equipment which the owner has more or less 'forgotten'. Naturally people vary in this matter, and some will even try to add in the price of the old tin kettle, but there's no doubt that there are always bargains to be had, especially in boats which are slightly unfashionable. So if you have been a little deterred by the prices of new boats send off for the full particulars of some secondhand ones, and add up what all the extras would cost if you had to buy them from scratch.

And quite apart from that, there are many things that the owner can avoid actually paying for if he is willing to make them himself. Instead of a stainless steel pulpit which would cost him about £25 he can make one of galvanized water barrel. I made one such for less than £2, and though I no longer own that particular boat I do know that the home-made pulpit was still giving good service ten years after I sold her.

Saving money by making your own gear

A reasonably handy man can improvise or make quite a number of items for his new boat, and when the cost of extras is mounting up anything at all that can be saved in this way is worth while. You can, for example, save a little by making up your own berth mattresses from the foam plastic material which is advertised regularly in the yachting magazines. It's easy enough to cover this stuff in some furnishing material from the top shelf of the linen cupboard at home. In this connection it's worth remembering that a 6-ft. man can sleep very well on a 4-ft. mattress—feet don't need much support and a folded jersey, or a kapok life-jacket can be used for the job. Apart from the saving in cost, a short mattress also saves a good deal of space, which is an important point if you have to pack some of the bedding away in the daytime.

On the subject of berths, it's important when choosing a boat to make sure that the berths are wide enough for comfort. The problem is likely to arise only in the smallest cruisers, but I would say that the absolute minimum width is 24 in., and that around 27 in. is to be preferred. For real comfort a bunk ought to be slightly concave: Maurice Griffiths, who was for many years editor of *Yachting Monthly* and the designer of many boats for sensible, comfortable cruising, says that the hollow should amount to 1½ in. at the centre of a berth 2 ft. wide. I can only add that I think it a pity that all designers and builders do not follow his precept.

There are so many things that are needed for a cruising boat—this second home— that it is a good idea to sit down and make a list: for one thing it helps to get the priorities right. I have mentioned in the previous chapter that a water tank and its associated pump are not really necessary. The builder may be willing to provide a built-in stainless-steel sink, but a 25p. plastic bowl does the same job and spares a good many pounds for other things. You can postpone the fitting of a stainless-steel sink until the season after next, but you can't postpone the buying of your anchors and chain.

Nowadays there is a great variety of fancy yacht fittings on the market. Often these have been developed for racing and did not exist before the war and therefore did not run away with our money. Many of these gadgets are jolly good, but don't fall into the trap of supposing that boats cannot sail without them. A sheet winch, for example, might cost you £10 or £20, but it is not a necessity. Boats have been cruising for hundreds of years, and still are, without the aid of these particular gadgets. The headsail should be sheeted home while she's luff to wind and there's no weight in her: in any case you can get an advantage by using a block or dead-eye at the clew of the sail and leading the sheet as a whip. It may be more effective to reeve pendants into the clew and to bring them down through fairleads to whips running along the deck; then there will be no heavy block to flog about with the sail. But however it is done, the point I am trying to make is that there were ways of handling headsails before winches were introduced. Many years ago I used to have the duties of foredeck hand on a 25-ton Dutch botter whose staysail was like a large but rather stiff genoa, but never a sheet winch was there. That powerful sail was kept under control (with occasional lapses) by a simple but effective lead of the sheet to an iron horse running athwart the deck.

For a small boat you can buy a worm-gear roller reefing attachment for anything between £7 and £20: on the other hand, it's much cheaper to use the good old method of a drum around the boom at the gooseneck with a line leading to the cockpit.

Unless you are very well off it is always worth thinking before buying gear, in case you can make up something just as effective by your own efforts. You may not be able to save a great deal of money in that way, but it can be satisfying work and the saving does help. Good strong cleats, for example, can be made without any great skill in carving, if you make them up as shown in the drawing (Figure 28). You need straight-grained oak or some similarly strong wood, of course, but if the wood is sound the cleats will be strong. Use Aerolite 306 glue.

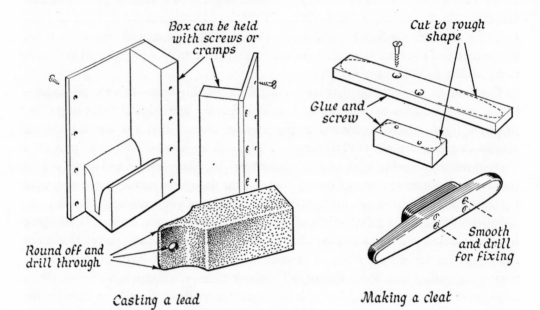

Casting a lead   Making a cleat

Figure 28. Two examples of the many items that a boat owner can make for himself. The mould to cast a lead, left, and a 'built-up' cleat, right.

You could make your own leadline too. The lead itself can easily be cast at home in a mould made by screwing four pieces of wood together—five to be exact, since you need one to close the bottom end of the short, square mould into which the lead will run (Figure 28). I have made several leads myself in the past, and I still collect scraps of plumber's pipe, lead cable covering, toy soldiers and farm animals for future use. All these bits and pieces are melted in an aluminium saucepan on the kitchen stove. As a precaution, I wear gloves, overalls and gum-boots when handling molten lead. If you are not a spectacle-wearer some sort of eye-shield seems sensible, too. In any case a home-made leadline is far cheaper than an echo sounder. . . .

Nowadays I like to make a leadline from a nylon filament line with braided outer sheath. This neither kinks nor rots. Natural fibre can rot without your noticing it—I lost a nice little lead like that only a few seasons ago. With a braided line you cannot slip the leather marks through the lay of the rope, but you can stitch them on with nylon thread. Don't throw away worn-out leather gloves: the leather is just the thing for marking the line.

With care, a good pulpit can be made from galvanized water pipe, using standard fittings and threaded joints. It isn't only the small things that can be improvised for economy.

Precautions with petrol

Proper cans for the storage of petrol and paraffin *are* an essential item: it's particularly worth while to take care with petrol.

Petrol leaks are very dangerous—petrol vapour in the bilges can result in explosion followed by fire (indeed, it far too frequently does). Since the most likely place for petrol cans to be stowed is under the cockpit seats, any smokers on board may find themselves actually sitting on top of a fuel store of a most dangerous kind, so use proper petrol cans with the brass screw caps that seal tight.

Petrol cans should be painted the usual bright red, and paraffin cans should be in blue or some quite distinct colour. I remember the owner of a small cruiser who was having trouble in getting his outboard to start. We looked to see if there was fuel in the tank—there was, but it was paraffin. 'How silly of me,' said he. 'I must have filled it from the wrong can.' He would have looked even sillier if he had filled his cooking-stove from the petrol can. This was a man who kept both kinds of fuel in plain galvanized cans with only a scratched-on 'Pet' and 'Par' to distinguish them.

There's nothing old-womanish in being cautious about petrol fumes: after all, there's no half-way house between complete safety and a real explosion, for a petrol fire is not something that you can expect to start slowly and gradually build up while you look at it and plan what to do. Anyone who has mistakenly tried to stimulate a bonfire with half a cupful of petrol will understand that. For example, it is not at all impossible for an explosion to result from filling a petrol tank at the after end of the cockpit while the cooker is being used in the cabin. Such a catastrophe is made the more likely by the fact that the airflow through a vessel lying head-to-wind is normally from aft forward. Petrol being sloshed gaily into a large funnel can give off enough vapour to be ignited by a naked flame several feet away, in which case it would probably flash right back to the filling point. The best rule is, 'No naked lights aboard while handling petrol.'

In support of this point I recall a most instructive account of a petrol fire in a small boat. This was described in a book of cruising reminiscences, and though I have forgotten the author's name I hope he will not mind my relating this very good example of the kind of thing that can happen. This owner had left his boat at her mooring with a small paraffin heater burning at the fore end of the cabin to create a bit of a draught and to dry the boat out. He came aboard in the dark and started to fill the petrol tank abaft the cockpit from a couple of cans: because he could not see properly some of the petrol overflowed and within seconds there was a 'crrump', followed by a sheet of flame and a roaring fire. Being a resolute and quick-witted man, he fought the fire and saved his boat, as well as getting away with his own life. When it was all over he sat down to think what could have ignited the petrol and came to the only possible conclusion: vapour from the spilled petrol had been drawn along the bilge under the floorboards, moved by the normal forward draught which was augmented by the uprising warm air at the paraffin stove. When the vapour reached the naked flame of the paraffin heater it ignited and flashed back to the cockpit.

Apart from the lesson about naked flames, that tale is also a reminder that the petrol filler on any boat should be arranged so that any overflow goes over the side and not into the bilges.

A similarly cautious attitude should be adopted towards bottled gas. As everyone knows, this is heavier than air and if it leaks it can sink into the bilges: mixed in the right proportion with air and in a confined space it can explode, an occurrence which will be followed by fire. The answer is to have the shortest possible pipe runs from the gas bottle to the cooker, to make sure that there are no leaks in the pipe or at any of the unions (test with a soap-and-water bubble mixture), and always to turn off the valve at the bottle after each occasion when the cooker is used.

When it comes to extinguishing fire aboard a boat the first thing to remember is that there is plenty of water quite handy, unless you happen to have had the double misfortune to have run aground! But water is no good for a petrol fire, in which lubricating oil floating on the bilge water may also play its part. Since both oil and petrol float on water, any extra water in the bilge is only likely to spread the fire. Thus vapours, such as BCF (bromochlorodifluoromethane), and various powders are recommended, and they are very good so long as one can be sure of getting the extinguishant to the fire itself . . . but that is not so easy. If you picture a typical engine installation in the cockpit of a small boat, either completely under the sole, or under some sort of wooden box-like cover, you will realize that the real problem with a fire is to get to the seat of it. Somewhere down there, beneath the box, and under the engine itself, there is perhaps a pool of oil burning in the bilge. Flames will be bursting out of every crack, of course, and the initial explosion may well have blown the engine casing sky-high. In any case it's not the sort of situation where you can get down on your hands and knees and look for the exact spot under the crankcase where you ought to direct the extinguishant. You need something that will get there of its own accord, that will go round corners and will permeate the bilges forward and aft of the seat of the fire.

The only thing that is really likely to permeate everywhere and not be obstructed in its work by parts of the engine or the vessel's structure which happen to lie in its path is a good blast of gas—either BCF or carbon dioxide. Dry powder extinguishant is very good, so long as you can be sure of delivering it in such a way that it will smother the fire wherever it happens to be. The same goes for foam. The outdated standby, the carbon tetrachloride (CTC) extinguisher, is not so effective as BCF and has the disadvantage of creating poisonous and corrosive fumes. In short, the best answer is BCF, yet all too few people carry enough on board.

Galley equipment

To turn from fire to cooking, your boat will need her consignment of cooking utensils, cutlery and crockery. Unless someone aboard is very careless there is no reason why ordinary crockery should not last just as long on the boat as it does at home. Cheap plastic ware is usually rather unattractive, and the best-quality stuff costs about as much as china and is still not so pleasant to use. Plastic *is* useful for tumblers, since thin glass is difficult to preserve in a small boat: Perspex 'glasses' for sherry and short drinks are very good, if you can track some down.

Although it is pleasant to have ordinary crockery for meals served at the cabin table, it is necessary to have some flat-bottomed mugs which won't turn over easily for use in the cockpit when under way.

Cookers themselves fall into three main groups: gas, spirit, and paraffin. Gas is very convenient and ranges from the small self-contained Bleuet or Camping Gaz type of stove, with a gas can about as big as a jam-jar, to full-scale cookers. One advantage of the pocket-sized camping gas stoves is that they can easily be swung athwartships. If you have a large fixed cooker, you may also like to have one of these little stoves in a swinging mounting for use when the boat is heeling. Again, if your main cooker runs on gas you may not wish to carry a spare 12 lb. bottle with you—they take up quite a bit of space. In that case a little picnic-type stove can be a useful standby, and it's easy enough to find room to stow a couple of spare canisters for that.

From the cook's point of view the main advantages of the gas cooker are its immediate readiness to light up, its controllability, and the fact that you can cook just as you do at home—one can have a normal grill, for example. By contrast the one drawback with the ever-popular paraffin pressure cooker is the fact that each burner has to be pre-heated before it can be lit. The excellent Taylor Para-Fin cookers, from which so many of us have had so many meals afloat, are basically similar in action to the Primus. Paraffin under pressure is delivered to a fine jet, and as it passes through the jet it is vaporized by the heat of the surrounding metal. If the metal is not hot enough, the paraffin is merely atomized—that is to say it comes out of the jet in fine droplets—and you get a big yellow flame flaring up. Then you have to release the pressure in the paraffin tank until the flame goes out, pump up and again go through the business of pre-heating with methylated spirits. In practice any sensible person will avoid flare-ups

117

by taking care to burn enough methylated spirit in the annular cup before attempting to light the cooker. It is not the flare-up that is the real drawback with the paraffin pressure stove; it is the need to re-heat the burner every time you want to light up again—half-way through breakfast perhaps, because you want some more hot water to put in the teapot. On the other hand, paraffin involves a much smaller fire risk than gas, and no risk at all of explosion. Moreover, if you are using paraffin for lighting there is the advantage of simplicity in having one fewer item on your stores list.

Wick-fed paraffin cookers, which are very good ashore, are not, as far as I know, well suited to boats. The trouble is that heeling of the boat makes the fuel slosh about in the tank, drives it up the wick and makes the flame go up and down in time with the sloshing.

The methylated spirit stove seems to be gaining in popularity: I have never used one myself, so I can say little about them, but friends who use them speak well of them. They are known as alcohol stoves in the trade, and have the reputation of being rather slow. But the fuel they use is inherently safe—unless you are foolish enough to drink it!

Bedding, and fluff in the bilges

Comfortable sleeping is as important as good eating, but there really isn't very much to say on the matter. In bigger boats you have sleeping-cabins where berths are properly 'made' with sheets and blankets, and very nice it is, too. In small boats sleeping-bags win every time. Very often it is helpful to have a blanket or two for extra warmth, and it's particularly valuable to have something extra to lie *on*. Generally speaking the foam mattresses which are supplied for small cruising boats are not as thick as they should be—they are generally 3 in., but 4 is the minimum for comfort and warmth in my view. Whatever kind of bedding you do adopt, try to avoid anything that will shed fluffs or feathers. A boat, being a closed shell, collects such things only too easily, a fact which will be very apparent when you come to clean out the bilges at the end of the season. The modern Terylene sleeping-bags are excellent in this respect, since they seem to shed no fluffs at all.

The same warning goes for warps and fenders: do not have coir or grass warps, nor rope fenders without canvas covers. After a season or two they will start to shed fibres, and no matter where you store them they will find their way around the boat. Of course, if you are going to bring your dog aboard you may as well give up worrying, though I believe that poodles are not so bad, because they do not lose the short curly wool that covers them. Still, any dog is sure to bring plenty of sand aboard sooner or later!

Tools and spare gear

The aim with a cruising boat is to be as far as possible self-sufficient, so one needs to carry a good supply of tools and spare components. Perhaps the greatest difficulty is knowing where to draw the line. At one extreme is the kind of man of whom I once observed a good example in a southern harbour: he arrived in a small modern cruiser powered by a single outboard motor, made fast alongside the quay and took his friends ashore for a drink. When they returned the outboard would not start, and after some minutes of frustrated pulling he called across to the skipper of a nearby boat, 'I suppose you wouldn't by any chance have a plug spanner I could borrow?'

If by any chance a cruising boat does not have a plug spanner on board, and some spare plugs, and other basic engine tools as well, then it is likely to be a pretty poor outlook for all on board.

Obviously one should not only have the spanners necessary to remove plugs, but also a feeler gauge so that the gaps can be correctly set. Spanners will be needed to remove petrol and water filters, and you may even need a spanner big enough to tighten the nut at the stern gland—something with a jaw width of between 2 and 3 in. perhaps. A set of gaskets is an obvious thing to carry, and perhaps a spare contact-breaker, or even a complete magneto if that component happens to be a troublesome item in your own particular engine. Obviously a good deal depends on the peculiarities of the boat and her equipment.

To be able to cope with repairs and improvements during three or four weeks cruising you need a good assortment of general-purpose tools. I say 'improvements', because it is during a cruise that one sees all manner of little things that might be changed for the better, and one has the opportunity to try out these new ideas. It seems sensible to try to choose tools that will serve a dual purpose: for example, I always have on board one of those Eclipse saws which can be used for either metal or wood. Shifting spanners and a Mole wrench are other items which can cover a range of jobs. I have a hand-drilling machine with a range of bits, screwdrivers, pliers, file, and also a small clamp-on vice which is invaluable. One needs at least one hammer—I have a brass-headed one, and I wish that all my tools were non-rusting—and some sort of plane. One of the Surform tools is quite good for the kind of rough-and-ready planing that one is likely to do on board. Other items are a rule, adjustable bevel, a chisel or two (protect the end with a finger from an old leather glove), and a carborundum stone. I carry an old-fashioned flat-iron which can actually be heated on the stove to iron clothes, but is more generally used as an anvil or riveting dolly.

Although one may not be able to have all non-rusting tools, nowadays one can tackle the problem another way by using the 'Ban-Rust' paper. This is coated with a compound which gives off a vapour which positively inhibits the oxidation reaction of rusting. Obviously the stuff works best in a closed space where the vapour is not quickly dispersed, but it's well worth using wherever possible. Not only can you line your tool-box with anti-rust paper each season, you can also use it in the cupboard where you keep galley equipment, as well as around the engine.

Apart from tools one needs screws in all sizes, copper boat nails and roves to suit, galvanized bolts and nuts, copper wire, brass split pins, lashing eyes, screw eyes and cup-hooks. If you shop at an ordinary ironmonger's for 'brass' hooks and eyes, take a small magnet along with you to be sure that you are not buying iron hooks brassed over. Brassed iron will serve well enough in a house, but on board a boat it very soon begins to rust: even worse is the fact that iron makes a firm bond to wood as it rusts, so when you try to remove the rusted hook it may well shear off, leaving a buried stub which will weep rust for years to come.

Chandlery to be carried aboard includes blocks, cod line, serving twine, needles and thread for repairs to sails and canvas covers, thimbles (for spliced eyes, not for use with the needles!), plenty of shackles. There is almost no limit to the variety of things one might carry: in order to keep the numbers down it is wise to discriminate between things that can be replaced by an improvisation, and those that cannot. A broken rigging screw, for example, can easily be replaced by a lanyard, in the old-fashioned way, though with Terylene and nylon available it is even easier to rig a lanyard, because the line is more slippery and the successive turns pull through easily. Moreover, the extra strength of these synthetic cordages means that fewer turns are needed.

Glue is obviously desirable: I carry Evostik for quick repairs to lightly stressed items, Aerolite 300 for wood joints which must be strong, and Araldite for the jobs that it alone can do, metal-to-metal repairs for example. Araldite, by the way, can be used instead of a whipping on the end of a light lanyard, the sort of thing you use to lace up a sail cover, for example. Ordinary flax servings can too easily be pulled off the end of a piece of cod line, so I prefer to make a rigid and permanent end with Araldite, not only because it lasts but also because it is so easy to push through an eyelet. The way to do it is to mix up the Araldite and spread a small amount on a scrap of waxed paper (from the cornflake packet). Fold the paper round the end of the line and work the resin well into the lay. Then twirl, as for waxed moustaches. The paper can be left in place until the Araldite dries. If your twirling wasn't very successful and the thing dries with a rather shapeless end you can cut and file it to a point. An ordinary whipping can be preserved and stiffened by soaking it with varnish: alternatively you may coat the rope's end with Evostik before serving. Although this can be a bit messy, it does keep the serving in place.

In the category of glue-like materials comes plastic stopping and sealing compound —always carry some on board, because the time to stop a leak in a deck or coaming is when you see it. Paint, varnish, white spirit and brushes are always worth having on board, so that you can touch-up during the season and protect scratched wood from moisture. Obviously you will need oils and greases. Apart from those specified for the engine, you will need light oil for hinges. Anhydrous lanolin is an excellent protective and lubricant for shackle pins, rigging screws and so forth.

This kind of list very quickly becomes tedious, and one could go on for ever. In any case I would not presume to tell anyone else what he ought or ought not to have on board: it is simply a matter of stimulating thought on the subject. Sooner or later one always wishes that one had thought to bring some obscure tool, such as a spokeshave or a soldering iron. The main point is that a cruising boat, unlike a dinghy or a day-boat, has to be equipped more or less as a second home, since you can hardly carry all your tools back and forth every week-end.

Finally, to get away from the tedium of the list, there is an important point of safety in connection with tools: *never go aloft with unattached tools*. When you go up the mast, knife, spanner, spike or whatever you take must be attached to you with a lanyard. If you don't take that precaution sooner or later someone below will have you to thank for a cracked skull. A marlin spike dropped from 20 ft. reminds one of what happened to poor Harold at Hastings. Of course, if you happen to knock out the chap who's hauling you up you'll probably get your deserts, too.

It is also worth attaching a lanyard to your tools if you are working over the side of the vessel—at a chain plate, for example, or at a rudder gudgeon. Perhaps because of the awkward angle, or because of the law of cussedness, tools are always dropped in such circumstances. They hardly ever float.

11

Taking care of sails

Dinghy sails are generally better treated than those of cruising boats; they are unbent at the end of the day, stuffed into bags and taken home to be stored in places where they can dry out. In cruising boats sails seldom get the attention they deserve: at the end of the day they are bundled up on deck, tied round the boom, or lashed to the pulpit, sometimes covered and sometimes not. Even when they are unbent they are stowed below decks in an atmosphere which is always damp and salt-laden.

I would be the last person to claim that I am without blame, though perhaps I should be more careful than most because I still prefer cotton sails (for their looks, for their feel, and perhaps because of nostalgic sentiments). Of course, nowadays there is the advantage that you can send your cotton sails to be professionally proofed against water and mildew. It's all so much more simple than the almost forgotten business of dressing with oil and ochre, which produced that wonderful tanned colour, and it's really quite cheap too.

But whatever the material, it is worth treating your sails properly, in part to get the best performance out of them and in part to get long life out of them; replacements will be quite expensive. The people who know best how sails should be treated are the sailmakers themselves, so I asked permission from Ratsey and Lapthorn Limited, of Cowes, to abstract information from their own guide to sail care, copies of which are available, by the way, to any yachtsman who cares to take the trouble of writing to ask. In other parts of this book I have expressed my own opinions on the way to go about things and the reader may feel free to disagree; but in what follows I do not think that there is much ground for dispute, because these are the views of 'Ratseys', and that should be sufficient in itself.

To begin with cotton sails, it is perhaps not widely recognized how much care must be taken in stretching a new cotton sail carefully before it is ready for hard use. A new cotton sail should be set for the first time on a fine sunny day when there is a moderate breeze blowing; Force 3, say, but not a full Force 4. If you can't find the perfect day you won't be surprised, but *never* set the new sail if it is blowing hard, raining, misty or just damp. And never reef a new sail unless it is a matter of life and death. On the other hand, Ratseys do not recommend setting a new sail on a day when there is little or no breeze, just flopping about with the weight of the boom on it is not a good thing.

The rule for setting is to hoist away on the luff until it is fairly taut, and the canvas is smooth and unwrinkled, but no more; then pull the sail out along the boom until it is just a little harder than hand taut. The way to gauge it is to pull until the wrinkles along the foot just disappear: the point is that the bolt rope is sewn on the sail fairly taut because the sailmaker knows that it is going to stretch more than the canvas, so when the wrinkles are gone the rope has been stretched to the point where the canvas is of the dimension to which it was originally cut. Obviously different thicknesses of bolt rope will need different tensions to stretch them out, so that the proper guide is not the amount of tension you have to put into the rope, but the disappearance of the wrinkles from the sailcloth.

The leech of a sail is seldom roped, except for large boats. It is usually cut with a convex edge, or 'roach' as it is known, and battens in their pockets are needed to hold the roach out to shape. A sail should never be hoisted without its battens, because the weight of the boom will tend to draw the roach out into a straight line, stretching the material forward of it. The unroped leech of the sail will stretch practically all it is ever going to stretch in the first day's sailing, but when hoisting take care to support the weight of the boom by the topping lift until the luff of the sail is up to the length of the canvas and the halyard is made fast.

When a new sail has been set the thing to do is to cruise around for an hour or two, not keeping the boat on any one point of sailing all the time, nor sheeting the sail in too flat—that will tend to overstretch the leech.

After a bit of sailing around sags and wrinkles will begin to appear along both the luff and the foot of the sail, and these should be taken up by further hauling, always sticking to the rule of applying just enough tension to smooth the canvas. The sail should be stretching slowly and naturally, due to the distributed pressure of the wind, and it is quite wrong to try and force things. On the other hand, an understretched sail will never set correctly, and if the sail does not seem to be getting near its marks after a reasonable stretching period in adequate wind, then more weight will have to be put on the halyard and outhaul. Although the rule is to go at it cautiously and steadily, never trying to pull out the bolt ropes bar taut, Ratseys say that more sails are, in fact, spoiled by understretching than the reverse.

There is no set rule as to the number of hours of sailing needed to break a sail in. It depends on the weight of the canvas and the weight of the wind, but about 5 hours of sailing in warm air and moderate breezes seems to be right before using the sail in a strong breeze.

With a gaff sail there is rather more work, though the principle is the same, because the head of the sail will have to be drawn out bit by bit, in the same way as the foot.

A staysail or jib which has a wire luff cannot be stretched along that particular edge: you can set the luff up as tight as you please, knowing that the sailmaker has already adjusted the canvas to the length of the wire.

Care of sails in rain or misty weather

Stretching a cotton sail is the first step to get good performance and long life out of it, but it must be cared for during its lifetime. For example, if you are out sailing and it begins to rain or a wet mist comes up, the canvas will begin to shrink before the roping does; unless the halyards and outhauls are slacked off bit by bit the sail will not be able to shrink evenly—the luff and the foot will be pulled hard flat while the rest of the canvas shrinks at a natural rate. So, unless you want to run the risk of causing permanent damage to your sails, ease off halyards and outhauls as soon as dampness begins to affect the sails.

Whether the weather is wet or dry the outhaul should always be slackened when the mainsail is lowered and covered, because sooner or later there will be damp weather and the foot-roping will absorb more moisture than the furled-up canvas. If the rope cannot shrink to its natural length, it may in effect be stretched beyond its elastic limit, with permanent distortion of the sail. It is important to realize that if a rope is prevented from shrinking to its 'wet' length the result is the same as if it were stretched mechanically to an excessive length when dry. Cotton sails, even though proofed, ought not to be furled up or stowed in their bags while they are wet; always try to hoist them up for an airing before furling them. Of course, this may not be so easy; if it happens to have rained all through Sunday and you were back on the mooring about midnight, with the drive home before you and the need to be in the office in the morning, then you just haven't much chance.

Sails can become impregnated with salt, left behind when spray evaporates. The trouble with salt is that it quickly absorbs moisture from the air, so that sails or parts of them can become almost permanently damp. That's not going to be good for the canvas, and if only certain parts are salted those parts will shrink and the sail will set badly. The thing to do is to wash the sails out in fresh water, if you have a big enough bath, or to hose them down. This should be done at the end of each season, or more frequently if you have been doing well for spray. This is another of those councils of perfection: you may not lay your boat up until well into October, and then somehow you have to find some really good drying days during the week-ends of November and December, because after you have rinsed them the sails must be thoroughly dry before putting away. Probably the simple and sensible answer is to send them to the sailmaker —he has the equipment to rinse and dry. Moreover, he can make any repairs necessary, and even alterations if you wish. Then you will have your sails back in perfect order in plenty of time for next season and you won't have to start thinking about that torn batten pocket or a started seam at fitting-out time when there are so many other things to do.

Terylene sails

Stretching a Terylene sail is a much less troublesome business than it is with cotton. It will not matter if the weather is damp, or even raining, and a couple of hours of sailing in any reasonable sort of breeze should be enough to stretch the sail so that it can be brought to its marks. As with cotton sails, the idea is to tension the bolt ropes until wrinkles in the canvas disappear; and the sail should not be sheeted down too hard until it has had several hours in which to stretch.

Terylene does not shrink when wet and it is resistant to mildew—even in those rare cases when mildew does form on a Terylene sail the material itself remains unharmed. Although Terylene sails have these advantages over cotton, and are also stronger and more resistant to chafe, they do have the slight disadvantage that they tend to collect dirt rather easily. So although you need not bother so much about covering your sails to protect them from the rain, it's worth putting covers on to keep the dirt off. When they do get dirty, Terylene sails can be washed in hand-hot water, with either soap or detergent.

Terylene and cotton have about the same degree of resistance to sunlight, which in both cases is pretty good. Nylon, on the other hand, is more susceptible to sunlight, though as it is normally used only for lightweight spinnakers it does not see the light of day as often as the working suit. Anyway, if a nylon sail is not actually hoisted, don't leave it lying around in the sun.

Headsails: stretching and care

With loose-footed headsails little breaking-in is needed: they usually have wire luffs, so that they may be set up taut from the start. Nevertheless it is better to begin by using them in light or moderate breezes, and in fine weather, so that the canvas gets a chance to find its natural shape.

Most headsails are cut with a mitre seam—if you look at a photograph of a cruising boat you will see this seam leading from the clew to a point roughly half-way up the luff. In fact, the mitre should bisect the angle at the clew. If the lead of the sheet is correct the line of it, prolonged forward and upward, should meet the luff at a point just above the mitre seam. This is typical for a working staysail. For a genoa with its longer foot the point would be a little below the mitre seam. The angle must vary slightly from sail to sail, of course, but the line of the mitre is a good guide.

The angle of the sheet from the centreline of the boat is almost as important as the angle in the vertical plane. Normally a genoa will need to be sheeted as far outboard as possible, so as not to get the angle too fine. Smaller headsails will vary according to the shape of the sail and the type of boat; the faster the boat the smaller the angle with the centreline. Ratseys say that the average is about 12 deg., but point out that only trial and error can determine the best headsail angle for any given boat. As you can't easily measure an angle of 12 deg. on your boat, here is a table of offsets showing how far the lead should be from the centreline of the boat for different distances back from the tack.

HEADSAIL SHEET LEADING AT 12 DEGREES

Distance back from tack—feet	6	7	8	9	10	11	12	13	14	15	16	17	18	19	20
Distance out from centreline—inches	15	18	20	23	26	28	30	33	35	38	40	43	46	48	51

Setting up halyards correctly

The tension in the halyard has its effect on the set of a mainsail: the sail itself should have a curve, which you could call convex or concave according to the side you view it from, but from the leeward side the greatest convexity is in the forward third. The shape is like the camber in the wing of an aeroplane—a slow-flying one, whose speed is not too far different from the natural speed of the wind over a sail. To sailmakers this convexity is known as the draught, and in a Bermudian sail it is kept to the forward part by setting up the halyard so that there is more tension in the luff rope than there is in the foot rope. The draught can be moved aft to a certain extent by decreasing the tension in the luff and increasing it in the foot.

In a gaff-headed sail the position of the draught is adjusted both by the tension with which the head of the sail is pulled out along the gaff, and also by the angle to which the gaff is peaked up. As this book is primarily concerned with the modern small cruisers, which all have jib-headed (Bermudian) mainsails, I shall not go any further into the setting of gaff-headed sails, leaving it to any reader who is interested to drop a line to Ratseys for their advice.

No sail will set properly if the spars are not holding their designed shape. Nearly all masts are meant to be straight, and they must be kept so by adjustment of the rigging screws. You will probably have to lie on your back on the deck to sight up the mast (with sails drawing, of course). Sight along the back edge because any taper in the mast will have been confined to the front so as to keep the luff straight. Your boom, too, should be as straight as possible, but as it is unstayed you may find it difficult to do much about it, even if you do think it is bowing too much. Short of getting a new, stiffer boom, you might either rearrange the run of the mainsheet, so as to distribute the downward pull along the boom, or you may have the sail itself modified by a sailmaker. To do the job properly he would need the best measurements you can give him concerning the bowing of the boom.

To get a really good idea of how your sails are setting and how your spars are standing, the best thing to do is to go ashore, or aboard another boat, while someone else sails your own boat around. This is a view we seldom see—it's common enough to see something definitely odd about another fellow's boat, something which he hasn't noticed himself. If he had the benefit of your viewpoint he would spot it at once. . . .

Care in reefing

Whether your boat has roller reefing or the now rather unfashionable reef points, it is worth taking care to make a neat job of reefing. If the sail is reefed badly it can be pulled out of shape when the weight of the wind comes on it; in fact, with a really badly made reef it can be torn.

If you are using reefing points, see that the weight of the boom is taken off the sail, by the topping lift or the boom crutch, then lower away on the halyard until the tack ear-ring can be lashed down. Next pull out the sail along the boom by means of the pendant through the leech ear-ring; it is important that the sail should be pulled aft along the boom, hand-taut. With tack and clew of the sail made fast the lower part of the sail can be carefully rolled up and the reef points tied round. The points are tied round the foot of the sail, not round the boom.

Some people do not keep reef points permanently rove through the eyelets in the sail, but prefer to reeve a lacing line through them, making a continuous spiral along the foot of the sail. If that method is used, no hitches should be made at the eyelets— the load can then spread evenly. When shaking out a reef under way, first take the weight of the boom on the topping lift; then undo the reef points and make sure that they are *all* undone before freeing first the tack and then the clew. Obviously if one reef point is accidentally left tied the sail will be torn when the weight comes on it.

To free a reef knot, take hold of either of the ends and of the standing part alongside it. Pull them apart, and the knot will unroll. Even so, on a cold wet day it can be quite a trial for the fingers.

Never leave a sail reefed after the need for it is over, especially if it is damp.

With roller reefing it is not always necessary to use the topping lift. The important thing is to be sure that the luff rope stows nicely around the fore-end of the boom: the extra thickness due to the rope can be a nuisance as the turns build up and a bit of hand guidance will probably be needed to make it snug down properly. The leech will also need attention; it may tend to come too far forward along the boom as it rolls up. Excessive use of the topping lift will make that tendency worse, but even if the topping lift is just right, or quite slack, it may be necessary to post a hand whose job is to coax the leech aft. He can also remove any battens which roll down as far as the boom.

On the subject of battens, Ratseys say that they prefer wood (hickory) to plastic, because it is lighter and because its thickness can be adjusted to give the right degree of flexibility at the right points. A batten should be an inch or so shorter than the pocket in which it goes.

12

A note on Thames tonnage

Thames tonnage is out of date, misleading, and quite irrational . . . but there's no sign that anyone is going to stop talking about '5-tonners', or '10-tonners', so the best thing one can do is to try and see what it is all about and to be aware how misleading it can be.

It was in 1854 that the Royal Thames Yacht Club adopted the formula for measurement which has since become so firmly established as Thames tonnage; the formula makes use of only two measurements from the craft herself—her length and her beam. These alone are not enough to give even the total volume of the hull, let alone that part which is immersed, so it is only by chance that any tonnage calculated from length and beam alone will happen to be near the actual weight (displacement) of the vessel. In boats of the past, with straight stems, deep draught, fairly narrow beam and short counters, the Thames tonnage did, in fact, work out at approximately the displacement. Nowadays things are quite different, as this short list shows:

	Displacement, tons weight	*Thames tonnage*
Westcoaster	1	3
Halcyon	1·25	4·5
Dauntless 22 ft.	2	5
Atalanta	2	6
Centaur	3	6
Vertue	4·5	5

The formula that produces these odd results is as follows:

$$\frac{(L - B) \times B \times \frac{1}{2}B}{94}$$

L and B, of course, are the length and the beam respectively. By 'beam' is meant the extreme breadth of the hull, excluding any protrusions such as rubbing strakes or chain plates. The definition of length is a bit more subtle: in the case of something like a Dragonfly or a Folkboat, which has a transom stern with the rudder hung outboard, the length is measured from the fore side of the stem at deck-level to the after side of the transom at deck-level.

But in a boat of more traditional construction which has a sternpost the measurement is made to the after side of the sternpost at deck-level. If by any chance the sternpost stops short of the deck, then the measurement is taken to the point where it would meet the deck if it were prolonged.

Finally, some boats have the rudder inboard, but are built without a sternpost: in that case the measurement is made to the centreline of the rudder stock at deck-level. The sketches in Figure 29 show what is implied.

The three hulls sketched in the figure show not only how differences in construction change the measuring point under this rule, they also indicate how three boats of the same 'tonnage' can have widely differing internal volumes. A 5-tonner, for example, could have a beam of 8 ft. on a length of 22 ft., or she could have a beam of 7 ft. on a measured length of 27 ft., which might be associated with an actual overall length of 30 ft. when one takes into account the overhang aft of the sternpost or rudder stock. The comparison between two such imaginary boats is shown in Figure 30.

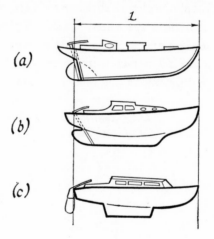

Figure 29. As explained in the text, 'length' for the purpose of calculating Thames tonnage has various meanings, and is less than 'length overall' for a boat with a counter stern.

It will be seen that the term Thames tonnage gives very little idea of the accommodation inside a boat—for one thing it ignores that most important dimension, the depth of the hull. It would seem that there is nothing to prevent an oversized sailing surf-board being described as a 3-tonner so long as she has sufficient length and beam. Moreover, the beam is merely the maximum beam and this makes no allowances for the shape of the sections or the fineness (or fullness) of the hull fore and aft of the maximum-beam section. In Figure 30 some sections are indicated to show how very important this point is.

Another obvious weakness is the fact that the beam appears twice in the formula as a multiplier, so that a small increment in that dimension has a disproportionate effect on the Thames tonnage. Of course, in a sense this is justified, because if you care to take any boat you can think of it has to be admitted that an extra foot on the beam makes much more difference to the accommodation than an extra foot on the length.

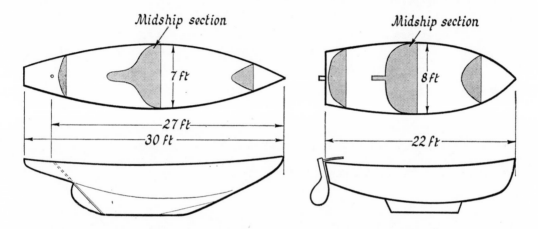

Figure 30. Two boats which seem to have only one thing in common—the fact that they are both '5-tonners'. The lean, deeper-draught craft on the left would almost certainly have the greater displacement, while the shorter, beamier craft has the larger usable volume inside.

But in spite of its very evident shortcomings Thames measurement is still widely used, but it only becomes meaningful if one has some other description. A 9-ton Falmouth Quay Punt is a meaningful phrase only if you have a general idea of what a Quay Punt looks like.

Another difficulty is that, according to the Royal Thames Yacht Club, the Thames tonnage should be stated to the nearest whole ton. This means that a boat of 9 ft. beam with a measured length of 26 ft. is a '7-tonner', because the formula works out at 7·3 tons; but a boat of the same beam and with a length of 27 ft. is an '8-tonner' (7·75 tons).

The table on page 133 shows the Thames tonnages that should be quoted for various lengths and beams, and it will be seen just what a variety of shapes of boat is embraced by the term '6-tonner', for example. Although the rule says that Thames tonnage should be expressed to the nearest whole ton, I have given the smaller boats the benefit of half tons, as is, in fact, customary for these sizes.

A note on Thames tonnage

TABLE OF THAMES TONNAGES

BEAM (Feet)

LENGTH (Feet)	6	6.5	7	7.5	8	8.5	9	9.5	10	10.5	11	11.5	12
16	2	2	2½										
17	2	2	2½										
18	2½	2½	3	3	3½								
19	2½	3	3	3½	3½								
20	2½	3	3½	4	4	4½	5	5					
21	3	3	3½	4	4½	5	5	5½	6	6			
22	3	3½	4	4½	5	5	6	6	6	6			
23	3½	4	4	4½	5	5½	6	7	7	7	8		
24	3½	4	4½	5	5½	6	7	7	8	8	8	9	
25	3½	4	4½	5	6	6	7	8	8	8	9	9	10
26	4	4½	5	5½	6	7	7	8	9	9	10	10	11
27	4	4½	5	6	7	7	8	8	9	10	10	11	11
28	4	5	5½	6	7	8	8	9	10	10	11	12	12
29	4½	5	5½	7	7	8	9	9	10	11	12	12	13
30	4½	5	6	7	8	8	9	10	11	11	12	13	14
31	5	5½	6	7	8	9	9	10	11	12	13	14	15
32	5	5½	7	7	8	9	10	11	12	13	13	14	15
33		6	7	8	9	9	10	11	12	13	14	15	16
34		6	7	8	9	10	11	12	13	14	15	16	17
35			7	8	9	10	11	12	13	14	15	16	18
36			8	9	10	11	12	13	14	15	16	17	18
37				9	10	11	12	13	14	15	17	18	19
38				9	10	11	12	14	15	16	17	19	20
39						12	13	14	15	17	18	19	21
40							13	15	16	17	19	20	21

Accommodation Plans

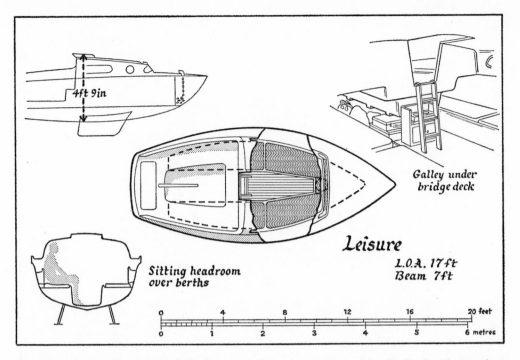

4ft 9in

Galley under
bridge deck

Leisure

L.O.A. 17 ft
Beam 7 ft

Sitting headroom
over berths

| 0 | | 4 | | 8 | | 12 | | 16 | | 20 feet |
| 0 | | 1 | | 2 | | 3 | | 4 | | 5 | | 6 metres |

The drawings on this and the following pages have been prepared by D. L. Jenkins to show typical accommodation arrangements in small boats. The examples are arranged in order of increasing overall length.

It is possible to provide sleeping berths for four people even in a boat which is only 17 ft. long. The major contribution to that achievement is the use of 'quarter berths' which is the term used to describe a berth running in a tunnel formed by the cockpit seat. Quarter berths have become especially popular since the introduction of boats moulded in glass-reinforced polyester resin, possibly because it is easier to make the cockpit seats leakproof in this material than it is with timber. Many of the boats described in this book have quarter berths on one or both sides of the boat, and some have more of their length in the main cabin and less under the cockpit seats than in this example. The difficulty in a boat so small as the Leisure 17 is to find stowage space for all the gear, bedding and food that four people would bring with them. Notice the way in which the space under the cockpit sole is used for stowage. ('Sole' is simply the marine word for what one would otherwise call a floor, by the way. Moreover, a 'floor' in a boat is a transverse member underneath the cabin sole and is not at all like a domestic floor.) The Snapdragon 600 is another boat which has this type of berth plan, but when one gets to a slightly longer boat, such as the Corribee, the two berths on each side of the boat can be separated by a small cupboard, a fitment supporting a cooking stove, or even a boxed-in w.c. The Vivacity 20 and the Four 21 are examples of boats which have fitments dividing their quarter berths from their forward berths.

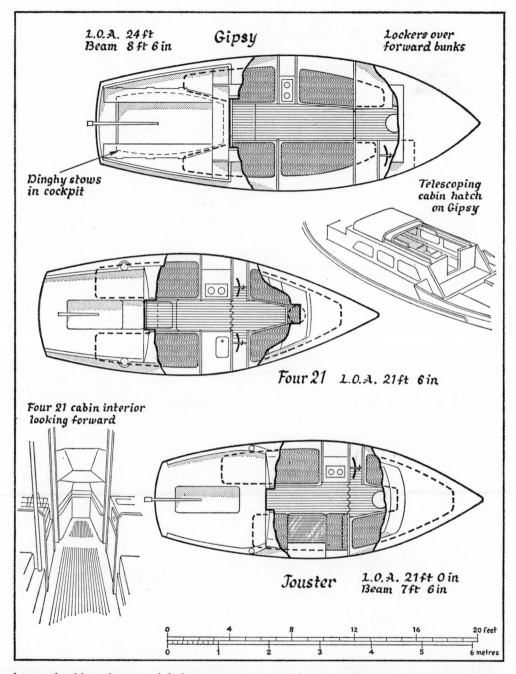

L.O.A. 24 ft
Beam 8 ft 6 in

Gipsy

Lockers over
forward bunks

Dinghy stows
in cockpit

Telescoping
cabin hatch
on Gipsy

Four 21   L.O.A. 21 ft 6 in

Four 21 cabin interior
looking forward

Jouster   L.O.A. 21 ft 0 in
Beam 7 ft 6 in

| 0 | 4 | 8 | 12 | 16 | 20 feet |
| 0 | 1 | 2 | 3 | 4 | 5 | 6 metres |

Among the things that a good designer must try to work in are cooking space, a hanging locker for clothes (and a separate one for oilskins if he can), and a suitable position for the w.c. The Gipsy has the w.c. right forward, beneath the forehatch and beyond a bulkhead, with the 'feet' ends of two berths running either side of it in tunnels. A table is provided. The Four 21 also has her w.c. forward, under a shaped cushion, while her galley is split with cooker to one side and sink to the other. Jouster has a small dinette scheme—that's to say a table-plus-seats on the starboard side. At night the table lets down and joins the seats to form a berth.

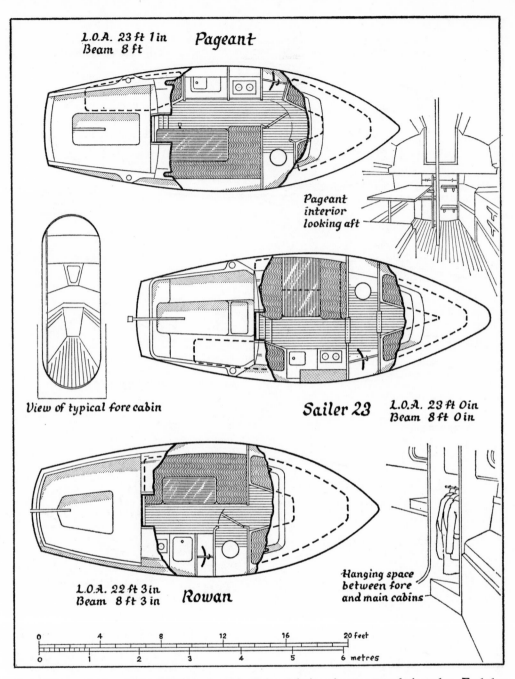

L.O.A. 23 ft 1 in
Beam 8 ft

Pageant

*Pageant
interior
looking aft*

View of typical fore cabin

Sailer 23

L.O.A. 23 ft 0 in
Beam 8 ft 0 in

L.O.A. 22 ft 3 in
Beam 8 ft 3 in

Rowan

*Hanging space
between fore
and main cabins*

| 0 | 4 | 8 | 12 | 16 | 20 feet |
| 0 | 1 | 2 | 3 | 4 | 5 | 6 metres |

Three boats of very similar dimensions, with slight variations in accommodation plan. Each has two berths forward, but Pageant has one quarter berth, and a dinette that makes a berth at night. It could even be used as a double berth, and the dinette does seat four. So does Sailer's, and that too makes a double. (In the daytime the table also folds along the dotted line.) Rowan, a slightly smaller boat, has yet another pattern of dinette which also seats four, and makes a double berth at night.

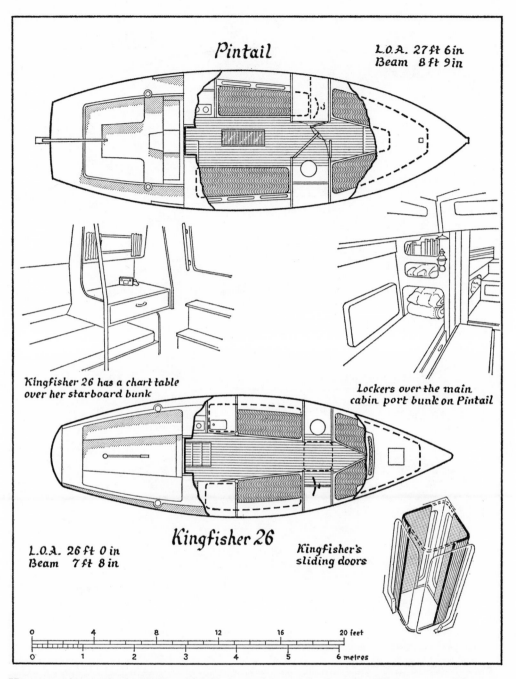

Pintail

L.O.A. 27ft 6in
Beam 8ft 9in

Kingfisher 26 has a chart table
over her starboard bunk

Lockers over the main
cabin port bunk on Pintail

Kingfisher 26

L.O.A. 26ft 0in
Beam 7ft 8in

Kingfisher's
sliding doors

0   4   8   12   16   20 feet
0'   1   2   3   4   5   6 metres

Here we arrive at a basic pattern which is repeated over and over again. With the mast stepped on deck a pair of bulkheads can conveniently be used to support its downward thrust. At the same time these bulkheads naturally form a w.c. compartment on one side of the boat, and a clothes locker on the other. In Pintail the cooking area pinches a portion of the space available for the port main berth, whose foot end extends through the bulkhead of the wardrobe. In the Kingfisher 26 doors like a roller-top for a desk run in tracks to separate the cabins or the w.c.

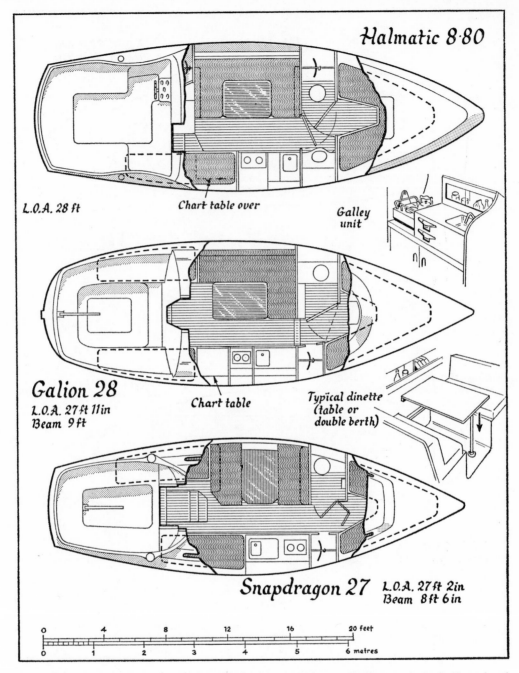

Halmatic 8·80

L.O.A. 28 ft

Chart table over

Galley unit

Galion 28
L.O.A. 27 ft 11in
Beam 9 ft

Chart table

Typical dinette
(table or
double berth)

Snapdragon 27 L.O.A. 27 ft 2in
Beam 8 ft 6in

Three larger boats, but showing the three basic forms of dinette—the U-shaped, the L-shaped and the H-shaped. Each of these boats makes use of the bulkheads under the mast to provide a w.c. compartment and a wardrobe. Each has a quarter berth, plus two berths in a fore cabin, and each has the galley opposite the dinette so that you have the convenience of short-distance serving but the disadvantage of contemplating the aftermath of the cook's art as well as the waiting washing-up when you have finished your meal. (The Galion 28 is a big sister to the 22, but is not reviewed in this book.)

Part Two

SOME STANDARD SMALL CRUISING BOATS

Looking back at the first edition of this book one sees that the most notable change that has come over the nature of small standard cruising boats concerns structural material. Less than ten years ago marine plywood was highly favoured, and the use of polyester resin reinforced with glass fibre was quite rare. Only half a dozen of the boats that took my fancy at that time were built in the material which now dominates all others. In fact the boats reviewed on the following pages are all built in resinglass, except where otherwise stated.

There has also been quite a change in the standard of fittings and finish. Stainless steel is now the standard material for standing wire rigging, for stanchions and pulpits and rudder hangings. Aluminium alloy spars are now the norm. Indeed the improvement in detail design of small cruisers has been most remarkable in the last three or four years, probably as a result of the stimulus of competition.

While the modern materials are very good, one cannot help wondering whether there are not many people who would prefer a plywood hull, or fittings in galvanized mild steel if that resulted in a lower price. For it is true that prices even as I write seem very high for quite small boats, and it is very likely that the few months between writing and publication will make nonsense of such figures as I have quoted. If that should be so there is nothing more I can do than to say I am sorry—not so much because my figures are wrong but because inflation is galloping away so swiftly.

To anyone who finds the prices of new boats a deterrent, I would earnestly advise a look through the small ads for secondhand craft. Many of the plywood boats I described in the first edition are still going strong. Many others are not—and the difference usually lies between those that have been well looked after and those that have not. A plywood boat that has been well cared for can be a very good buy, and even if she is not in perfect condition an average handyman can usually put her to rights quite easily.

And do not suppose that because resinglass boats have now come into vogue that wood is a suspect material. Traditionally planked boats, whether carvel or clinker, can be expected to last a very long time. There are plenty currently in service which are more than fifty years old, so for many of us a secondhand wooden boat can be expected to last more than our own lifetime.

In my opinion there is no quick and easy way of choosing the right boat. It is a task that takes a certain amount of time, and a good deal of tallying up with pencil and paper. You have first to decide what level of equipment you want your boat to have. Very often a secondhand boat will include a great deal of useful gear in her price—mooring warps, a second anchor, an oil lamp or a fire extinguisher, a cockpit cover and a couple of spare sails. . . . But the list price of a new boat may not include even one anchor, and may even exclude sails in some cases. There is no uniformity and even different boats by the same builder may be equipped to different specifications for the 'basic' price. So the only true answer is to take pencil and paper and tot up the final cost, including any extras, of the boat with the equipment you want.

A point to remember is that wooden boats built by the small family yards are still, as I write, among the cheapest of new construction. And there is also the advantage that you may be able to get the builder to arrange the internal accommodation to your choice. That is not possible with a resinglass boat—unless you buy a bare shell and finish her off yourself—because such craft are built on a production line, and the flow cannot be interrupted.

Internal accommodation has in fact become somewhat stereotyped in recent years, especially among the resinglass craft. I should have liked to show accommodation drawings of all the boats described, but it would have made the book excessively costly. Nevertheless, Dave Jenkins has drawn a variety of typical accommodation arrangements covering the most popular patterns. Among them the 'dinette' arrangement is currently in vogue. By that is meant the grouping of seats around a table at one side of the cabin instead of the older convention of a central table with settee-berths on opposite sides of the boat.

Most small craft with a dinette have the galley on the opposite side of the cabin from the table, and though that is convenient it does have the disadvantage that the pots and dishes are right under your nose just when you want to relax after a meal.

Another feature that has become almost standard is the siting of the w.c. in the middle of the boat, between a pair of bulkheads which support the downward thrust of the mast. There is logic in such an arrangement, but I think that there is more logic in trying to place the w.c. right forward, under the fore-hatch. With a little ingenuity that can be arranged to give full headroom in port, when the hatch can be opened and some kind of canvas cover can be rigged. If at sea the hatch must be shut and there is only sitting headroom, but I would think that a fair price to pay for having the loo in a well-ventilated position that is also as remote as is possible from the main cabin. Neither the sounds nor the scents associated with the loo can be considered to contribute to a pleasant life.

There will be readers who are disappointed that this or that boat has not been included. Well, I had to make a choice somehow, and went primarily for those which I have sailed, or which seemed to me to be good examples of their type. But the truth is that there are many more that could have been treated, and that the number is swelling each year. The only way to keep track, as I said in the first edition, is to watch the yachting magazines. And it will be noticed that I have made no mention of the multi-hulls—the catamarans and trimarans—which have shown a marked increase in popularity since the first edition. The reason for that is that they would have needed a whole book to themselves, not because their variety is so numerous but because their character and the handling methods that are appropriate require careful exposition. It is not safe to go to sea in a catamaran, say, using the same philosophy and the same techniques that one uses with a monohull.

Completing a boat yourself

Many of the boats I have described can be had from the builders in part-completed form, and a good deal of money can be saved by the man who is willing and able to finish the job at home. Some of the builders will also supply a kit of wooden parts, roughly cut to shape on the band-saw. With the aid of such a kit I have known people who could hardly warrant the title of 'handyman' to make a perfectly good job of completing a hull. And they enjoyed the work itself almost as much as the saving of money.

On the other hand there are some moulded boats which have entirely moulded interiors, and in such cases there is little that can be done by the home-finisher. Nevertheless, he is not forced to accept a stainless steel pulpit, fitted by the boatbuilder, at a figure of £50. He can make one himself from galvanized water barrel for less than a fiver, including the cost of welding at the local garage. I am not handy at metal-work myself, but I made a pulpit from water barrel some ten years ago for less than £2, using threaded plates and T-junctions from the local builders' merchant. That little piece of amateur 'engineering' is still going strong and will give a good many years service yet.

Certainly anybody who is competent in metalworking could save himself quite a bit of money. From the list of 'extras' for a current 23-ft. boat I see that the total cost of pulpit, pushpit, stanchions and guard wires, would amount to around £80. A small fitted compass is quoted at £35, yet I know that I could buy one just as good and fit it myself for less than £12. It certainly is not hard to fit the round Tannoy ventilators, and it's not a very big job to fit an echo sounder, yet by tackling a few jobs of that nature instead of 'buying' them built-in you could quickly save £100.

Rather more advanced but still possible is the conversion of an automobile engine to marine use, followed by installing it yourself. The result may not be so good as a pukka marine engine, but there may be a difference in cost of £300 or more. A half-way stage is to look through the classified advertisements for a secondhand marine engine and to fit that yourself. Work of this kind *is* pretty ambitious, but the principle remains the same—to analyse the costs carefully and see if you can reduce some of them.

The prices I quote on the following pages are really round figures, given for purposes of comparison at this point in time. Changes are bound to occur, and one can assume that they will be upward and not down. Therefore a serious buyer will have to write to the makers of the boats that interest him so as to get the latest figures.

When it comes to *paying* for the boat you may find that it is not quite the same as buying a motor-car, for example. Traditional yards, building each boat to a customer's order, are accustomed to asking for progress payments. In effect you pay for materials and labour as the job progresses, though you don't pay over the final instalment of perhaps as much as 25 per cent, or perhaps as little as 10 per cent, until you have conducted a successful acceptance trial.

With series-produced boats a similar system may still hold good—a substantial deposit, perhaps 25 per cent with order, a further large amount when the decked hull is completed and the balance after acceptance trial. There are all manner of variations, and in some cases it may be a straightforward case of 'walk in and buy it'. But wherever money is being paid in stages or in advance the customer is quite right to take every care in checking the soundness of the company, and also that his boat has reached the stage of completion that is claimed. Boatbuilders are by an overwhelming majority honest, but in every profession there is always the possibility of being cheated.

Raising the money is usually the biggest problem, and there are plenty of people who make a nice living from lending others the means to buy boats. The classical method is to raise a marine mortgage, which is in principle just like a house mortgage, though at a the time of writing it is not possible to claim income tax relief on the annual outgoings for interest.

Another method is hire purchase, which tends to be more expensive if the repayment is made over the same period as a marine mortgage. A personal loan from your bank may prove the cheapest of all, and there is no reason why you should not raise a mortgage (or second mortgage) on a house if that is more economical. The costs of these various methods vary from time to time, and there are often government restrictions which make one or the other method more attractive. For example, H.M.G. may limit the repayment period for hire purchase to two years, but allow an indefinite period for a marine mortgage. That would open the possibility of smaller monthly payments for a marine mortgage, but over a longer period. The rate of interest might be lower but the total cost higher, because long repayments always cost more.

There are always firms advertising for your custom when it comes to finance, and the best advice one can give is (as usual) to shop around. Don't take the first one that comes along. And if you can manage without borrowing, then that will almost certainly be the cheapest way of all.

CENTAUR

Designer Laurent Giles & Partners
Builder Westerly Marine Construction Ltd.,
  Aysgarth Road, Waterlooville, PO7 7UF,
  Hampshire

Thames tonnage	6	
Displacement	3,000 kg.	6,150 lb.
Ballast	1,270 kg.	2,800 lb.
Length O.A.	7.92 m.	26 ft.
Length W.L.	6.5 m.	21 ft. 4 in.
Beam	2.57 m.	8 ft. 5 in.
Draught	0.91 m.	3 ft.
Sail area	27.4 sq. m.	294 sq. ft.
Sail area with genoa	31.9 sq. m.	341 sq. ft.

Looking at the above table of figures after I had typed them I was conscious of the difficulty of giving full and precise details in a book of this kind. For example, the sail area of this boat can be extended to over 400 sq. ft. by the use of a bigger genoa, and of course it can be much smaller with the heavy weather staysail of only 45 sq. ft.

But one tries to give a representative picture, and to think of a reasonable sort of wardrobe that might be carried by a cruising boat. And Centaur *is* intended for family cruising. With her twin keels she is big sister to the Pageant, just as the

single-keeled Tiger is big sister to Cirrus. She offers six berths, in fact, of which two are formed when the dinette table is lowered to make a double. Now since the dinette will not accommodate six people to a meal, and since six people are likely to be something of a crowd in a 26-ft. boat, I would suggest that this is an ideal boat for four. Two can sleep in the fore cabin and two in the quarter berths aft. Then the table can be left in place and people will have a reasonable amount of breathing space.

Like all Westerly boats, this one is nicely finished, and one gets a feeling of wellbeing as soon as one goes below. Resinglass lacks any appeal in itself, but with care the interior of a resinglass boat can be made attractive, even though some of us think that she will never have the same charm as a wooden boat. The interior of the Centaur is all lined out, the galley is properly equipped with stowages for plates and so forth, there are opening scuttles to ventilate the midships area around the loo, and all is neat and trim. The galley occupies the starboard side of the main cabin, opposite the dinette table.

Structurally, too, the boat maintains Westerly's high standards, with strong stanchions and winch mountings, a well-designed mast step, and so forth. In the boats I have seen the points I would criticize are the too-low fitting of the navigation lights, and the shortage of stowage space for six people. (And it is unfortunate that even when one has only four on board real stowage space does not become available in the way it would have done if the boat had been *designed* for four.)

One thing that makes life pleasant aboard any boat—especially in the English climate—is the ability to sit down below and see what is going on around. That can be done in Centaur (and in her sisters in the Westerly fleet).

A boat of this size needs an inboard engine as an auxiliary, and for my choice not less than 10 h.p. would be needed for an average family boat which must get everybody home in time on Sunday evening. The makers offer a selection of engines, petrol or diesel, and it is a matter of pocket and preference for each individual to decide. But all the firm's engine installations that I have seen have been well done, with flexible mountings and shaft couplings that reduce vibration to a low level.

What may not be immediately apparent from

CORRIBEE

Designer Robert Tucker
Builder Newbridge Boats Ltd.,
   New Zealand Works, Bridport, Dorset

Thames tonnage	$3\frac{1}{2}$	
Displacement	820 kg.	1,800 lb.
Ballast		
Length O.A.	6.4 m.	21 ft.
Length W.L.	4.88 m.	16 ft.
Beam	2.08 m.	6 ft. 10 in.
Draught	0.81 m.	2 ft. 8 in.
Sail area	16.26 sq. m.	175 sq. ft.
Sail area with genoa	19.04 sq. m.	205 sq. ft.

From the board of a designer who was one of the main contributors to the upsurge of small cruising boats in the years around 1960, this boat is a real contribution to the needs of the not-so-wealthy family. She is a pretty boat, with overhangs fore and aft, and a curved sheer. Under water she has a fin keel and a spade rudder. She *is* a small boat and she *looks* a small boat, yet her accommodation below decks is not so cramped as one expects.

There is in fact a standard plan with four berths, two of which run under the cockpit side seats and extend to within about 50 cm. of the forward berths. That leaves room on one side for a cooker, and on the other for a w.c. or a bucket concealed in a fitment whose top forms a small chart table. A difficulty, of course, in cruising with a boat of this size is to find enough stowage space for clothes, food, ropes, sails, fuel, water and all the rest. Yet that it can be done I am able to confirm from personal experience.

One reason why Corribee's cabin seems surprisingly large is that the cockpit is on the small side, and it is difficult to see how the four people for whom there are berths could for long enjoy that cockpit. In fine weather one can go on the fore-deck, of course, and a favourite place on many a boat is to stand in the main hatch.

Aft of the cockpit there is a sizeable after-deck which contrasts with many modern boats whose cockpit extends all the way back to the transom. And in the centre of this after-deck is a rectangular cut-out to accommodate the outboard. When the motor is not needed it can be lifted upward and slanted forward so that the propeller comes out of the water, and it can remain in that position ready for use yet without encroaching on the cockpit. This seems a very sensible and practical arrangement, which perhaps compensates in convenience for the loss of space in the cockpit.

The side decks are too narrow to be of much use, but it is only a couple of steps to get forward over the cabin top, and there is the mast to cling to on the way.

The sailing performance of this boat is really very good for her size, and she will reward a fastidious helmsman. Where just two people want to cruise they could rearrange the interior to the best advantage. Then they would have a boat which could really be cruised without the use of an engine at all because Corribee will sail in very light winds, especially if she herself is not overladen.

One could buy a new resinglass Corribee for under £1,000, and fit her out with home-made mattresses and other D.I.Y. gear. Some wooden clinker-built Corribees have also been built by other yards (some of them slightly smaller and with centreboard).

ELIZABETHAN 23

Designer Peter Webster
Builder Peter Webster Ltd.,
   Ropewalk Boatyard, Lymington, Hampshire

Thames tonnage	4	
Displacement	1,600 kg.	3,550 lb.
Ballast	760 kg.	1,680 lb.
Length O.A.	7.01 m.	23 ft.
Length W.L.	5.64 m.	18 ft. 6 in.
Beam	2.16 m.	7 ft. 1 in.
Draught plate up	0.76 m.	2 ft. 6 in.
Draught plate down	1.49 m.	4 ft. 11 in.
Sail area	17.79 sq. m.	191.5 sq. ft.
Sail area with genoa	23.13 sq. m.	249 sq. ft.

Peter Webster himself is an enthusiastic sailing man, and an enthusiastic racing man. So it is not surprising if the boats he designs and produces tend to accord with the demands of the racing rules.

This one, the smallest of the family, is a sporty little craft, with very attractive lines and limited accommodation. (Compare her beam and the shape of her ends with some of the more commodious family cruisers of similar length and you will see why her accommodation has to be more constricted.)

But though it is simple, her accommodation is nicely done with teak joinery and vynide-covered deckhead and other areas so that there is no naked resinglass. The whole cabin is open plan with two

quarter berths and two berths forward, leaving just sufficient space in the centre of the boat for a cooker fitment on one side and a sink with small working top on the other. The marine w.c. stands unashamedly open to view between the forward berths.

The Mk II version of the boat has a raised coachroof so as to give extra headroom for those who feel the need.

The hull is moulded to a good standard, and the fittings are strong. In the standard boat there is a low pulpit and stanchions and lifelines along the side-decks, but not enough security in the cockpit for my own taste. For English weather at least I would also have been glad to have the protection of weather cloths, or 'dodgers' around the cockpit.

The cockpit itself is rather small for a full complement of four. It is self-draining and the drains have a seacock. (Seacocks are fitted to all through-the-hull fittings, including the sink drain.) The rudder is inboard, well forward under the counter stern and hangs on the trailing edge of the keel where it is well protected against either damage or fouling.

For many people the special attraction of the boat will be that she has the advantage of a centre-plate without the great beam normally associated with shoal-draft boats. Liz 23's plate is operated through a cable and winch, the cable rising through a pipe just aft of the companion ladder. It retracts into the ballast keel, and remains always below the level of the cabin sole.

The boat can be fitted with the 5 h.p. Stuart inboard, and there is a well in the counter where an outboard of 6 to 9 h.p. can be shipped. In this position it is aft of the rudder, of course.

This is a lively boat which I feel is more suited to the young than to the middle-aged—but perhaps I am commenting more upon myself than upon the boat when I say that! Prices of everything are moving rapidly upward as I write, but for under £2,000 you would get a boat with w.c., water tank, bilge pump, sheet winches, anchor and (rope) cable, cooking stove, three sails and other bits and pieces.

FANTASIE

Designer Robert Tucker
Builder Aquaboats Ltd.,
   261 Lymington Road, Christchurch,
   Hampshire

Thames tonnage	2½	
Displacement	660 kg.	1,450 lb.
Ballast	200 kg.	450 lb.
Length O.A.	5.79 m.	19 ft.
Length W.L.	4.82 m.	15 ft. 10 in.
Beam	1.91 m.	6 ft. 3 in.
Draught	0.61 m.	2 ft.
Sail area	13.9 sq. m.	150 sq. ft.
Sail area with genoa	16.7 sq. m.	180 sq. ft.

There is a wide variety of the smallest sailing cruisers from which one may choose, and each owner will have his own idea of priorities. It may be accommodation that appeals, or it may be the advantage that a centre-board has over bilge keels, or it may be some indefinable quality that brings on love at first sight.

The first thing that one notices about Fantasie is that she is a fairly lean boat by modern standards, with slight beam. Therefore she is a boat which one would expect to go over to a noticeable angle of heel quite early, and generally to sail at a relatively steep angle. On the other hand she would not be so baffled by short seas as beamier boats of the same length.

This boat is among those which have a central ballast keel, plus a pair of bilge keels designed to give them sufficient underwater area within the limits of their small draught. A point which appeals to me is that there is a skeg ahead of the rudder, with a cut-out section to accommodate the propeller of an outboard motor. With this arrangement the propeller does have some protection against mooring ropes, polythene bags and logs of timber.

But in practice it would be easy to clear a fouled propeller on this boat because the outboard auxiliary is shipped in a well at the after end of the cockpit. In that position it is easily accessible, protected from being douched by following seas, and easy to ship and unship without risk of its being dropped overboard.

The cockpit is big enough for three, which is as many as there are berths for, and is self-draining. One feature that is found usually only on small boats is that halyards can be worked while you are standing securely in either the fore-hatch or the main hatch. That can also be a comfort when it comes to reefing.

Below decks Fantasie has two full-length quarter berths and a third running forward on the port side of the cabin. But this one is only 5 ft. 8 in. (173 cm.) long so it would be suited to many women and most children. At the head of the quarter berth on the starboard side is the galley, which is quite sizeable. The w.c. is under the fore-hatch and is concealed beneath a seat cushion.

Originally the Fantasie was designed for building in marine plywood, and that is why she has a hard chine hull, even though the hulls are now moulded in resinglass by Robert Ives of Christchurch. But hard chine boats, if well designed, can be remarkably good sailers, and the Fantasie is certainly a responsive little boat, and a speedy one for her size.

A complete boat which could be sailed away if you didn't mind going without anchor, compass or the many other little items that really are necessary would be about £700 at the time of writing. On the other hand, one could save a great deal by completing a hull, and that would mean an initial investment of less than £300.

FOUR 21

Designer **John Powell**
Builder **Aquaboats Ltd.,**
    261 Lymington Road, Christchurch,
    Hampshire

Thames tonnage	4	
Displacement	1,630 kg.	3,600 lb.
Ballast	510 kg.	1,130 lb.
Length O.A.	6.55 m.	21 ft. 6 in.
Length W.L.	5.94 m.	19 ft. 6 in.
Beam	2.2 m.	7 ft. 3 in.
Draught	0.83 m.	2 ft. 7 in.
Sail area	20.4 sq. m.	220 sq. ft.
Sail area with genoa	24.9 sq. m.	268 sq. ft.

Most small boats nowadays reflect their designers' determination to provide a separate w.c. compartment if that is at all possible. But there is much to be said for putting the marine w.c. in the fore-cabin as John Powell has done on this boat. In that position its use is restricted when everyone is in bed, but during the remainder of the twenty-four hours it benefits from being in a bigger compartment than it would have to itself alone, *and* it can be under the fore-hatch. When I had a boat built for myself with this layout some years ago (she was also about 22 ft. long) I made a small square canvas tilt which could be rigged over the open fore-hatch in harbour. That gave extra headroom and air in the fore-cabin and was well worthwhile.

Right forward in the Four 21 there is a chain locker, then come the two fore-cabin berths with the loo between, and then there is a pair of bulkheads under the mast, making full-length hanging lockers port and starboard.

The main cabin is devoted to the needs of the cook at forward end, the galley being split port and starboard. To port you have a twin-burner cooker, while to starboard there is a sink with stowage space beneath.

The siting of the galley units at this point means that the length available for berths in the main cabin is severely limited, and the result is that these become quarter berths with only about half their length in the cabin. Thus there is not room to sit the ship's complement of four people at the table which hitches on to the engine box.

The latter is just inside the companionway and takes up quite a large amount of the cabin space. Indeed, if I were buying one of these boats I would give very careful thought to the alternative of using an outboard auxiliary, thus saving both capital expenditure and valuable volume on board. The boat, which is available with either twin keels or a single keel, is a good performer under sail in either version so that one might not use an engine so very often.

Incidentally, if one wants to minimize the use of engine power then it is essential to have plenty of sail area for those days when frustratingly light winds bring a finish to one's patience and a start to the motor. If one chooses an outboard instead of an inboard the money saved may well be spent on buying an extra large genoa or 'drifter' for light winds.

A starting price for this boat is around £1,500. But you could start with the mouldings, part-completed from about £600 and have a lot of pleasure in completing her yourself.

GALION 22

Designer Ian Hannay
Builder Deacons Boatyard Ltd.,
　Bursledon, Southampton, Hampshire
　SO3 8 AZ

Thames tonnage	4	
Displacement	1,550 kg.	3,400 lb.
Ballast	700 kg.	1,500 lb.
Length O.A.	6.7 m.	22 ft.
Length W.L.	5.5 m.	18 ft.
Beam	2.21 m.	7 ft. 3 in.
Draught	1.0 m.	3 ft. 3 in.
Sail area	20.44 sq. m.	220 sq. ft.
Sail area with genoa	246.2 sq. m.	265 sq. ft.

When the Galion first appeared she was thought to be a strange looking boat. The designer had managed to get four berths, and 175 cm. (69 in.) of headroom in a boat of only 18 ft. waterline length. She seemed to be carrying too much top hamper in her high cabin top.

But when it came to the proof she was seen to be a sailing boat which could hold her own against opposition that *seemed* likely to perform better. It then became apparent that the designer had known what he was doing.

Considering the small size of the boat, the deck

arrangement is quite fair for movement, which in any case is minimized at sea by the designer's sensible scheme of leading the halyards back to the cockpit. The reefing line, which turns a drum at the forward end of the boom, also leads aft so that the mainsail can be reefed from the cockpit. But when it comes to changing headsails, of course, somebody has to go forward.

The boat can be had in two versions, one known as the Bay model, the other as the Coastal. They are the same as far as hull, deck and rig are concerned, but different in their internal finish and deck fittings.

The actual arrangement of the accommodation in the two boats is very similar, but the Galion Bay makes use of more wood and fewer mouldings for her furnishings, and that makes her more suitable for completion by the owner. Part-complete boats, with kits for home completion, are available, and that can save a good deal of money.

But even without home construction the Galion Bay is about £200 less than the Coastal.

Accommodation is naturally fairly tight when four berths are fitted into a boat of this size. There are two quarter berths, then a galley fitment to starboard and a chart table to port. In the Bay model there are then a pair of narrow hanging lockers port and starboard, making the division before you come to the fore-cabin with its two berths and w.c. between-and-under. Galion Coastal is designed without these two hanging lockers, but with one to port as an option. A home-completer, working on his own rather than from a kit, could please himself, of course, so long as he ensured that there was some sort of bulkhead or pillar to take the mast thrust.

Underwater the boat has a fin keel separated from the rudder by a large gap in which the propeller is situated when an engine is fitted. The 6 h.p. Vire petrol engine is an appropriate power plant. The rudder itself is a balanced spade type.

One notable characteristic of the Galion is the thought that has gone into details, such as the positioning of the pulpit, the provision of mooring cleats, ventilation below decks, hand-holds and so forth. In short she is a well thought-out boat of her type. At the time of writing a Galion Bay costs about £1,600, ready to sail but without anchor, cooker, w.c., pushpit and guard rails, engine and other items. As usual one can only make one's list of requirements and tot it all up.

GIPSY II

Designer R. Warington Smyth
Builder Penryn Boatbuilding and Engineering
   Co. Ltd.,
   Ponsharden, Penryn, Cornwall

Thames tonnage	6	
Displacement	1,750 kg.	3,900 lb.
Ballast	450 kg.	1,000 lb.
Length O.A.	7.32 m.	24 ft.
Length W.L.	5.79 m.	19 ft.
Beam	2.59 m.	8 ft. 6 in.
Draught	0.84 m.	2 ft. 9 in.
Sail area	22.67 sq. m.	244 sq. ft.
Sail area with genoa	26.75 sq. m.	288 sq. ft.

Boat designs can easily become stereotyped because there is not much that a designer can do within the modest dimensions of the sort of craft that this book treats. But the Gipsy shows a fresh approach, and I was sorry that she made her first appearance just too late to be included in the first edition of this book.

Originally designed to be built in marine plywood, and thus of hard chime form, the Gipsy is now being built in resinglass. Her general character is of a 'motor sailer' designed for real family pleasure boating. I take the term motor sailer from the builder's own literature, but you will see that her working sail area is not really much smaller than that of comparable 'sailing' cruisers. For my part I think that it would be well worthwhile to give her a bit more, but that is a personal view.

The boat has a sturdy look about her. Notice the straight-sided cabin and the similarly rectangular yet comfortable cockpit. These two features in turn lead to wide side-decks which make it easy to get about the boat safely. The deck area is quite a remarkable feature of this boat and surrounded as one is by pulpit, pushpit and double lifelines there is a great feeling of security. All these items are strongly fitted, by the way.

The cockpit has a large-sized drain and plenty of stowage, with a special compartment for the gas bottle. When one turns to go below the first thing that draws your attention is the very large double sliding hatch cover. This opens the whole of the main cabin to the sky, which is a really delightful experience on a fine day, and perhaps even better on a warm starry night.

There are quarter berths port and starboard, and then two more berths with their feet-ends running forward either side of a w.c. compartment. Between the heads of the sleepers to port is the galley fitment with a cooker on top and a slide-out sink beneath. The stove itself is also on slides so that it can be pushed under the side-deck and out of the way when it is not in use.

There is ample stowage in the main cabin, and in the forward part of the w.c. compartment there is a fine broad shelf for sails and suchlike gear. The interior of the boat is lined so that one does not get the impression of naked fibreglass, and a sufficient amount of timber is used at strategic points to achieve a pleasing result. I don't think anybody can go aboard a Gipsy II without feeling attracted. (Sketch-plan on page 137.)

She is not at all a bad sailing boat (and as I have said, I think she would be better with more sail area), and she is certainly a reliable sea-going craft that inspires confidence.

Underwater, Gipsy has twin keels and a skegless, transom-hung rudder. Her shallow draught, and her ability to take the ground, make her a versatile boat for family cruising, since one can go close into beaches or up into bird-haunted creeks in search of one's pleasures.

With one of the excellent 8 h.p. Sabb diesels, electric starting, electric lighting, marine w.c., anchor, chain, mattresses, pulpit and pushpit, cooker and many other items the price at the time of writing stands at about £2,600.

HALCYON 27

Designer Alan Buchanan
Builder Offshore Yachts Ltd.,
   Mill Road, Royston, Herts

Thames tonnage	6	
Displacement	3,000 kg.	6,600 lb.
Ballast	1,500 kg.	3,300 lb.
Length O.A.	8.23 m.	27 ft.
Length W.L.	6.17 m.	20 ft. 3 in.
Beam	2.34 m.	7 ft. 8 in.
Draught	1.22 m.	4 ft.
Sail area	26.7 sq. m.	287 sq. ft.
Sail area with genoa	31.8 sq. m.	343 sq. ft.

First a word about the name. There is also, from the same designer and the same builder, a smaller boat, the Halcyon 23. And that is a development of a boat formerly called Crystal, of which details may be found in the first edition of this book. In passing I feel it worth saying that the Halcyon 23 is still one of the nicest small family cruising boats being produced in resinglass to this day, and *one* reason is the amount of tasteful wood trim that is used for coamings, bulkheads and so forth.

The same comment applies equally well to the Halcyon 27 which is not merely a different boat but also a boat of different character. The 27 is really a cruiser-racer with fairly fine lines, so that her accommodation is not so much larger as one might expect from a jump from 23 to 27 ft. in boats of the same concept.

Her accommodation is in fact pretty straightforward. The engine obtrudes a little into the cabin space, with the result that the top step of the companionway is in fact the front end of the engine box. Nevertheless, there is enough room below the step to house the galley sink. To port there is the galley itself and to starboard a chart table; then two settee berths; forward again are the more or less conventional transverse bulkheads which take the downward thrust of the mast and for the w.c. compartment and the wardrobe on opposite sides of the boat. Forward of them are two berths in a fore cabin which has two fixed windows and a ventilator in the hatch.

Neatly made wooden lockers abound, and in the boats I have seen there has never been any shoddy workmanship. Since a matt finish, rather than a very glossy one, has been the aim those who admire the art of the French polisher may be disappointed, but a fit is a fit, whether glossy or not, and for myself I prefer the matt.

There is also a possible fifth berth—a quarter berth which must be a bit cramped for a full-sized adult, and the space would be better used to store gear unless the family consists of five and the only alternative is to leave one behind! Apart from the timber work, the interior of the boat is lined out, which improves the appearance and the feel and also avoids the condensation which naked resinglass so easily collects.

Spars, stanchions and deck fittings are substantial, as they are on the other boats built by the same firm. Within the limits of the beam of the boat the side-decks are quite wide—certainly wide enough for easy and safe movement, especially as the guard rails are sufficiently high to do their proper job. Add to that a good sailing performance and a roomy cockpit with a good-sized drain, and you have a very satisfactory cruising boat firmly in the English tradition. The price at the time of writing is somewhat under £3,000 including navigation and interior lights, pulpit and guard rails, anchor and chain, working sails, an inboard engine, etc.

HALMATIC EIGHT 80

Designer Camper & Nicholsons Ltd.
Builder Halmatic Ltd.,
  Brookside Road, Havant, Hampshire

Thames tonnage	8	
Displacement	3,550 kg.	7,850 lb.
Ballast	1,050 kg.	2,330 lb.
Length O.A.	8.53 m.	28 ft.
Length W.L.	7.0 m.	23 ft. 1 in.
Beam	2.74 m.	9 ft.
Draught	0.9 m.	3 ft.
Sail area	27.3 sq. m.	293 sq. ft.
Sail area with genoa	38.0 sq. m.	409 sq. ft.

Halmatic is not very well known as a boat-building company, yet it has great experience in moulding resinglass hulls which are completed by other builders and sold under other names.

One thing that can reasonably be assumed for this boat is that she is well built, and that leaves one free to turn one's thoughts to the philosophy underlying her design. According to the makers she is intended to be used as a sailing boat when the wind is favourable, but as a power craft when you have to make progress against headwinds. Because the makers did not anticipate that a typical Eight 80 owner would want to spend much time sailing to windward they gave the boat a rather small sail area for her weight, and especially a small mainsail.

Potential buyers must make up their own minds whether or not that argument seems reasonable to them. All I can say is that starting from the same premise (that I don't much like sailing to windward) I provided my own boat with the largest sail area I could reasonably afford. And I had a pretty large proportion of it in the main because a middle-aged crew (which I assume to be the target of Halmatic's enterprise) can easily start up the engine, sheet the main in flat and head to windward if need be. But handling a large genoa can be quite a difficult task for one middle-aged gentleman (or a ditto lady).

Some people may take a different view of the ease of dealing with mainsails or headsails, but it cannot be argued that for sailing with the wind free you need a larger area than for going to windward. In the one case the boat decreases the speed of the relative wind by sailing away from it: in the other it increases the speed by sailing towards the wind. It is for that reason (among others) that I believe a motor-sailer should have a larger sail area than a pure sailing boat.

Enough of that subject which will provide food for thought and discussion for a long time. The Eight 80 is a twin-keeled craft with a full-width cabin carried right forward to give headroom within and an unorthodox appearance without. The accommodation plan, with its U-shaped dinette, is shown on page 140. Berths are provided for five people, following the conventional plan of two forward, two in the dinette-double, and one in the quarter berth. The internal fittings are to a high standard, and with her full headroom and ducted ventilation she makes a very comfortable boat. The galley is in the main saloon.

The cockpit is spacious, self-draining and right aft. As a result the forward end of the engine extends into the main cabin, where it is fully encased and concealed alongside the companion steps. Typically, a 48 h.p. Perkins diesel would be fitted —more than ample power for a boat of this size.

Steering is by wheel on the main bulkhead at the forward end of the cockpit, where the steersman has additional shelter from a fixed windscreen.

The decks are surrounded by strong guard rails, and movement about them is easy enough, though the transition from cockpit to deck requires a firm grip and a long stride.

With full equipment a boat like this would cost you around £5,000.

L

HURLEY 18

Designer Ian Anderson
Builder Hurley Marine Ltd.,
   Valley Road, Plympton, South Devon

Thames tonnage	$2\frac{1}{2}$	
Displacement	1,100 kg.	2,350 lb.
Ballast	450 kg.	1,000 lb.
Length O.A.	5.63 m.	18 ft. 6 in.
Length W.L.	4.42 m.	14 ft. 6 in.
Beam	2.03 m.	6 ft. 8 in.
Draught, fin keel	0.99 m.	3 ft. 3 in.
Sail area	16.72 sq. m.	180 sq. ft.
Sail area with genoa	20.25 sq. m.	218 sq. ft.

All the Hurley boats designed by Ian Anderson are real sailing boats with real sailing hull forms. In consequence they all sail fast (for their size) and they all go to windward very well. It is also important that a cruising boat should have a comfortable motion at sea, since she is to be sailed for pleasure, and it is therefore noteworthy that Mr. Anderson has avoided the extremely small under-

water areas commonly found in offshore racing boats and commonly the cause of unpleasing movements at sea.

Although the two larger boats in this family are available with twin bilge keels, this smallest member can be had only with the single keel. It is of a form which moulds easily into the well-faired hull and it carries a worthwhile weight of ballast.

The self-draining cockpit has a trunking over the port quarter for an outboard auxiliary, and forward of that is the rudder head and tiller. The rudder is of the inboard, spade type, and balanced.

The small cabin top is well proportioned and shows what can be done in resinglass to get an elegant shape.

Below decks the accommodation is limited by the size of the boat, whose waterline length is no more than that of a large dinghy. She is laid out with three berths, two forward and one quarter berth. The space corresponding to the head end of the quarter berth on the opposite (port) side of the boat is devoted to the galley. A folding table can be brought into use above the port forward berth and forward of the galley. Considering the size of the boat a very useful selection of lockers (or cubby-holes) have been worked into the boat.

A marine w.c. or a bucket can be housed in the vee between the forward berths, where it is normally concealed by a removable section of the mattress cushions.

For sails, warps, fuel cans and the like there is a locker under the port cockpit seat (the side where there is no quarter berth) and a smaller locker in the starboard half of the counter (the side where the outboard trunk is not).

With a simple suit of sails a Hurley 18 is nudging £1,000 at the time of writing. To add berth cushions, anchor and chain, anti-fouling, gas cooker and cylinder, pulpit and guard rails, a ventilator, and bilge pump would put on a further £150. And then you might well want a w.c. and an outboard motor. . . .

HURLEY 20

Designer Ian Anderson
Builder Hurley Marine Ltd.,
   Valley Road, Plympton, South Devon

Thames tonnage	3	
Displacement	1,030 kg.	2,275 lb.
Ballast	450 kg.	1,000 lb.
Length O.A.	6.09 m.	20 ft.
Length W.L.	4.88 m.	16 ft.
Beam	2.16 m.	7 ft. 1 in.
Draught, twin keels	0.79 m.	2 ft. 7 in.
Draught, single keel	0.99 m.	3 ft. 3 in.
Sail area	17.18 sq. m.	185 sq. ft.
Sail area with genoa	22.3 sq. m.	240 sq. ft.

Like her bigger sister, the 22-footer, this member of the Hurley family is available with either a single keel or with twin keels. The twin keel version carries her ballast on those keels and there is no central keel—a form of design that should please the purists because in a boat of this size especially there would be hydrodynamic interference if three keels had to share such a small space. The ballast, incidentally, is moulded into the resin of the keels.

Like the other members of the family, this one is a good sailing boat, with a proper seagoing sailing hull form. Being a bit larger all round makes a great deal of difference to living aboard when you compare her with the 18. Below decks she offers berths for four, two forward beyond partial bulkheads, and two quarter berths. On the port side there is a cooker position at the forward end of the quarter berth, and a folding table which can be used by either the cook or the navigator, drops into position over the berth, and at the cook's left hand.

A w.c. can be fitted between the junction of the forward berths, where it benefits from being near, though not exactly under, the fore-hatch.

As much stowage space as possible has been worked in, but if one is going to have four berths in a 20 ft. boat with a well-shaped hull then there cannot be much room to spare. In the same way that the 18 would make a nice little cruising boat for two, the 20 would be nice for three—and even better for two of course.

All the Hurley 18s I have seen have their windows held in place by moulded rubber surrounds with special inserts. That is not a type of installation that I would choose for myself in a small boat where one is fairly near the sea because there have been cases where such windows have been pushed in by a heavy sea. The larger Hurley sisters, on the other hand, have metal-framed windows which are much to be preferred.

Like the 18, the 20 has a trunk for an outboard in the port half of the counter. But unlike the 18 her rudder is carried aft of a skeg, and has no balance area.

The basic price, as I write, is £1,150, but several hundred pounds' worth of equipment and fittings would be needed before you could enjoy a comfortable cruising holiday aboard.

HURLEY 22

Designer Ian Anderson
Builder Hurley Marine Ltd.,
  Valley Road, Plympton, South Devon

Thames tonnage	4	
Displacement	1,770 kg.	3,900 lb.
Ballast	1,040 kg.	2,300 lb.
Length O.A.	6.7 m.	22 ft.
Length W.L.	5.18 m.	17 ft.
Beam	2.22 m.	7 ft. 5 in.
Draught, twin keels	0.91 m.	3 ft. 0 in.
Draught, single keel	1.14 m.	3 ft. 9 in.
Sail area	22.29 sq. m.	240 sq. ft.
Sail area with genoa	23.97 sq. m.	258 sq. ft.

There's something about the Hurley 22 that makes one think of a beautiful model yacht—she looks like a thoroughbred in miniature both below and above the waterline. In fact with her very high ballast ratio, modest beam and deep keel she does follow the English tradition of yacht design to some extent. (Incidentally the figure quoted for displacement by the makers seems hardly likely to be her normal laden displacement, and as the designer has quoted a ballast ratio of 40 per cent the working displacement is more likely to be around 5,500 lb.)

Although this boat is available with twin keels, one feels that she really is by nature a single-keeled craft. Her underwater lines need not be marred by the propeller and shaft of an inboard motor because a special trunking for an outboard is built into the counter stern. What is more, when the motor is not in use the bottom of the trunk can be blanked off by a moulded plug which restores the underwater form of the boat perfectly.

The rudder is inboard, and is of the unbalanced type, set behind a skeg. In contrast with an inboard-engined boat, it is worth noting that with the Hurley 22 and similar craft the propeller of the outboard is astern of the rudder. Thus when manœuvring under power at low speed the rudder does not get the beneficial effect of the propeller slipstream, and may therefore seem somewhat 'soft'.

The cockpit is self-draining with large-sized drains, a point on which many otherwise satisfactory cockpits fall short. At the after ends of the cockpit side seats there are lockers, but the greater part of the volume under each seat is taken up by a quarter berth.

These berths run forward into the cabin as far as a partial bulkhead which marks the beginning of the two-berth fore-cabin. The w.c. is in this fore-cabin, between the berths and not too far from the fore-hatch, though it would have been better if the one could have been directly above the other.

There are plenty of lockers and stowages. The sink is under the bridge deck—which is the raised forward end of the cockpit that stops water from running down into the cabin. The sink is tucked under it, so that you step clear as you move down into the cabin. The cooker, on the other hand, is under the forward end of the port main berth, a section of which is removable for access. (Earlier models had a different arrangement.)

The windows are set in metal frames, and the hatch covers have a simulated wood appearance which is achieved by bonding an imitation teak veneer beneath a surface of glass tissue and resin. This gives the appearance of wood (almost) without the need for maintenance, and whether or not you like it is a matter of personal taste.

Like other Hurley boats, this one has a rather bare inventory for her basic price of £1,650. But it does include a w.c., sheet winches, a bilge pump, stemhead roller and cabin table. Nevertheless, if I were planning to pick up one of these boats and sail her along the coast a matter of 50 or 100 miles to get her to my home port, I would expect to spend at least another £200 on her before setting off.

JOUSTER

Designer Laurent Giles & Partners Ltd.
Builder Westerly Marine Construction Ltd.,
Aysgarth Road, Waterlooville, PO7 7UF,
Hampshire

Thames tonnage	4	
Displacement	1,000 kg.	2,200 lb.
Length O.A.	6.4 m.	21 ft.
Length W.L.	5.6 m.	18 ft. 3 in.
Beam	2.29 m.	7 ft. 6 in.
Draught	1.07 m.	3 ft. 6 in.
Ballast	430 kg.	950 lb.
Sail area	19.5 sq. m.	210 sq. ft.
Sail area with genoa	24.8 sq. m.	266 sq. ft.

This is a boat which I immediately felt to be suitable for younger people, or at least for people who are still young in spirit. She is small and handy, with a sufficient sail area to keep her going in light winds, the same area as the heavier Cirrus, in fact. She sails more like a dinghy than a cruising boat, and her accommodation corresponds. . . .

Jouster has a single keel, a clean-running hull and a modest displacement with a sail area sufficient to keep her going in light winds. On the other hand, if you hold on to that sail area (especially in the main, of course) as the wind strength rises you will find the weather helm increasing until the boat finally takes charge and luffs up into wind. And a good thing too, because I feel sure that she must follow the general rule with all boats that a timely reef increases the speed made good to windward. (Never fall for the longshoreman's suggestion that the really 'press-on' skipper sails with his 'lee rail under'. That is a concept which springs from ignorance.)

A Jouster owner is likely to want at least three headsails, and probably four, and he will need to be ready to reef the main without delay, so it is a real asset that it is so easy to move around on this boat. (Though on the boat I sailed too little of the deck area was treated with non-slip paint for my liking—I would wish to cover any area where a person *might* be expected to put a foot.)

The fact that the genoa is cut low in this boat gives me the opportunity to mention the advantages and disadvantages of such an arrangement. On the credit side it is aerodynamically efficient to have the smallest possible gap between hull and staysail, especially when going to windward. But on the other side it can be a nuisance and even a danger to cut off one's view forward. My own choice is for safety, which is the ultimate expression of efficiency, over the limited aspect of aerodynamic efficiency.

Below decks Jouster has a plain but just about adequate arrangement for four berths. The headroom is only 144 cm. in the main cabin (4 ft. 9 in.), and there is a dinette scheme on one side which allows only two people to sit at table in the daytime or makes one berth at night. Then there are two berths forward and one quarter berth. There is a galley flat opposite the dinette, and the w.c. is in the fore-cabin between the berths. In sum, not at all good for four people, reasonable for three and fair enough for two. When one sees a boat like this one wishes that the makers would offer an alternative plan for people who positively need only two berths—then they could have something really comfortable.

The construction is to Westerly's usual good standard, and so is the finish. The price is around £1,200 with a rather basic inventory which leaves the owner to add berth cushions, cooker, w.c., outboard motor and so forth.

The boat pictured opposite was photographed while hove-to off the Sussex coast.

KINGFISHER 26

Designer R. A. G. Nierop
Builder Westfield Engineering Ltd.,
  Creekmoor, Cabot Lane, Poole, Dorset

Thames tonnage	5	
Displacement	2,200 kg.	4,800 lb.
Ballast	900 kg.	2,000 lb.
Length O.A.	7.92 m.	26 ft.
Length W.L.	6.4 m.	21 ft.
Beam	2.34 m.	7 ft. 8 in.
Draught	0.96 m.	3 ft. 3 in.
Sail area	25 sq. m.	270 sq. ft.
Sail area with genoa	32.7 sq. m.	352 sq. ft.

In the first edition of this book, some eight years ago, I drew attention to the Kingfisher 20. At that time the world was changing, and the idea of building boats from polyester resin with glass-fibre reinforcement was still rather new. In fact about four-fifths of the boats reviewed in that edition were built in timber, and only one-fifth in resinglass. What a difference now!

And at that time I felt it necessary to advise people not to be put off by the unusual appearance of the Kingfisher 20. Since then she has become popular and recognized as a very well thought-out and strongly built little boat. And now she has two sisters, the 26-footer shown here and also a 30-footer with a centre cockpit.

All the Kingfishers were designed primarily as twin-keeled boats, but since the 20-footer first appeared the designer has arranged for an alternative single-keeled version to be available for those who prefer it.

The 26 is a bilge-keeler which is a real pleasure to sail. Her handling, her windward ability, and her general feel avoid the faults of some of the beamier and more commodious cruising boats which (regrettably) do not always carry extra sail area in proportion to their bulk.

The Kingfisher has a nicely proportioned hull, hydrodynamically shaped keels, a ballast ratio of about 41 per cent, and a modest beam. There is no central keel, but there is a fixed fin or skeg ahead of the rudder and protecting the propeller. It is a strongly held opinion of mine that this is a very valuable feature in a cruising boat since there are so many fishing floats, nets, balks of timber, polythene bags and other things around our coasts nowadays which can positively cripple a yacht if they foul either her propeller or her rudder.

The deck layout is straightforward, making it easy to get about and do one's work. In spite of the distinctly high look of the cabin top, the helmsman's view forward is good enough. The designer, who is also the builder, is an engineer, and all the deck fittings reflect the engineering approach in their robustness—strength is a notable characteristic of all the Kingfisher family.

Rather a nice deck detail on these boats is the provision of a draining well in the fore-deck which houses anchor, cable, fenders and suchlike. This has a lid to close it, leaving a perfectly smooth and clear deck when the ground tackle is stowed away. It is an idea which is beginning to be copied in other boats.

The interior accommodation is very attractive —at least it was to me—in spite of the fact that there is no timber to be seen and everything is 'plastic' or metal. In fact, I think it fair to say that in going all out for resinglass and metal, the designer has achieved a pleasing and effective way of using the materials.

Of course, one is not looking at the rough interior of a resinglass hull when one goes below in this boat. What you see is the smooth side of a separate inner moulding which may, for example, embody a complete galley, berth, bulkhead, and hull ceiling in a single piece. The galley is to port as you enter, and on the opposite side is a large chart table with stowage under. This is all moulded in resinglass, and with a very good finish. The chart table, incidentally, tends to get used as an additional working surface by the cook when in harbour.

Forward of this section there are berths port and starboard, with their after (feet) ends running under the galley and chart table respectively. This still leaves plenty of room for four people to sit and chat—or eat.

Moving forward the next item is one of a pair of bulkheads which run athwart the ship under the mast step and serve the usual purpose of making a w.c. compartment on one side of the boat and a hanging locker on the other. And in the fore-cabin there are two berths. The whole effect is light, clean, and not so cold as one might imagine.

The boat is full of good detail design that makes for a carefree life. Fuel is stored right down in the keels; there are useful shelves and stowages for small items; the hull is ringed by a moulded pvc rubbing band; the tiller comes in a position which allows the helmsman to sit at the forward end of the cockpit with his crew behind him and not blocking his view; tubular steel pillars give a good handhold when you go below; and so forth.

For many people the appearance is against her, but if you want a strong, easily maintained twin-keeler for four people it makes sense to have a look at this boat before finally deciding.

The price stands at around £3,000 with sails, anchor, mattresses, cooker, w.c. and other gear, but without engine. Although you can use an outboard, a boat like this really needs an inboard, and that means another £300 or £400. One thing that you cannot do with this boat is to buy a part-completed hull and finish her yourself. That's because all the interior furnishings are moulded and must be assembled in the factory.

KELPIE

Designer C. S. J. Roy
Builder West Kirby Marine Services Ltd.,
  40 York Avenue, West Kirby, Cheshire

Thames tonnage	$1\frac{1}{2}$	
Displacement	550 kg.	1,000 lb.
Ballast	200 kg.	450 lb.
Length O.A.	4.57 m.	15 ft.
Length W.L.	3.66 m.	12 ft.
Beam	1.68 m.	5 ft. 6 in.
Draught	0.61 m.	2 ft.
Sail area	10.6 sq. m.	115 sq. ft.

There are two Kelpies. One is an open, or half-decked dayboat, the other is properly named Kelpie Weekender, and she has a small fore-cabin in which there are two berths whose feet ends extend aft under the cockpit seats.

The thing to recognize about the Kelpie is that she is a ballasted keel boat. Nowadays there are many day-sailing dinghies which depend on the liveliness of their occupants to avoid a capsize. They use what might be called live ballast. But there are many people who do not want to indulge in that kind of sailing—and that does not mean only the middle-aged and above.

People who want to go for pleasure-boating, who like to take their cameras and spare clothes; people who have small children for whom they have too much respect to wish to frighten them; people who don't find any pleasure in getting wet on a cool and windy day: for such people the best type of boat is something akin to a cruising boat proper, and the Kelpie comes in that bracket.

She is moulded in resinglass, and the clever thing about her is the arrangement of her ballast. This is in iron pigs which weigh only 28 lb. each (13 kg.) and can therefore be quite easily removed from the depths of her hollow keel. That means that the boat can be stripped down to a weight of only about 350 lb. (160 kg.) for loading on to a trailer.

Whether one has the open or the cabin version the Kelpie is a very attractive boat to sail. You sit in a well-protected cockpit and sail her like a *boat*. But, like capsizable dinghies, she does have built-in buoyancy which will support twice the weight of the boat and her crew. So you have perhaps the best of all worlds—unless you want to be able to plane.

The Weekender's cabin has a fore-hatch, and standing in it I found that it made a very secure position from which to set both jib and mainsail, to reef the main or to pick up a mooring. Certainly one is more secure standing in that hatch than on the deck of some bigger, though still small, cruising boats.

If one wanted to use this version for more than a week-end it would be a good idea to have a simple tilt-type tent over the cockpit to provide a bit more sheltered space. I can picture a very pleasant cruising holiday in the waters of the Solent and Poole, for example, in this mini cruiser. If an auxiliary were felt to be really necessary, and I am not sure that it would, then an outboard can easily be fitted.

The price for the open boat, with main and jib, stands at about £430. The Weekender version would be around £450.

LEISURE 17

Designer Arthur Howard
Builder Cobramold Ltd.,
    Bassingbourne Hall, Stansted Airfield,
    Essex

Thames tonnage	2½	
Displacement	540 kg.	1,200 lb.
Ballast	250 kg.	550 lb.
Length O.A.	5.18 m.	17 ft.
Length W.L.	4.27 m.	14 ft.
Beam	2.13 m.	7 ft.
Draught	0.66 m.	2 ft. 2 in.
Sail area	12.1 sq. m.	130 sq. ft.
Sail area with genoa	14.3 sq. m.	165 sq. ft.

This is a good example of cruising-boat design on the smallest scale. She has twin ballasted bilge keels of sufficient weight in proportion to the displacement to ensure against capsize or knock-down. Although it is true that the total weight of a boat so small as this can be very much increased by the relatively high weight of her crew and stores, one has to take into account that the crew weight will be used to good advantage as dynamic ballast. In other words, people will tend to sit to windward, as in a dinghy.

It is perhaps worth noting that the righting effect of two people sitting about 3 ft. to weather of the centre of buoyancy in this boat is about three times as great as that produced by the ballast keels when the boat is heeled to 30 deg. At very steep angles of heel the ballast keels have an increasing effect and that, of course, is what distinguishes this type of boat from an unballasted dinghy.

Below decks it is possible to sleep four, though with very little space to spare. In effect each side of the boat is one double-length berth on which one person can sleep with his feet towards the bows, the other with his feet to the stern. Their heads may then be almost touching if they are full-sized adults.

There is just sitting headroom, and in the vee between the forward ends of the berths there is space for a w.c. bucket. Good temper, good discipline and good weather are needed if four people are to spend more than a week-end aboard. With small children it may be easier, and I know from experience that it can be done—at least in a boat only a foot longer and a foot beamier than this one.

Within the limits of her size this boat offers some good design points. There is a stowage for anchor cable right forward which is isolated from the rest of the interior by a bulkhead and has drains so that water brought in with the cable goes back out again. But there are in fact ventilation holes high up in the bulkhead between this locker and the cabin, and these provide a means of ventilation. The main hatch slides forward but also hinges up, the cockpit is self-draining, the rudder is protected behind a fixed fin or skeg, and proper provision has been made for mounting an outboard motor as an auxiliary.

A small boat like this is bound to be lively, and it is therefore important to have good guard rails around the cockpit, especially when sailing with children. At a price of about £650 for the boat with rig but without much else this is one of the cheapest ways of buying a *new* boat for cruising. For the same money one could get a roomier, better-equipped secondhand boat, but she would demand more time to be spent on maintenance.

MIRROR OFFSHORE DIESEL

Designer E. G. Van de Stadt
Builder Dell Quay Productions Ltd.,
    Itchenor, Sussex

Thames tonnage	7	
Displacement		
Ballast	170 kg.	380 lb.
Length O.A.	5.79 m.	18 ft.
Length W.L.	4.8 m.	15 ft. 9 in.
Beam	2.05 m.	6 ft. 9 in.
Draught	0.57 m.	1 ft. 10 in.
Sail area	10.96 sq. m.	118 sq. ft.

Most of the boats in this book are sailing cruisers with 'auxiliary' engines, though if one were to examine the facts closely one would find that many of them have more engine power available than sail power.

A statement like that one demands some qualification because although a 10 h.p. engine is always a 10 h.p. engine (one hopes!) the power available from a suit of sails varies very much with the wind speed. But in pleasant weather where winds are between force 2 and 4 there are nowadays many sailing cruisers which can draw more power from their engines than from their sails.

On the other hand, it would be reasonable to call the Mirror Offshore Diesel a motor cruiser with auxiliary sails. And that is a very sensible type of boat to have because it is always risky to go to sea trusting in the power of a single engine.

Obviously a boat like this is aimed at the couple who are not dedicated to sail, but who appreciate its uses when the wind is fair or when the engine is out of action. And it has been designed with such people in mind providing a roller-furling staysail. This has a tubular aluminium alloy spar to its luff, and it can easily be furled or unfurled from the cockpit. Unlike the Wykeham Martin gear, for which your jib has only a luff wire, the use of a spar allows the system to be used for *reefing* a sail.

Below decks the arrangement is simple, with two berths, a simple galley to port inside the companionway, and an enclosed lavatory to starboard. There is a fore-hatch which helps with ventilation and gives access to the fore-deck if you don't feel like clambering over the top.

The cockpit is big enough to sleep two more people, and appropriate mattresses form back rests to the cabin seats in the day-time. For sailing (or motoring) the cockpit is big enough for four, but it is rather exposed and does need a pushpit and guard rails in my opinion.

The standard engine installation is a Volvo Penta single cylinder diesel of 7 h.p., and the last time I was aboard one of these boats I felt that some more attention could well be given to its silencing and vibration-damping—after all, this is a boat in which the engine is to be used a good deal.

The boat can be trailed behind a car, which has obvious advantages in offering new cruising grounds, and she may be fitted (as an extra) with twin keels as well as the single central keel so that she will take the ground upright. A starting price for a usable boat would be about £1,300.

One last word about the name—on the whole I think that these boats are in fact mainly used in *inshore* waters, rather than *offshore*.

MACWESTER 30

Designer C. S. J. Roy
Builder Macwester Marine Co. Ltd.,
   River Road, Littlehampton, Sussex

Thames tonnage	9	
Displacement	4,100 kg.	9,000 lb.
Ballast	1,220 kg.	2,700 lb.
Length O.A.	9.3 m.	30 ft. 6 in.
Length W.L.	7.2 m.	23 ft. 6 in.
Beam	2.74 m.	9 ft.
Draught	1.0 m.	3 ft. 3 in.
Sail area	36.2 sq. m.	390 sq. ft.

At the time of writing this is the largest of the Macwester family and she is likely to appeal to someone who wants the comfort—in terms of sea-keeping as well as of accommodation—that can be had in a 30 ft. boat, but who wants to achieve it as economically as possible. A tally of the advertised prices of boats of similar size will show that the Macwester 30 is good value.

The boat is very similar in general form to the 26 and 28 (and probably to the 27 which is projected but not in production as I write). In fact she has the same beam as her smaller sisters, but with her greater length is therefore more slender. This shows itself to advantage in her superior speed and her greater ease in dealing with head-seas.

Two versions are available—the conventional sloop with aft cockpit, and the yawl which has a centre cockpit. (The sail area quoted above is the working rig of the yawl—the sloop would have about 10 sq. ft. less.) The advantages of a central cockpit are several. In the first place the crew is better protected from spray and from menacing following seas. Secondly there is the fact that the sole in a central cockpit is higher, so that one gets a better view, and that is very valuable when docking or picking up a mooring. The extra height of the sole, plus the forward position, makes it possible to install a big engine below, with plenty of space around. For example, a 4-cylinder diesel such as the B.M.C. Captain is the standard power unit for the yawl, but a twin-cylinder such as the Volvo Penta MD 2 is the biggest that can be fitted to the sloop. That extra power can make a notable difference in a hurried passage.

Finally, the after cabin gives a privacy that is rare in small boats. It is especially useful for children who have to be tucked up early or for guests who are not fully accustomed to the rough and tumble of boat life.

It is, of course, rather difficult to arrange direct tiller steering with an after cabin, so boats of this layout are normally fitted with a wheel. In the case of the Macwester the wheel is on a pedestal towards the after end of the cockpit. At this position the helmsman has the mainsheet close at hand, as well as the engine gear lever and throttle. There is plenty of room in the cockpit for the remainder of the crew, which could amount to five people if all the six berths have been allocated. Two of these berths are in the after-cabin, two in the fore-cabin, and two in a double that is formed by the dinette table—when it has been lowered, of course. . . .

The galley is usually located opposite the dinette in the main cabin, and forward of that is the usual athwartships compartment with w.c. and wardrobe. In fact the arrangement of the boat is very similar to that of many others, but with the addition of an extra cabin aft of the cockpit. There is headroom of 6 ft. 6 in. (198 cm.), and the accommodation is simple, sensible, but not fanciful.

At the time of writing the price is below £5,000 for a well-equipped boat including galley, w.c., all cushions, full interior and exterior lighting, sails, pulpit and guard rails, anchor, and virtually all the gear necessary for a sea passage except a compass and bed 'linen'. The price includes a B.M.C. Captain with its 40 gallon (180 litre) fuel tank. In short a good moneysworth.

MACWESTER 26 (and 28)

Designer C. S. J. Roy
Builder Macwester Marine Co. Ltd.,
   River Road, Littlehampton Sussex

Thames tonnage	6 (7)	
Displacement	3,040 kg.	6,700 lb.
	(3,550 kg.)	(7,850 lb.)
Ballast	1,030 kg.	2,265 lb.
Length O.A.	7.92 m.	26 ft.
	(8.61 m.)	(28 ft. 3 in.)
Length W.L.	6.4 m.	21 ft.
	(6.94 m.)	(22 ft. 9 in.)
Beam	2.74 m.	9 ft.
Draught	0.84 m.	2 ft. 9 in.
Sail area	27.96 sq. m.	301 sq. ft.
	(30.66 sq. m.)	(330 sq. ft.)

This boat exists in two very similar versions, the larger having that extra 2 ft. which gives her more spacious accommodation both in the cockpit and below decks, plus the advantage of a greater waterline length. But to a considerable extent one can talk of them as if they were one.

At the time of writing the new Macwester 27 is expected soon to come on the market. Whereas the owner of a 26 or 28 could not look for any great turn of speed, I found the first 27 much better, for the hull-and-bilge-keel form has been improved by tank-testing at Southampton University.

Be that as it may, hundreds of owners have found what they wanted in a Macwester, and it can be stated they have had a good moneysworth. The original Macwester philosophy was to sell the customer a basically simple but well-constructed boat so that he could devote his money to getting the biggest amount of boat. Sprucing up could come when his bank balance had recovered from the original purchase.

That always seems to me, as a buyer, to be a sound philosophy: so many people find after a year or two that they really need a larger boat than they thought. In the event, Macwester's original idea seems to have undergone a slight change, perhaps because a too-bare interior suffers in competition with lush-looking interiors. But a Macwester is still remarkably good value for money and a good sea boat.

In either boat I have always felt very much at home. There is something about the proportions of the cockpit, the view forward, the proportions of the side decks and the height of the coamings you have to step over to reach them that seems right to me. As a result, a Macwester is an easier boat to sail and handle. In addition to the clear decks which are non-slip over almost their entire area, a long (and strong) handrail down each side of the cabin top makes going forward easier and safer. The stanchions and guard rails are of a sensible height, the deck fittings are strong and properly attached, and it is easy to work whether on the fore-deck or around the foot of the mast. Both versions have an after deck of useful size.

The underwater form is rather burly, with twin keels sharing the ballast between them, and a rudder which is protected by a skeg. The skeg is of large area and almost certainly helps directional stability at sea, as well as bringing some underwater lateral well aft to minimize weather helm. (Nevertheless those Macwester owners who have fitted a bowsprit and jib have been glad of the reduced weather helm as well as of the extra sail area for light winds.)

Below decks the accommodation centres on the usual two bulkheads which support the decks in the region of the mast step, and also serve to make the toilet compartment. In the fore-cabin, which is made lighter by the translucent hatch, as well as its fixed windows, there are two berths, each with a shelf alongside for small personal gear. The w.c. compartment is spacious enough and is faced by a hanging locker.

Aft of this hanging locker is the galley area with cooker and sink which can be tidied out of sight by dropping wooden flaps to make a flat covering surface. There are good stowages, and a wooden post from cabin sole to deckhead at the after corner of the galley area where it is useful to hang on to. There are also handrails along the under side of the deckhead—most valuable items when moving around while under sail.

On the same side as the galley, and immediately aft of it is a quarter berth with at least half its length in the cabin—plenty of room for two to sit. On the opposite side of the boat is the dinette table which can sit four people, though elbow room is pretty tight. There is a good view out.

Although not lavishly fitted out, the boats have pleasant and practical interiors, and of course judgement must take into account the very reasonable prices for these boats. With a 10 h.p. Stuart Turner engine the price of a 26 at the time of writing is just under £3,000. And that figure

includes w.c., bunk mattresses, anchor, built-in water tanks, electric lighting, cooker, anchor, bucket and boathook, and other items. It is a very complete inventory and includes anti-fouling the bottom, launching, bending on sails and getting the boat in every way ready for the owner to take away.

The 28-footer, which is generally similar but with more space inside because the cockpit bulkhead moves aft, would cost about £3,400 to the same specification. This boat is also available with a fin keel instead of twins.

NANTUCKET

Designer Alan Buchanan
Builder Offshore Yachts Ltd.,
  Mill Road, Royston, Herts

Thames tonnage	7½	
Displacement	3,750 kg.	8,300 lb.
Ballast	1,525 kg.	3,350 lb.
Length O.A.	9.65 m.	31 ft. 8 in.
Length W.L.	6.4 m.	21 ft.
Beam	2.78 m.	9 ft. 1.5 in.
Draught	1.3 m.	4 ft. 3 in.
Sail area	33.6 sq. m.	362 sq. ft.
Sail area with genoa	45.2 sq. m.	486 sq. ft.

Here is a very attractive boat whose design provides the text for a sermon on one shortcoming of many modern small cruisers, and how it may be cured.

Below decks Nantucket has an accommodation plan that can be found over and over again in small cruisers of this sort of waterline length—two berths forward, transverse bulkheads making w.c. and hanging locker, main cabin with dinette/double berth plus galley, and one quarter berth. That is the content of the package, but the shell in which it is wrapped is extended by a clipper bow and a short bowsprit.

Thus the base on which sails can be set is extended, and that makes it possible to fly a good area of canvas without an excessively tall rig. By contrast, the type of boat which crams the maximum possible accommodation (which means weight) into the shortest possible hull (for economy) cannot set enough sail area to make her go on those days when the sun is warm, the wind is light, and sailing is as heaven intended.

Quite apart from all that, the clipper bow and bowsprit result in a line which has a considerable appeal for some owners, and in this case those traditional features are married quite nicely into a modern underwater hull and a modern cabin top. And whether or not the short bowsprit has any emotional appeal, the fact that it is of the broad, 'plank' type makes the fore-deck effectively much more spacious. Furthermore it is a favourite place from which to enjoy the sun and a little spray (when the water is not too cold).

The boat is offered in two versions, as a sloop and as a yawl, with the same total sail areas. Either, in my opinion, would look better and be more satisfying to handle if she were cutter rigged with a roller furling jib and a staysail. That makes the sails smaller and easier to handle, and when the biggest staysail has to go up or come down the boat can be kept sailing under good control with the mainsail and the jib.

In common with many other modern standard boats built in Britain, Nantucket is well made, well finished and well fitted. I think that anyone who steps aboard will find that she creates feelings of pleasure and confidence in equal measure. The self-draining cockpit is secure and comfortable, with a good view and easy access to the sheets. Sufficient use of iroko for coamings, seats and handrails, gives an air of workmanlike elegance, and the clincher is the well-proportioned side decks and the general ease of movement around the boat.

Below decks the main fault was a rather narrow dinette seat, where elbows in too-close proximity might send a fork into an eye. Another weakness in the early boats was the narrowness of the companionway steps on which feet could hardly be expected to find a firm purchase even in a flat calm.

But for the rest the boat is well and tastefully fitted, with no nasty bare resinglass to be seen anywhere. As with so many boats, my taste would be for a couple of opening windows in the main cabin (think of the cooker in there) and a scuttle, or porthole if you prefer, in the w.c. compartment.

In a boat like this, with berths for five people, the main 'living-room' and the 'kitchen' are combined in a space smaller than the average bathroom. The main ventilation in muggy weather is through the fore and main hatches, neither of which can be open more than a crack if it is actually raining. So although the designer has provided the boat with quite sizeable ventilators, it does not seem unreasonable to me to ask for more.

At the time of writing Nantucket is a newcomer, and she carries a remarkably low price-tag for a boat of this size and this standard of equipment. With an 8 h.p. Sabb diesel engine, basic sails, winches, stainless steel rigging, electrics and so forth, the price is below £4,000. Long may it remain there—or at least in that vicinity!

PINTAIL

Designer H. T. Rossiter
Builder Purbrook Rossiter Ltd.
  Bridge Street, Christchurch, Hampshire

Thames tonnage	$7\frac{1}{2}$	
Displacement	5,200 kg.	11,500 lb.
Ballast	1,700 kg.	3,750 lb.
Length O.A.	8.38 m.	27 ft. 6 in.
Length W.L.	7.01 m.	23 ft.
Beam	2.67 m.	8 ft. 9 in.
Draught	1.07 m.	3 ft. 6 in.
Sail area	33.73 sq. m.	363 sq. ft.
Sail area with genoa	38.46 sq. m.	414 sq. ft.

Some readers may remember other Purbrook boats, the Heron in particular perhaps, and they will recognize a family likeness in Pintail. She is in any case in the English tradition though with a goodly beam to balance her modest draught. Although you would not guess it from her topsides and her general appearance, she has twin bilge keels in addition to her central ballast keel, and these allow her to take the ground upright.

To my eye she is one of the most pleasing cruisers of her size, and I still wonder that the full-width cabin with 'shoulder'-type doghouse and almost flat full-width deck is not used more often by other designers. It gives a very fine deck space, avoids the problem of having to decide how wide to make the side decks, and also pays off in extra usable volume below.

Pintail's accommodation is fairly conventional, as may be seen from the drawing on page 139. From forward there is a chain locker, then the fore-cabin with two berths and a hatch above. Then comes the usual athwartships compartment between bulkheads which support the thrust of the mast. In the wash compartment there is a Baby Blake and a hand basin that slides out from beneath a shelf and drains into the w.c. Doors isolate this compartment from both the cabins.

The main cabin has standing headroom, since it is all under the doghouse, which might be called the coachroof—I can't make up my mind which is the better word for it. The main cabin is just long enough to take a berth, with a bit to spare for lockers. But the galley is inside the companionway on the port hand, and there is not quite enough length to spare for that. So the berth on that side is extended forward through the bulkhead to provide space for the occupant's feet.

Extra berths may be fitted, though this is really the right size for cruising with four people. An extra small berth, for a child, can be worked in forward, while in the main cabin a full-length roll-up canvas root berth can be fitted above the starboard settee. This stows away very neatly behind the panelling when not in use.

The galley itself is simple, with a two-burner swung stove and moderate but well-planned stowage spaces.

Everything in the boats is really beautifully made and finished, and it is a real delight to go aboard. As the designer is an enthusiastic cruising man himself the details are appropriate to sea going. Handholds below decks, which are so important at sea but which are often forgotten by landlubberish boat manufacturers, are an example of the seamanlike approach which is combined with high craftsmanship throughout the Pintails.

The cockpit is particularly well designed, so as to give both comfort and protection. The coamings, for example, are angled outward at a sympathetic angle to your back. And the seating arrangement is both sensible and unusual in that space is provided where the sheet hands can stand close to the coamings and work the winches.

The cockpit has been made deep, for shelter and ease of working, and as a result it cannot be fully draining. But by a very sensible compromise it drains overboard until about 6 in. of water are left. This amount does not weigh very much, and can be removed by the pump.

This is a particularly pleasant boat to sail, and handling in harbour, or sail-changing at sea, is much helped by the clear deck layout. Typically, a 16 h.p. Albin diesel engine is fitted, and the remainder of the standard inventory is pretty extensive. Pulpit, pushpit, lifelines, two bilge pumps, fresh-water tanks with pumps to galley and wash-hand basin and so forth.

Originally all Pintails were built entirely in wood, but now their hulls and decks are being made in glass-reinforced resin, with extensive use of timber for the cockpit seats, coamings and so forth. The result is still a really lovely and desirable boat. And that is the reason why I have permitted myself to include her in these pages, because her price should really have ruled her out. Still, I suppose I can break my own rules, and if you have something over £6,500 and want to undertake some sensible family cruising, do look at a Pintail.

PAGEANT

Designer Laurent Giles & Partners Ltd.
Builder Westerly Marine Construction Ltd.,
  Aysgarth Road, Waterlooville, PO7 7UF,
  Hampshire

Thames tonnage	4½	
Displacement	1,950 kg.	4,300 lb.
Length O.A.	7.0 m.	23 ft. 1 in.
Length W.L.	5.8 m.	19 ft.
Beam	2.4 m.	8 ft.
Draught	0.85 m.	2 ft. 10 in.
Ballast	950 kg.	2,100 lb.
Sail area	21.95 sq. m.	236 sq. ft.
Sail area with genoa	25.1 sq. m.	270 sq. ft.

It was a wintry day when I sailed a Pageant for the first time, with fresh squally winds and alternating sunshine and snow showers. Quite a good day in fact to discover whether one really feels happy aboard a boat. And I did. In fact I came to the conclusion that the Pageant was one of those boats destined to enjoy a long and popular life. Accommodation, finish, ease of handling, and sailing performance were all pleasing to me, though I am the first to recognize that tastes differ.

And tastes may change with time. Like several other boats of her size (and some bigger ones too) Pageant has a dinette on one side of her cabin, faced by the galley on the other. In 1970, as I write, this seems to be popular, but I wonder if people will get tired of a plan which offers a seating pattern rather too formal for a relaxed evening chat with friends, and which keeps the dishes and débris of supper too much in view. . . .

But given that one likes the dinette idea, Pageant offers a comfortable interpretation of it. In the main cabin that rough and unattractive surface offered by naked resinglass is not to be seen. Moulded lockers with Perspex sliding doors, closed lockers with wooden doors, stowage bins with smooth gel-coated inner linings of resinglass, and the use of foam-backed vinyl headlining under the deck—all these things make life pleasant. Furthermore, a sensible use of wood and wood veneers on bulkheads and other parts adds warmth and sets off the lightness of the resin. There is full headroom in the main cabin, and excellent visibility to the outside world. The fore-hatch has a translucent cover, which cheers up the fore-cabin.

In the usual manner, the mast thrust is supported by bulkheads which form the w.c. compartment between the two cabins, with a hanging space opposite. A slightly unusual shift of one bulkhead on the hanging locker side increases the space in the fore-cabin and shows a trend which I would expect to be followed elsewhere—namely not to have all bulkheads symmetrical or all companionways central.

One has two berths forward, then there is a quarter berth to port (aft of the galley) and of course the dinette table makes up into a double berth. There is also a sail stowage tunnel on the starboard side which is in effect a short quarter berth which I think could be used for a child. Indeed this would be a very nice boat for a party of three, or perhaps two adults and two offspring if one of the latter were small enough to sleep in the mini-berth. Then that dinette table would not have to be disturbed each night and morning.

One of the most notable characteristics of the Pageant, I thought, was the cleanness of her decks and the ease with which one can get about. Moving to and from the deck and cockpit, reefing and changing headsails were all made easy. The cockpit I found to be a convenient working place, with pretty good visibility forward when sitting aft where the designers intend you to sit. Remembering that the cabin is high enough to give full headroom below, this is another of those boats where I think that there is a case to be made for sitting the helmsman at the forward end of the cockpit. There he is snugged against the bulkhead protected from wind and spray (I still remember those snowstorms) and of course the headsail sheet hand does get into his line of sight. A slip-on tiller extension meets this case very neatly and cheaply, and anybody who bothers to make one will gain a big improvement in forward visibility.

I thought the sailing and handling qualities of the Pageant delightful. She is a twin-keel boat, and has a balanced rudder. That's to say, some of the rudder area is forward of the pivot line, so that the water pressure helps the helmsman and balances the water pressure aft of the pivot line which resists him. The result is a very light helm, and that is matched by an easily turned hull, so that the boat is very responsive. Yet she is steady on the run, even with a quartering wind and sea, and she will sail herself on the wind, either close or on a broad reach, with the helm lashed.

In other words, Pageant seemed to me to combine several virtues, and of course her bilge keels make her easy to beach or to trail.

She is designed for an inboard engine, such as 6 h.p. Vire petrol engine (about £400 installed) or a Volvo Penta MD 1 diesel of 7 h.p. which is rather more. A price of about £1,800 is quoted for a boat with sails, roller reefing, w.c., berth cushions and not much else. But one would need an anchor and its cable, a cooker, pulpit and pushpit, headsail sheet winches, cabin lights and nav lights, and a few other bits and pieces. And there's that engine of course, so that £2,500 would be a more realistic starting point.

ROWAN

Designer	C. S. J. Roy	
Builder	Macwester Marine Co. Ltd.,	
	River Road, Littlehampton, Sussex	
Thames tonnage	4	
Displacement	1,850 kg.	4,100 lb.
Length O.A.	6.8 m.	22 ft. 3 in.
Length W.L.		
Beam	2.5 m.	8 ft. 3 in.
Draught	0.83 m.	2 ft. 9 in.
Ballast	610 kg.	1,350 lb.
Sail area	18.11 sq. m.	195 sq. ft.
Sail area with genoa	20.88 sq. m.	225 sq. ft.

Rowan is a single-keeled boat with a traditional sort of underwater profile and of modest draught. The keel proper begins just aft of the cabin front and the leading edge rakes back to achieve almost the full depth at a point approximately under the mast step. From that point it runs back almost as far as the transom, with only a very slight increase in depth as it does so.

So one has a long, shallow keel, presenting plenty of area well aft, and although I have seen the opinion expressed by at least one famous designer that such an arrangement does not achieve directional stability, I can only answer that in the Rowan it does. At least something does, for this is a boat which holds her course, and which will sail hands off for useful periods of time—both valuable characteristics in a cruising boat.

In fact I would say that Rowan is a very pleasant boat to sail, though in these modern times she is reminiscent of earlier generations of sailing cruiser. Her cockpit is like those of other Macwesters in that it is a comfortable place from which to sail the boat—at least it suited me. It is easy to get about on deck, the stanchions and lifelines are firmly attached, and there are twin backstays, a feature which I favour both for the security of the mast and as a useful handhold when moving about. The fact that the lower shrouds come to the cabin sides means that it is easy to walk along the side decks. In all a boat which makes it easy to move about safely.

The cabin-top is necessarily high, as the designer has provided 6 ft. of headroom in quite a small boat. Yet to my eye she looks nicely proportioned, and not at all top-heavy.

The rudder is hung on the transom, which keeps the cockpit clear, and makes the rudder hangings accessible for maintenance. The tiller is of Rowan wood, or mountain ash, from which the boat gets her name—Scottish folklore endows this wood with a mystical protective property against the perils of the sea, apparently.

Below decks there are berths for four, with two in the fore-cabin and a double berth in the main cabin. This double is made by dropping the dinette table. With the table erected you can seat four people to a meal, and there is still good space to get to and fro past the cook whose galley area is opposite the table on the starboard side. Visibility from the cabin is good.

The w.c. compartment is forward of the galley area on the starboard side, and is just adequate but not ample. A hanging locker stands between the w.c. bulkhead and the galley, which is simple but practical.

The standard auxiliary is a 5 h.p. single-cylinder Stuart Turner two-stroke, with electric starting. This is situated under the sole of the self-draining cockpit, and access to it is from the cabin after the steps and other bits of structure have been removed. This is quite simply done, and then if you lie down it is possible to get at all parts of the engine without too much trouble. Engine accessibility may fairly be summed up, I think, as adequate, but not ideal.

The structure of the boat is in resinglass with integrally moulded wooden stringers to increase strength and stiffness where desirable. To keep the price down the interior finish is plain and unadorned, the idea being that the owner may embellish the boat when he has recovered from the initial expenditure. At the time of writing the price is £1,500 with sails, engine, pulpit, pushpit and lifelines, anchor, bunk mattresses, w.c. and cooker, and other bits and pieces. If you check the inventory against other firms' extras you will find that it is a highly competitive price, and if you want to use an outboard as an auxiliary then you could knock off £225 and add the price of the outboard.

Macwester hulls are available in literally 101 colours, and if the thought of taking the ground on a single keel is a deterrent you can have a version with a pair of galvanized steel bilge plates which allow her to stand upright. Alternatively the builder will supply legs designed for the boat with proper attachments.

A smaller sister, the 3.66 m. (15 ft.) Kelpie, is very similar in hull form and character, and is available as an open day sailer or with a small cabin which will sleep two.

SABRE 27

Designer Alan F. Hill
Builder Marine Construction (Woolston) Ltd.,
   Whites Shipyard, Woolston, Southampton,
   Hants

Thames tonnage	7	
Displacement	3,100 kg.	6,800 lb.
Ballast	1,400 kg.	3,100 lb.
Length O.A.	8.24 m.	27 ft. $0\frac{1}{2}$ in.
Length W.L.	6.75 m.	22 ft. $1\frac{3}{4}$ in.
Beam	2.74 m.	9 ft.
Draught	1.37 m.	4 ft. 6 in.
Sail area	26.75 sq. m.	288 sq. ft.
Sail area with genoa	33.16 sq. m.	357 sq. ft.

It is quite interesting to compare this boat with another 27-footer, the Halcyon. Though in many respects similar, Sabre has about 15 per cent more beam, and as she can obviously carry it I would have wished to see her equipped with a bit more sail area to make her go in light winds. (For a cruising, as opposed to a racing boat, there is no restriction on the amount of sail that is carried other than purely practical ones.)

It is also perhaps worth noting that if the Sabre had a transom-hung rudder as Halcyon has, the peculiarities of the Thames Measure formula would rate her as an '8-tonner' against Halcyon's 6, and I think that those two figures would in fact be more representative of the amount of space to be found on board.

In a sense, Sabre is a successor to the Trident, an earlier Hill design which was new when the first edition of this book came out. Trident continues in demand and in production, but Sabre simply provides a step forward. Apart from her extra beam and length she has 6 ft. of headroom. Like the Trident she is available with twin keels or a single keel—but not with a centreboard I regret to say.

With her beam, Sabre has a handsome if not a pretty appearance, and gives that chunky sense of a stout sea boat. Her beam has made possible good side decks while leaving space below to work in a fair-sized dinette plan. The trouble with dinettes is always the same in smallish boats—to find enough width for two people to sit side by side without the risk that one chap's elbow will drive the other's fork into his eye.

The boat has six berths, including two quarter berths and the dinette-double. That is fine for a six-member family (to whom one feels like offer-ing simultaneous congratulations and sympathy) but for pleasant cruising four would be a far better number. In that case the dinette table could stay as it is . . . in any case it is not big enough for six.

The galley is opposite the dinette and is very big by boat standards. There is a good view of the world outside as you slave over the stove or sink, and the same goes for those lazing at the table. With a monotony that must begin to affect the reader as it is now affecting the writer, we come to the thwartships bulkheads which support the mast and make space for w.c. compartment and wardrobe. A logical arrangement but nowadays absolutely stereotyped.

With aluminium spars, stainless steel rigging and deck fittings Sabre has that extra beam and comfort that take her slightly out of what I call the English tradition of yachts. She can be had in kit form, following the success of the same idea with the Trident, and therefore prices are rather variable. But they range from about £2,000 for the kit to nearly double that for a well-equipped and fully finished boat.

SEAFARER

Designer Alan Buchanan		
Builder Small Craft Ltd.,		
Blockley, Gloucestershire		
Thames tonnage	3	
Displacement	725 kg.	1,600 lb.
Ballast	330 kg.	730 lb.
Length O.A.	5.46 m.	18 ft. 3 in.
Length W.L.	5.05 m.	16 ft. 7 in.
Beam	2.18 m.	7 ft. 2 in.
Draught, plate up	0.46 m.	1 ft. 6 in.
Draught, plate down	1.45 m.	4 ft. 9 in.
Sail area	13.0 sq. m.	140 sq. ft.
Sail area with genoa	15.8 sq. m.	170 sq. ft.

This is a type of boat which I happen to like personally. I found that I was enjoying myself as soon as we set sail and dropped the mooring, because she is a forgiving boat. Very likely that will suggest to some that she could carry more canvas, and I certainly think she could—in the hands of an owner sensible enough to reef down in good time. For this is a family day-boat, with a very limited accommodation for cruising, and the whole point is that she will never get her passengers wet.

Although she is reminiscent of Alan Buch-

anan's very pretty little Dragonfly which was described in the first edition of this book, she is in fact rather beamier. And it is her beam, her hard bilged sections and her ballast that obviate the need for anyone to engage in gymnastics to keep the boat the right way up. The ballast is mainly fixed, but the heavy centreplate makes a big contribution. You sit *in* this boat, and sail along like gentlefolk. It doesn't much matter which side you sit (unless the wind is very strong), and as I said when I reported her for *Practical Boat Owner*, she is just the boat in which to take your aged parents out for a really enjoyable sail.

The centreplate is of $\frac{1}{2}$ in. steel (12 mm.). It weighs 190 lb. (86 kg.), but is very easy to raise and lower by means of a simple winch. The cockpit is very roomy—it would easily seat six—and the seats are comfortable. The flat cockpit sole itself is raised several inches above the bottom of the boat so as to keep your feet well clear of any loose water that happens to be around.

The fore-cabin would better be termed a cuddy, it is so small. Yet there is enough room for two to sleep, while for cruising one would obviously rig a simple tent over the boom, to give extra space and headroom. The sole of the cuddy is in fact below the sole of the cockpit, but there is a water-tight bulkhead across the boat so that the cuddy stays dry.

With a resinglass hull (and a light aluminium mast that is easily raised or lowered by one man) she is a simple boat to maintain and a simple boat to handle. Kits for home completion are offered by the makers, and that is a sensible way to cut the bill by £100. I can well imagine that some 'home-finishers' would be attracted by the idea of enlarging the cabin somewhat, at the expense of that huge cockpit—it's all a matter of what one wants.

An outboard would make a good auxiliary, and although a figure of about £650 for the boat with two sails but without such things as an anchor or warps cannot be called cheap, she is certainly a strong, stable and thoroughly serviceable boat for any family.

SAILER 23

Designer Laurent Giles & Partners Ltd.
Builder Seamaster Ltd.
   20 Ongar Road, Great Dunmow, Essex

Thames tonnage	5	
Displacement	1,020 kg.	2,250 lb.
Ballast	900 kg.	2,000 lb.
Length O.A.	7.01 m.	23 ft.
Length W.L.	5.84 m.	19 ft. 6 in.
Beam	2.44 m.	8 ft.
Draught, fixed keel	1.07 m.	3 ft. 6 in.
Draught, c.p. up	0.76 m.	2 ft. 6 in.
Draught, c.p. down	1.68 m.	5 ft. 6 in.
Sail area	23.3 sq. m.	250 sq. ft.
Sail area with genoa	27.5 sq. m.	307 sq. ft.

As may be seen from the above table, this is one of the relatively few modern boats which can be had with a centreboard if that is what you want. And there are good reasons for wanting it. The figures show the advantage in draught when you are going to windward in broken water, and on the other hand you can raise the plate when the wind is free and gain a marked advantage in speed over a similar fixed-keel boat. For inshore pilotage there are special advantages with a stout steel drop-plate. You can avoid the worst of the tidal stream or take short cuts by feeling your way over the shallows, always comforted by the knowledge that the bumping plate will both warn you and slow the boat down before she is firmly on.

Yes, there is much to be said for centre-plates, even though their construction is rather crude and seldom rises to the standard of engineering shown by the Fairey Atalanta of an earlier generation.

In other respects the two versions of the Sailer 23 are identical and may be treated as one. The arrangement below decks is one that had become conventional before this particular boat came on the market—a fore-cabin with two berths, then a w.c. compartment and a hanging locker between a pair of bulkheads which take the downward thrust of the mast, and then the main cabin with galley to starboard and dinette opposite, and finally a quarter berth.

The dinette, as usual, converts to a double berth, so that there are five in all, and one can only make the usual comment that this would be a very nice boat for three people to cruise in, so that the double berth did not *have* to be used. This is an example of a point I have made in the first part of the book that the difficulty with people is not when they are lying horizontally, but when they are getting dressed or trying to cook in a confined space. The point bears repeating, though it is not specifically related to this particular boat. In a sense it is we, the customers, who are to blame for the many small boats which have too many berths. The makers say it is a good selling point, which is the same as saying it is a good buying point.

Coming back at last to the boat itself, I thought her very well fitted out. The galley fitment with its lockers and its two foot pumps which supply the stainless steel sink with fresh and salt water is a good example. The cabin table itself is another since it folds or unfolds to make a small or large table according to choice. That may not sound very important, but in a small boat one needs a permanent small table for most of the day, while at mealtimes one needs a large table.

The dinette seats four in comfort, and the visibility of the outside world is good. No bare resin-glass is visible, the whole is lined, or concealed by lockers and fittings. An important detail is the provision of handholds and no fewer than four Tannoy ventilators in the deck. (Early models had no opening portholes which caused me to complain, but when I last inquired the builder was seriously considering the provision of at least one in the w.c.)

The self-draining cockpit provides seating for the helmsman at two levels—low down for open sea work and biting weather, higher up for close-quarters work and in harbour. The deck is well arranged, with three strong cleats on each side of the boat for mooring, plus a stout samson post forward for the anchor cable. It is easy to get about on deck, and with her strong guard rails I rated this boat as one in which deck work is safe and easy.

One can summarize by saying that Sailer 23 is a good sailing boat; built, finished and equipped to a high standard. Few people would find her unattractive, I am sure, but a high-quality package such as this with an extensive inventory cannot be cheap. At the time of writing the price is in the region of £2,500 with a Volvo Penta MD I diesel engine installed, sails, cooker, w.c., mattresses, interior lights and nav lights—in fact pretty well everything you need to go cruising with the exception of those two essential elements, an anchor and a compass.

SEA KING

Designer R. H. Patten
Builder Sea King (Boatbuilders) Ltd.,
  High Street, Leigh-on-Sea, Essex

Thames tonnage	6½	
Displacement	1,800 kg.	4,000 lb.
Ballast	450 kg.	1,000 lb.
Length O.A.	7.32 m.	24 ft.
Length W.L.	6.7 m.	22 ft.
Beam	2.66 m.	8 ft. 9 in.
Draught	See below	
Sail area	27 sq. m.	290 sq. ft.

The boat illustrated opposite is our own Sea King, 29 ft. hull length, with the bowsprit and bumkins which I adopted so that I could get the extra sail area I wanted. The one shown on this page is a 24-footer with more conventional rig, but notice that the owner has had the after end of the cabin raised to give him the headroom he wanted.

Now we are dealing with something very different. Most of the boats described in these pages are built in polyester resin, reinforced with fibreglass, inside a standard mould. Many of them have standard interiors, though a few are furnished in wood and may therefore be adjusted to suit an owner's wishes.

But Sea Kings are built to individual order, and though they all show a likeness in hull form, I doubt if any two are precisely the same. Thus the figures shown above are probably not accurate for any one boat, but are fairly typical of a 24-footer. A customer may specify a 24-footer 'similar to that one out on the mooring', but then he may ask for deeper draught, a bigger rudder and a different shape to the bow. He may ask for more or less headroom, and an entirely different arrangement below decks. All the things he wants he will get, though if he is sensible he will be guided by the builder's long experience and perhaps modify some of his more extreme ideas.

But the remarkable thing is that the customer will get a boat that embodies many of his own ideas and wishes, a boat that is distinctly his own, for a price notably lower than that of a standard fibreglass boat. Furthermore, his boat will be strongly built of best-quality materials—grown oak crooks for the stem and sternpost. Oak frames and hefty oak beams under the mast, with durable iroko planking copper-fastened.

Unless he particularly wants an aluminium mast he will get a hollow wooden one, and his interior joinery will be of mahogany cut from a single log to achieve matching grain and colour. It is true that the builder normally has a waiting list of two or three years, but there is pleasure to be had from a visit to the yard in that period and the sight of 'your' log, and 'your' crooks weathering slowly the natural way. (If the reader detects a note of enthusiasm here it is because my wife and I now own our second Sea King.)

But to look at the other side of the picture, although one gets more boat for one's money, a wooden craft needs more upkeep than a resinglass one, and that means an extra £50 to £75 a year for boatyard assistance, or more work for the owner and his wife. It is a matter of personal choice.

Sea Kings are built in sizes between 23 and 30 ft. in length. Some have had a single deep keel, but most are shoal draught boats with either a drop-plate or bilge keels, though I believe that

one owner had a drop-plate *and* twin keels fitted. But it will be clear why I have given no figure for draught—it can be anything from 18 in. to 5 ft., though a figure of 2 to 3 ft. would be more usual.

Similarly, it is not possible to describe a standard accommodation plan. Some have large families and want many berths, others fancy a 26-footer with a sleeping cabin for two and a comfortable saloon for day use. One can have pretty well what one wishes within the space available, and even that can be varied by having wider or narrower side decks—or no side decks at all. As these are by nature beamy boats they do have a good deal of room inside, but there are some things that I would not really advise—quarter berths for example are not easily made absolutely leak-proof in a wooden boat.

But with this type of boat-building you have to make your own decisions. For example, my own criticism of most of the Sea Kings was 'too little sail area and too little ballast', and I had my boat equipped accordingly. In a series-produced resin-glass boat it would have been a matter of 'like it or lump it'.

Taking as an example a 24-footer the current price, ready to go, would be about £1,900. For that you would get a boat with sails, inboard engine, mattresses, w.c., cooker, pulpit and life-lines, sheet winches, anchor and sail cover, electric lighting, anti-fouled and in the water. For fuller details the best thing is to visit the yard and look at some of the boats that lie there on their moorings.

SNAPDRAGON 21

Designer Thames Marine Ltd.
Builder Thames Marine Ltd.,
   Charfleet, Canvey Island, Essex

Thames tonnage	$3\frac{1}{2}$	
Displacement	1,000 kg.	2,200 lb.
Ballast	430 kg.	950 lb.
Length O.A.	6.35 m.	20 ft. 10 in.
Length W.L.	5.5 m.	18 ft.
Beam	2.2 m.	7 ft. 3 in.
Draught, twin keel	0.76 m.	2 ft. 6 in.
Sail area	17.2 sq. m.	185 sq. ft.
Sail area with genoa	22.3 sq. m.	240 sq. ft.

This member of the Snapdragon family shows the same sound engineering as her bigger sisters, and with the same attention to interior detail and finish. She provides berths for four people, but without the separate w.c. compartment. Instead, that vital piece of equipment is installed in the vee-junction of the two forward berths, approximately under the fore-hatch. This always seems to me to be the best solution for a small boat, since the fore-cabin is free during the daytime, and at night a bit of organization (and possibly the use of a bucket in the cockpit) will solve most problems. Although a *contretemps* may occasionally arise at night, for the rest there is the advantage of having the thing under an opening hatch. In harbour it is easy enough to rig a bit of canvas so that this hatch can be left open, and then you get standing headroom in a small boat.

The headroom in the main cabin of the Snapdragon 21 is in fact 4 ft. 10 in. There are two quarter berths and two berths in the fore-cabin, all of them well over 6 ft. long. On the port side of the main cabin is a galley area, and the berth on that side has about half its length under the cockpit seat. But the berth on the other side is really not a true quarter berth at all, because three-quarters of its length is inside the main cabin. The only other thing to take up space on that side of the boat is a hanging locker.

The galley is well fitted, with stowages for food and crocks, and with a sink supplied by pump from a tank under one of the forward berths. There is a great deal of stowage space, considering the total size of the boat and because there is no attempt to divide the boat into two cabins with bulkheads there is quite a roomy feel about her when you are below.

The cockpit is roomy enough for a family of four, and the coamings and seats give protection and comfort. The visibility forward is good. At the after end there is a special well to take an outboard motor, which is the most sensible auxiliary power plant for a boat of this size, I think. The well has a moulded folding cover over it, and when this is hinged back the engine is very accessible. There is plenty of non-slip finish on the decks and moving around can be very safe if you have the pulpit, pushpit, stanchions and lifelines that make a fence all around the boat. That little package, to be fitted yourself, is quoted at £72 at the time of writing, and of course they *are* very desirable items. But the price quoted is for parts in stainless steel, and I guess that the whole job could be done for £20 using galvanized steel water barrel, stock fittings and a bit of ingenuity.

For those who really want to get the price down Thames Marine offer part-completed boats. These are available at a variety of different stages, and fittings and equipment can be bought subsequently from the makers. Thus you save labour charges, or you may improvise some items for yourself and thus save even more. But a typical figure for a complete boat, with basic seagoing equipment, would be about £1,500 as I write, excluding the outboard.

Last point: a boat of this size is trailable, with obvious advantages.

SNAPDRAGON 27

Designer	Thames Marine Ltd.	
Builder	Thames Marine Ltd.,	
	Charfleet, Canvey Island, Essex	
Thames tonnage	$6\frac{1}{2}$	
Displacement	2,500 kg.	5,500 lb.
Ballast	1,000 kg.	2,200 lb.
Length O.A.	8.28 m.	27 ft. 2 in.
Length W.L.	6.93 m.	22 ft. 9 in.
Beam	2.59 m.	8 ft. 6 in.
Draught	0.84 m.	2 ft. 9 in.
Sail area	25.08 sq. m.	270 sq. ft.
Sail area with genoa	31.59 sq. m.	340 sq. ft.

The Snapdragons form a distinct family, with a common character. In fact they may be called a family of real family boats, each one for its size offering a degree of comfort that reflects the tastes and experiences of the managing director and his wife when cruising with their children.

When I was writing the first edition of this book boats built in resin and glass were rare, and it was a new experience to visit Thames Structural Plastics (as the firm was then called) and see the managing director with a bucket of resin and his sleeves rolled up. I thought the Snapdragon of that day, a 23 ft. centreboarder, to be a particularly attractive boat and even then her accommodation was notable. Since then public tastes and expectations have changed, assisted by the efforts of designers to offer something better.

Basically, all the current Snapdragons are twin-keeled boats, and each in its price bracket offers a high standard of comfort and interior finish. The 27-footer is really so commodious that when I went aboard for a trial sail I had the feeling that I was aboard a craft of 30 ft. With her full headroom and light interior she certainly seemed very much larger than the 26 ft. boat of an earlier era which I owned at the time.

There are four permanent berths in the boat, and the dinette table converts into a double berth some 46 in. wide (116 cm.). The galley is neatly arranged opposite, and shows a very high degree of workmanship. The whole of this cabin is very attractive indeed because double mouldings are used to give a smooth and creamy interior to many parts, and this is embellished by the use of wood for various parts and of leathercloth or similar 'headlinings'.

There is a grabrail under the deckhead—a very important thing when it comes to moving about a boat at sea. As it happens, this is a boat in which it is easy to move about below decks, and that is one of her charms I think, even though one does not at first consciously appreciate it.

Moving forward there is the w.c. compartment to port and a clothes locker opposite, between the conventional mast-supporting bulkheads. The loo compartment is designed to be used also as a shower, which is typical of this company's attitude to the needs of a cruising family. Again, it is well finished and conducive to that pride of ownership without which a boat is really not worth having.

In the fore-cabin the headroom is 5 ft. 10 in. (178 cm.), and this is a place where one could with complete confidence house a couple of middle-aged guests and expect them to be very much at home.

There are very good lockers and stowages, and the outlook from all the cabins is good. In short, I rate this one of the most attractive boats of her size in the matter of accommodation.

In the cockpit the same careful attention to detail design is evident. There are both large and small lockers, an important point in my view, one sits comfortably, feels secure and has a good view forward. But when it came to getting forward along the side decks I found it difficult if not impossible to put one foot before the other, and that must be accounted the penalty that is paid for such excellent accommodation below.

Examination of the boats under construction in the factory, and of the one I sailed, showed the engineering to be sound, with strong attachments for all the stressed parts such as stanchions, shroud plates and the like.

Sailing performance I would rate as respectable if not rapid, but it is hard to be fair in a field which is so subjective and where one really needs weeks of different seas and winds to form a soundly based opinion. But one can say that this is a very commodious, comfortable and seaworthy family cruiser. In a fully equipped form, with auxiliary engine installed, I doubt if she can cost less than £3,500.

SNAPDRAGON 24

Designer Thames Marine Ltd.		
Builder Thames Marine Ltd.,		
Charfleet, Canvey Island, Essex		
Thames tonnage	5½	
Displacement	1,700 kg.	3,700 lb.
Ballast	700 kg.	1,550 lb.
Length O.A.	7.32 m.	24 ft.
Length W.L.	6.25 m.	20 ft. 6 in.
Beam	2.44 m.	8 ft.
Draught, twin keel	0.75 m.	2 ft. 6 in.
Draught, single keel	1.1 m.	3 ft. 6 in.
Sail area	20 sq. m.	220 sq. ft.
Sail area with genoa	26 sq. m.	280 sq. ft.

As I have remarked in an earlier chapter, Thames tonnage is a most peculiar measure. Because the length that is taken into account in the formula is the length from stem to rudder head, boats with inboard rudders (like the Snapdragons) show a smaller T.M. than those with transom-hung rudders. The figures I give are worked out as nearly as possible in accordance with the old, revered, yet slightly ridiculous formula. Boatbuilders, with some justice, may bend the rule a little and take the overall length of the hull for their calculations. In the case of the Snapdragons that does in fact give a more meaningful figure, and a more sensible one, even if it is less 'accurate', because these *are* roomy boats.

This 24-footer, for example, offers very good accommodation for her size and, like her sisters, her innards are well done. There is a 6 ft. 4 in. quarter berth on the starboard side, and forward of that in the main cabin is the galley area.

On the opposite side there is a dinette, which makes up into another 6 ft. 4 in. berth for two. Then comes the usual athwartships compartment with w.c. and hanging locker, but this one is unusually spacious for the size of boat, and it is ventilated. The clothes locker is nicely made, and the whole compartment, including the fore-cabin, can be shut off from the rest of the boat by a folding door.

The fore-cabin berths are big enough for comfort, and forward of them again is a hopper for the anchor chain. This is beyond a partial bulkhead and therefore open to view, which can be a very valuable feature, for chains have a habit of getting themselves twisted and knotted. . . .

There is plenty of stowage, notably under the dinette berths and the forward berths, but these large spaces are approached from the top, which means lifting the mattress and whatever happens to be on it. This is not an arrangement which appeals to me, but it is very common. There is a water tank under the head of the quarter berth, supplying the galley sink which is right alongside.

Indicative of the high standard of thought and workmanship that goes into Thames Marine's boats is the ventilation system that they use. This brings air in through ducts and leads it close to the inner skin of the hull bottom, where the temperature is always low. As the air passes over these cool surfaces a proportion of the moisture it contains condenses, so that the air which finally reaches the cabin itself is drier than it would otherwise be.

Another indication is the care that they take with their engine installations. In the 24 one could fit either a Volvo Penta MD 1 diesel or a Vire petrol engine. In either case the installation is well engineered, but whether the soundproofing will have been improved by the time these words appear in print I do not know. I can only hope so.

For this well-built, tastefully finished and seaworthy boat the price at the time of writing is around £2,500, with Vire engine fitted, cooker, w.c. and pretty well everything one would need to go cruising.

SNAPDRAGON 600

Designer	Thames Marine Ltd.	
Builder	Thames Marine Ltd.,	
	Charfleet, Canvey Island, Essex	
Thames tonnage	4	
Displacement	1,000 kg.	22,000 lb.
Ballast	450 kg.	1,000 lb.
Length O.A.	6.0 m.	19 ft. 8in.
Length W.L.	5.18 m.	17 ft.
Beam	2.29 m.	7 ft. 6 in.
Draught, twin keels	0.76 m.	2 ft. 6 in.
Sail area	16.72 sq. m.	180 sq. ft.
Sail area with genoa	20.44 sq. m.	220 sq. ft.

Before commenting on the smallest member of the Snapdragon tribe, one may take a passing glance at the peculiarities of the formula for Thames measure. Although a smaller boat than her 21 ft. sister, this one rates a large Thames tonnage, partly because she has an extra 3 in. of beam and partly because her rudder is hung on the transom instead of being mounted inboard.

With such a small amount of space to play with

the designers have reduced the accommodation plan to its essential simplicity. The cockpit has not been cramped in the attempt to get sufficient cabin space, with the result that two of the berths are quarter berths with half their length under the cockpit side seats. But in fact each side of the boat is effectively one long berth, since the quarter berths run forward to join the forward berths, so that sleepers lie end-to-end, or at least head-to-head.

And talking of 'heads' reminds one of the peculiar fact that in naval parlance the same word is used for the w.c., or the non-U, but nowadays almost universal, 'toilet'. Call it what you will, that useful item of domestic equipment is right forward in this boat, close to but not immediately under, the fore-hatch. In my opinion that is the right place for it.

The makers say that a curtain provides privacy, but I think a practical-minded owner could fit bulkheads and a folding door.

There is no elaborate provision for a galley. Just a portable cooker, in one with its gas bottle so that you can use it where you wish—in the cabin or out in the cockpit if the weather allows.

There is a chain locker right forward in the peak, stowages under the berths, moulded lockers above them against the cabin sides, and cockpit lockers aft. The cockpit is self-draining, and extends right to the transom where there is provision for mounting an outboard motor as an auxiliary.

The boat is available with either a single keel, or with twins. The basic price (fin) is £1,070, or you can have twin keels for £75 less. Those prices include sails, berth mattresses, wiring ready for internal and nav lights, and that's about all. A cooker, a 'heads', an anchor and its chain and a few other items would augment that figure quite quickly by a further £100, and then you might need an outboard motor which could soak up £75 to £100. Kits for home completion are available, too.

And if you wonder how she gets her name—well that '600' is the result of the metric invasion. It's her length in centimetres.

TANKARD 23

Designer Brian D. Tankard
Builder Brian D. Tankard
  Parkwood Road, Tavistock, South Devon

Thames tonnage	3½	
Displacement	1,200 kg.	2,650 lb.
Ballast	540 kg.	1,200 lb.
Length O.A.	7.01 m.	23 ft.
Length W.L.	5.46 m.	18 ft. 3 in.
Beam	2.13 m.	7 ft.
Draught, twin keel	0.76 m.	2 ft. 6 in.
Draught, single keel	1.17 m.	3 ft. 10 in.
Sail area	20.44 sq. m.	220 sq. ft.
Sail area with genoa	26.94 sq. m.	290 sq. ft.

A boat of a very distinctive appearance, the Tankard 23 offers something of a different character from the general run of boats of her size. Her deck arrangement, for example, yields a large clear space for work or relaxation, though the absence of an extended coach-roof naturally limits the headroom over a considerable part of the cabin. Headroom has its attractions, but so does a large and almost flat deck space, so one simply has to decide which is the more important.

With a very shapely underwater form and a sufficient sail area she is a fast boat for her size, and one that gives zestful sailing. The hull mouldings that I have seen have all been very fair and well finished, and to look at them out of the water is to visualize the clean stream lines that the water will make when she moves.

The look of the boat is made by her sharply raked stem, the use of timber for her upper topsides, and the unusual moulded doghouse. Though whether the latter makes or mars her looks may be a matter of opinion.

Timber is also used for the cockpit, and it is worth pointing out that the designer-builder has integrated timber and resinglass so as to get the best functional and structural result. In other words the timber is not merely decorative.

The boat is available with either a single central keel with a ballast torpedo at the bottom, or with twin keels similarly ballasted. The fin keel is kept small in area, as in modern racing designs, but the rudder is behind a skeg which gives support and protection to its lower end. That is a sensible provision, in my view.

There is headroom of 5 ft. (1.52 m.) under the doghouse, and sitting headroom elsewhere in the boat. The normal layout is to have two berths forward, then bulkheads which can be fitted with a curtain for privacy. Aft of the bulkheads is a galley fitment to starboard and a locker to port. Then come two quarter berths. Other arrangements are possible for the man who completes his own hull, but the cabin space available in a boat of this shape with long overhangs fore and aft is very limited and she pays for her performance by squeezing her occupants. Therefore it might be better to arrange the boat for fewer than four people if one were free to do so.

An outboard motor makes a suitable auxiliary, and a trunking is moulded into the counter to take one. Without the engine, but rigged, with sails, mattress cushions, sink, pulpit, anchor and chain, and deck fittings the price approaches £1,900 at the time of writing.

TIGER

Designer John Butler
Builder Westerly Marine Construction Ltd.,
   Aysgarth Road, Waterlooville, PO7 7UF,
   Hampshire

Thames tonnage	6	
Displacement	2,400 kg.	5,300 lb.
Ballast	1,000 kg.	2,200 lb.
Length O.A.	7.7 m.	25 ft. 1 in.
Length W.L.	6.8 m.	21 ft. 10 in.
Beam	2.7 m.	8 ft. 9 in.
Draught	1.3 m.	4 ft. 3 in.
Sail area	26.8 sq. m.	288 sq. ft.
Sail area with genoa	35.6 sq. m.	381 sq. ft.

This boat is the big sister to the Cirrus and shows many similarities—her beam, for example, is 40 per cent of the waterline length and she has the same sort of profile with similar cabin windows. Indeed, without a glimpse of the sail marks it can be as difficult to tell a Cirrus from a Tiger as to distinguish between those other Westerly sisters, Pageant and Centaur.

Naturally the greater waterline length gives Tiger a potential speed advantage over Cirrus, and there is an even more important gain in accommodation. This boat has the L-shaped dinette which really does give space for four people to sit down and eat together. It makes into a double berth, though I would think that the happiest Tigers are those in which that facility is rarely used; there are two berths forward plus two quarter berths, and four people are enough to fill a boat of this size for any period longer than a week-end.

The galley, opposite the dinette, is well fitted, and the cabin windows are situated so that you get a good view while slaving over the cooker, or while sitting at the table to enjoy the results.

The w.c. compartment is quite roomy and has an opening scuttle (porthole), the merit of which must be obvious. One point which is worth noting is that the tubular stanchion which supports the table extends from cabin sole to deckhead, and offers a useful handhold when going below in lumpy weather. In my opinion that is something of real importance.

Tiger's decks are clear, with strong stanchions and pulpit (included in the basic price), and the cockpit is roomy, deep and comfortable. In all, she is a boat which makes deck work as easy and safe as it can ever be.

Although the lifelines and pulpit are included in the basic price, the pushpit aft is an extra at a price of about £35. And though the loo has an opening scuttle, to have the pair in the fore-cabin made openable would cost you about £20. In my view that is something to be desired. You would probably also want some electric lights, a fire extinguisher and some other items, but the basic price of around £2,600 embraces a much more comprehensive inventory in Tiger than in some of Westerly's other boats.

The most important extra of all is an auxiliary engine—say about £400 for a 6 h.p. Vire petrol engine or about £600 for a 7 h.p. Volvo Penta MD 1. With registration charges, echo sounder and a few other bits and pieces you would have to be careful not to exceed £3,500. But you would have a comfortable and durable boat which is a pleasure to sail.

VIVACITY 20

Designer D. C. Pollard
Builder Russell Marine Ltd.,
   Calvia Works, Prince Avenue, Southend-on-
   Sea, Essex

Thames tonnage	3½	
Displacement	800 kg.	1,800 lb.
Ballast	360 kg.	800 lb.
Length O.A.	6.1 m.	20 ft.
Length W.L.	5.23 m.	17 ft. 6 in.
Beam	2.13 m.	7 ft.
Draught	0.71 m.	2 ft. 4 in.
Sail area	16.25 sq. m.	175 sq. ft.
Sail area with genoa	22.3 sq. m.	240 sq. ft.

Boatbuilders follow various policies in the naming of boats. Some like to have a different name for each design, others stick to a family name and add a number to represent the length or some other dimension. Russell Marine come into this second group, but strangely enough their various Vivacities do not show much family resemblance.

In fact the Vivacity 20 is much more like the 18 ft. Alacrity which was reviewed in the first edition of this book. Indeed she began as an enlarged development of the Alacrity and as such was very successful. But after nearly 1,000 Vivacity 20s had been sold, the model was substantially improved and it is this developed version which I consider here.

The original Vivacity had an open-plan cabin (and this version remains available) but there is now the two-cabin version with doors to close off the fore-cabin. But some people prefer the benefits of the 'open-plan' during the daytime so Russell Marine have devised the very novel idea of *removable bulkheads*. In short the bulkheads, and the doors that hang on them, can be stowed away in the daytime to give the maximum cabin space through the boat—though they must be re-shipped I suppose whenever someone wants privacy at the loo.

The w.c. is in fact fitted just forward of these removable bulkheads, beneath the fore-hatch. On either side of it are the two forward berths. Then, moving aft there is a sink fitment on one side and a galley locker on the other whose top makes a useful put-down place or even a mini chart-table. But the cooker is farther aft. It is stowed under the companion entrance and slides out when wanted. Russell Marine favour methylated spirit

cookers which are well suited to being moved about and are certainly clean and easy to use.

The two main cabin berths are in fact quarter berths, and as each has only about half its length in the main cabin they do not really provide adequate seating for four. That, of course, is where the removable bulkheads can prove valuable since they allow the cabin to be enlarged.

These boats are well built and are available with either twin or single keels. The company has for several years put forward its Standard Cruising Inventory policy which allows the buyer to get a sensibly equipped boat at a reasonable figure. At about £1,300 this would give you a Vivacity 20 with anchor, chain, flushing w.c., bilge pump, cooker, pulpit, lifelines and so forth. But the company has other schemes to enable people to get afloat with the minimum cost, and then to bring the boat up to full cruising standard by easy stages.

VIVACITY 650

Designer Russell Marine Ltd.
Builder Russell Marine Ltd.,
   Calvia Works, Prince Avenue, Southend-on-
   Sea, Essex

Thames tonnage	4	
Displacement	1,150 kg.	2,500 lb.
Ballast	500 kg.	1,100 lb.
Length O.A.	6.48 m.	21 ft. 3 in.
Length	5.87 m.	19 ft. 3 in.
Beam	2.18 m.	7 ft. 2 in.
Draught, single keel	1.0 m.	3 ft. 3 in.
Draught, twin keels	0.71 m.	2 ft. 4 in.
Sail area	21.4 sq. m.	229 sq. ft.
Sail area with genoa	22.3 sq. m.	240 sq. ft.

Here is a boat in which the designer has found a quite novel solution to the problem of fitting four people into a tiny space. He has devised a retractable galley unit.

In the place which would normally be the starboard quarter berth—that's to say the tunnel extending aft from the cabin under the side seat of the cockpit—there is a moulded box which contains a cooker and an ice box or food store. When the cushions have been removed from the berth this box can be slid forward into a position which is well ventilated by the wide main hatch.

This solution seems a sensible one, since one does not need to cook when the berths are occupied, and if it is a matter of serving early morning tea in bed to three members of the party the fourth must get up to make it.

As a result of this idea, the two berths in the main cabin of this boat are wholly within the cabin and there is no need for either of them to extend under the cockpit. Furthermore, it has been found possible to provide a separate w.c. compartment between two bulkheads which support the mast. As one might expect, there is a small hanging locker opposite the w.c., and then there are two berths in the fore-cabin. These can be made into a double with a fitted cushion. The w.c. is pretty cramped—but then what can one expect if one wants four berths in a boat of this size?

Back with the galley arrangements, there is a sink unit under the step as one enters from the cockpit. It is covered with a board when not in use, and perhaps it is worth remarking that this position for a sink has successfully been used in other small cruisers, yet as far as I know very few people have put their foot in it!

This boat has a number of other good ideas which contribute to a very effective result for her size. There is an unusually large hatchway which makes the cabin light and airy. There is also a fore-hatch which can be arranged to hinge along any of its four sides, and to complete the ventilation there is a ducted system taking air from scoops in the topsides and exhaling it through grilles in the fore-cabin, the w.c. and the main cabin. Much use is made of double mouldings and linings, yet thought has been given to the accessibility of such things as the bolts holding the shroud plates.

There are no side decks, but that is a perfectly acceptable arrangement where the cabin top is kept reasonably flat and is treated against slip. Furthermore on this boat there are stanchions and safety rails leading from the cockpit to the pulpit, and although they are low they give protection to anyone going forward on hands and knees—which one need not be ashamed to do on a small boat when the going gets lively.

Forward on deck there is a well for the anchor, with a lid so that the deck is clear when the anchor is stowed. The well drains overboard. In general it is easy to get about on this boat and the shrouds do not impede movement along the deck.

Russell Marine have worked out a standard cruising inventory for their boats—a very sensible idea, even though it is not possible to get everyone to agree what should be included in such an inventory. For example, the 650 with sailing gear, galley unit, cooker, cushions, pulpit, pushpit and lifelines and w.c. would cost about £1,400 at the time of writing. (But the 'time of writing' also happens to be a time of rapidly rising prices in all sectors of industry, so there is likely to be some difference by the time of reading.)

A 5 to 10 h.p. outboard motor would make a good auxiliary power plant for this boat, and the design is arranged to accommodate such a unit. Most outboards are not efficient in slow-moving craft, but they have other advantages and a high fuel consumption is not important if the engine is being used only as an auxiliary.

VIVACITY 24

Designer Alan Hill
Builder Russell Marine Ltd.,
    Calvia Works, Prince Avenue, Southend-on-
    Sea, Essex

Thames tonnage	5.3	
Displacement	1,900 kg.	4,200 lb.
Length O.A.	7.31 m.	24 ft.
Length W.L.	6.34 m.	20 ft. 9 in.
Beam	2.44 m.	8 ft.
Draught, single keel	1.12 m.	3 ft. 8 in.
Draught, twin keels	0.76 m.	2 ft. 6 in.
Ballast	794 kg.	1,750 lb.
Sail area	23.7 sq. m.	255 sq. ft.
Sail area with genoa		

I think it interesting to compare this 24 ft. boat with the Trident of the same length which was also designed by Alan Hill and was treated in the first edition of this book. I thought Trident a very attractive boat at the time, and to judge by the numbers sold other people felt, and still feel, the same about her. But since those days, almost ten years ago, headroom has been steadily increased in small family cruisers, and whereas the Trident has 5 ft. 5 in., Vivacity 24 has just over 5 ft. 10 in. (178 cm.), which is a much bigger difference than it sounds.

The amount of space down below is also very much increased by the fact that side decks have been omitted, so that the cabin top extends almost to the full width of the hull. Whether or not you think that this makes the boat look boxy I cannot tell, but my own opinion is that she looks better than just acceptable, and I think that that is due to the way in which the designer has proportioned the windows, the step down in the cabin top, the vestigial side decks and other details.

Of course one has to go forward over the high cabin top, and that is also a working platform. When I sailed the boat I found both the cabin top and the fore-deck convenient places on which to work. One result of the layout is that there has to be a high lifeline and stanchions along the cabin sides, but people seem willing to accept that nowadays. Of course the benefits of the full-out cabin become apparent as soon as you step below decks. My own immediate impression, even though it was a cold blustery day in winter, was of a light, bright and 'liveable' cabin. The entrance hatch is large, and on summery days I know that it will be a delight to be on board such a boat.

But in common with many other resinglass boats, the forward cockpit bulkhead slopes forward, so that with the washboards removed it is very much open to any rain (or even hail or snow) that may be falling. In boats with that feature I think it is indisputable that the sliding hatch cover should be able to slide aft so as to make an overhanging 'eave' above the entrance. Oddly enough Vivacity 24 has just such a hatch cover at the other end of the boat, designed with a large overhanging lip that will allow the hatch to be partly open during a warm night without danger of being soaked by a sudden shower.

But back into the cabin . . . there is a dinette arrangement to starboard, two facing forward and two aft, with the table between them. It is really quite roomy, and can be numbered among the more successful dinettes in craft of this size.

On the opposite side of the boat there is a quarter berth extending aft under the cockpit side seat, and then the galley opposite the dinette. This is moulded in resinglass, satin smooth yet not cold and clinical. There are two sinks, a place for a cooker at a sensible height and good stowages. The whole effect of the interior of the boat I saw was clean, bright and yet friendly, with plenty of double mouldings to give smooth inner surfaces to lockers, yet with enough wooden trim around to give warmth.

Bulkheads under the mast tabernacle make an athwartships compartment, as they do on so many boats. Between them is the w.c. to starboard, and a hanging space to port. Forward of this area again is a small cabin with two berths and a chain locker right forward. A sliding door closes the hanging locker–loo area from the main cabin, though in the boats I have seen there was no special provision to close off the fore-cabin. A curtain could very well be adequate.

On the sloping front face of the cabin top a labyrinth-type ventilator has been moulded into the structure. That is a very good idea, though whether my belief that the boat in her standard form could do with still more ventilation is correct could be discovered only by living aboard for some time.

The extreme after end of the cockpit is arranged as an outboard well, and although an outboard motor is not an ideal auxiliary as far as running costs are concerned, it saves on capital cost. It also saves space inside the boat herself.

The cockpit itself is laid out conveniently for single-handed or fully crewed sailing, though, as is the case with several other boats, my preference would be for a longer tiller so that the helmsman could sit right forward.

Vivacity 24 is available with single or twin keels, the single-keel version costing about £100 more. With a basic inventory of sails, settee cushions and deck gear the twin-keeler is priced at about £1,900. With anchor, cooker, w.c., outboard motor and other gear the cost could quickly approach £2,500.

VOYAGER (and REDSTART)

Designer	M. R. Redman	
Builder	Juxta Mare Marine	
	Burnham on Crouch, Essex	
Thames tonnage	1	
Displacement	235 kg.	520 lb.
Length O.A.	4.06 m.	13 ft. 4 in.
Length W.L.		
Beam	1.55 m.	5 ft. 1 in.
Draught	0.41 m.	1 ft. 4 in.
Ballast	68 kg.	150 lb.
Sail area	7.43 sq. m.	80 sq. ft.
Sail area with genoa		

To find the figure for Thames tonnage in the table above I had to work it out specially, in spite of the fact that I had done dozens of such calculations for the chart which appears elsewhere in this book. When I calculated the chart I did not have in mind the concept of a cruising boat so small as the Voyager, though many cruises have been undertaken by enthusiasts in the right type (i.e. non-racing) of dinghy.

Voyager has twin bilge keels and is a development of a successful little design called Barbel. Later, Voyager was further developed into a very similar-looking boat called Redstart which has the advantage of very much more ballast (about 280 lb. in fact). This makes her a very much stiffer boat and one which I believe is much preferable for coastal and estuary cruising, because the chance that she might be capsized is virtually eliminated.

Accommodation in a boat of this kind is naturally severely limited. In the tiny cabin there are two bunks each 6½ ft. (198 cm.) long, a shelf for a cooker and a modest space right in the bows where kit can be stored. The only way to stand up in the cabin is with the hatch open, and that does indeed offer a sheltered position when sailing as well as a good place from which to reef the mainsail. There is room for a w.c. bucket under the fore-hatch.

Voyager is in effect a dinghy with a lid on, and she must be treated as a dinghy. For example, she can be capsized, though not very easily. On the other hand, she can be taken into water shallow enough to allow the crew to step ashore in thigh boots (or with trousers rolled) so in that respect too she is her own tender. And she is small enough and light enough for two people to get her on and off a road trailer.

As the photograph shows, there is no cockpit to sit *in*, though there is a well for the feet. I would think it sensible to have a rail around the after end of the boat, and for my comfort and protection I would rig a canvas dodger on it (and blow the extra windage!).

Complete and ready to sail the price is £400 or so. That includes bunk mattresses, sails, anchor and warp and fenders. A small outboard motor would be useful, but in my opinion it would be more sensible to arrange for rowlocks to be shipped because a boat of this size can be rowed quite well.

Finally, I think it bears repeating that in my opinion this boat is different from all the others I have reviewed in this book because she is capsizeable, in the course of ordinary cruising. She is therefore not the sort of boat that an inexperienced or un-agile couple should plan to take to sea.

The well-ballasted Redstart, on the other hand, though cramped is a more sensible proposition for cruising.

WARWICK

Designer Laurent Giles & Partners
Builder Westerly Marine Construction Ltd.,
  Aysgarth Road, Waterlooville, PO7 7UF,
  Hampshire

Thames tonnage	4½	
Displacement	1,680 kg.	3,700 lb.
Ballast	740 kg.	1,630 lb.
Length O.A.	6.55 m.	21 ft. 6 in.
Length W.L.	5.7 m.	18 ft. 9 in.
Beam	2.35 m.	7 ft. 9 in.
Draught	0.84 m.	2 ft. 9 in.
Sail area	19.5 sq. m.	210 sq. ft.
Sail area with genoa	24.8 sq. m.	266 sq. ft.

The smallest of Westerly's twin keelers, Warwick is evidence of the company's determination to cover the range of what may be called typical family boats—that's to say the range lying between 21 and 31 ft. in length. It is approximately the same range that some other British manufacturers think it desirable to cover, presumably on the basis that a customer who starts with one of the smaller boats is likely to come back for a bigger one.

Warwick follows the style of the very successful

Pageant, on a smaller scale. She is just a little longer and a few inches beamier than the single-keeled Jouster, and she differs from Jouster in having a separate and enclosed w.c. compartment. Whether or not that is really worthwhile is a matter of personal preference.

The accommodation arrangement allows two berths in the fore-cabin, with mingling feet. One of these berths is length-limited by the presence of the aforesaid w.c. compartment. In the main cabin there are two quarter berths. The forward end of the berth on the starboard side breaks down (and then builds up) to form a dinette-style table at which two people can certainly sit face to face, and where four are unlikely to be able to sit unless they are of special proportions and temperament. Forward of the dinette there is still space enough for the galley sink before you come to the bulkhead of the loo compartment.

On the opposite side of the boat the space forward of the berth-head is given over to the cooker with stowage below, and a hanging locker. There is good visibility from the cabin through the strong metal-framed windows. Fixed round portholes, one of which is in the loo, can be supplied as opening scuttles at an extra cost of £21 the pair. (That would be my first essential extra.)

The cockpit is 6 ft. long and is self-draining. The rudder is got out of the way by hanging it on the transom, where you can also ship an outboard motor as an auxiliary if you wish. On the other hand, a Vire petrol engine can be fitted as an inboard for about £400, which is twice the cost of a more or less equivalent outboard.

Warwick's decks are well planned for easy and safe movement, and her fittings are strongly made and attached, as they are in all this company's boats. The basic price is just under £1,600 as I write, and that includes the w.c., sink and water pump, berth mattresses, a two-piece suit of sails, anti-fouling and other useful items, but *not* anchor, sheet winches, pulpit and so forth. With those items plus an echo-sounder, an outboard motor, electric lights, better ventilation, a cooking stove, a bilge pump and some other things I estimate that she would cost me about £2,200 before I felt like putting to sea.